THE LIES OF THE LAND

THE
LIES
OF THE
LAND

SEEING RURAL AMERICA
FOR WHAT IT IS—AND ISN'T

STEVEN CONN

The University of Chicago Press
CHICAGO AND LONDON

The University of Chicago Press, Chicago 60637
The University of Chicago Press, Ltd., London
© 2023 by The University of Chicago
Published 2023
Printed in the United States of America

32 31 30 29 28 27 26 25 24 23   1 2 3 4 5

ISBN-13: 978-0-226-82690-5 (cloth)
ISBN-13: 978-0-226-82691-2 (e-book)
DOI: https://doi.org/10.7208/chicago/9780226826912.001.0001

Library of Congress Cataloging-in-Publication Data

Names: Conn, Steven, author.
Title: The lies of the land : seeing rural America for what it is—and isn't /
    Steven Conn.
Description: Chicago ; London : The University of Chicago Press, 2023. |
    Includes bibliographical references and index.
Identifiers: LCCN 2022061280 | ISBN 9780226826905 (cloth) |
    ISBN 9780226826912 (ebook)
Subjects: LCSH: United States—Rural conditions. | United States—
    Social conditions.
Classification: LCC HN57 .C594 2023 | DDC 306.0973—dc23/eng/20230206
LC record available at https://lccn.loc.gov/2022061280
♾ This paper meets the requirements of ANSI/NISO Z39.48-1992
(Permanence of Paper).

CONTENTS

THAT EMPTY FEELING

A book about rural America is preposterous on its face.

There is no such thing as "rural America," because there are many rural Americas, each with its own history, culture, and dynamics. There are "rurals" in every state and in every region of the country; rural Americans come, just like urban Americans, in every stripe and flavor politically, ethnically, religiously: Quebecois timber workers in northern Maine, shrimpers from Southeast Asia in coastal Louisiana, Central American slaughterhouse workers in rural Iowa and Kansas. And, of course, Native American reservation land remains overwhelmingly rural. We know from the novels of Willa Cather and Sinclair Lewis, from the diary of Rachel Calof and other such sources that women have long experienced rural life differently than men and have often felt its hardships more acutely, and still do.

Economically, rural America relies on agriculture, and it relies on extractive and manufacturing industries; it also depends on tourism and recreation. Depending on where you look, rural America is either desperately poor or awash in money. Any list of the nation's poorest counties includes mostly rural ones—places like Wheeler County,

Georgia, and McCreary County, Kentucky. At the same time, Teton County, Wyoming, inhabited at a sparse five people per square mile, can stake a claim to being both the wealthiest in the country, home to some of America's superrich, and the place with the nation's most yawning wealth gap. No single book—no single word—could pretend to do justice to all that diversity of experience.

Likewise, there have been any number of attempts to define exactly what rural America is in the first place. Researchers at Ohio State University recently announced five different kinds of "rural" in Ohio alone![1] Once, rural people were classified on the basis of the work they did, the assumption being that those people made their living directly from the land in one way or another. That is certainly not true anymore, and it hasn't been for some decades. Rural people drive long-haul trucks and they work for the state or county (though many might explain that this isn't the same as working for "the government"), and some commute long distances for office or factory work in a metropolitan area.

In 1987, the W. K. Kellogg Foundation funded the National Rural Studies Committee, to promote the study of rural America. Yet even this group of scholars "struggled with the term 'rural,'" and wound up using *rural, nonmetropolitan, countryside,* and *hinterlands* more or less synonymously. John Fraser Hart, a geographer who was on the committee, turned the definitional dilemma into something of an inadvertent koan: "The need to understand and define the concept of rural becomes all the more urgent as that concept becomes ever less clear."[2] At roughly the same time, the Bureau of the Census had more or less given up altogether, deciding that *rural* meant anything left over after counting urban and metropolitan regions. "The urban population consists of all persons living in urbanized areas and in places of 2,500 or more inhabitants," the bureau announced in 1985; "all other population is classified as rural."[3] The welter of definitions and the very precision they struggle to achieve underscores their arbitrariness in the first place. I'll say here that I have neither fixed on one definition nor attempted my own, though the bulk of this book focuses on the space between the Appalachians and the Sierras. This space includes much of what is commonly considered rural America, though certainly not all of it.

Still, most of us feel a rural place when we stand in one or when we drive through it. The spaces are bigger, the traffic is lighter, the houses fewer and farther between. We have the sensation—an illusion, really—of leaving all the artifice of the "urban" behind and entering something closer to nature. We can find ourselves alone, or nearly so. Indeed, that's often the reason metropolitans go out to the country in the first place.

I took my first trip to China in the summer of 1997, and among my most vivid memories of it are of the countryside as I traveled between China's big cities. Rural China struck me as a vastly different place than rural America because it bustled with people and activity. Chinese agriculture, I quickly came to see, remained small scale and thus still relied on human (and other animal) labor to wrest food from the land.[4] In this sense, rural China seemed the opposite of rural America, where fewer than 2 percent of us are now engaged in agriculture.[5]

I shared these memories with a dear friend from China. She responded that many who come to the United States from China refer to it as "the Big Empty." For the Chinese people, she went on to explain, the place feels like there's no one there. Accustomed to sharing a country roughly the same size as the United States with approximately four times as many people, many in China find much of this country to be almost literally disembodied. The lack of people strikes them as quintessentially American.

Maybe that's pop sociology, but the phrase sticks with me. The Big Empty seems as good a label for rural America as any developed by demographers, sociologists, political pundits, or anyone else.[6] It captures something both literal—there aren't many people there—and more visceral about the way it feels to be in a rural place. More than that, it describes the cultural expectation that so many Americans (few of whom actually live in rural America anymore) seem to have of what *rural* means: spacious rather than crowded; "natural" rather than artificial. The opposite of *urban*. And it applies equally to the vast variety of rural places in this country. However else Kansas wheat farms, North Dakota fracking operations, southern cotton fields, and denuded Appalachian coal country may differ, to stand in any one of them is to feel the emptiness and to know that you are in a rural place.

There is something contradictory or even paradoxical about that empty feeling. The evidence of human activity in all those places is easy enough to see. In fact, those places are no less shaped by our ambitions and desires, technology, and greed, than any city skyline. We just rarely see the people responsible for this shaping because there are so few of them—or because they are somewhere else. Far from being local and small scale, the forces at work on these landscapes are usually huge and remote. It takes only a solitary driver piloting a combine roughly the size of a two-story house to gobble up hundreds and hundreds of acres of that Kansas wheat. He may own that land, or he might rent it from some distant absentee landlord—but either way, he's paying constant attention to wheat prices in Chicago or some other global commodities market as his GPS pilots the highly sophisticated piece of farm technology with a precision that would have made the Apollo crews envious. Yet to watch him he appears solitary, out there all alone.

That sense of emptiness obscures. It prevents us from seeing what is really at work in rural America, and it veils what has been hiding in plain sight.

CRISIS AND MYTH

Today the rural mind . . . begins to retake its earlier place
as the dominant American mind.

CHARLES MORROW WILSON, 1940

When we talk about rural America, we find ourselves caught between
the language of crisis and the language of myth.

The two languages mirror each other. We can measure a crisis by
how far it seems to carry us away from an imagined idea of normal—
that is, from a myth. John Brinckerhoff Jackson, one of our foremost
writers about landscapes, noted some time ago that when Americans
look at a particular landscape, we "tend to see it not as it is, with
its own unique character, but as a degenerate version of the traditional landscape." We look, Jackson asserted, and what we see is "a
long drawn-out backsliding."[1] Trapped in this circular discourse, we
haven't been able to see rural America as clearly as we ought to, and
we have been blindered to things as they are.

But we can think differently about the rural. We can sidestep the
tropes of crisis and myth by looking instead at how four of the major
forces that propel modern America have shaped rural spaces to the
same extent as they have formed the rest of the country, and especially since the end of World War II: militarization, industrialization,
corporatization, and suburbanization. These forces aren't discrete

or independent from one another, and there is considerable overlap among them. But we can see rural spaces and those who live in them more clearly if we look military bases, not family farms; national corporations, rather than Main Street shops. The rural world as it actually is rather than what we expect it to be.

But first I want to dispense with the ideas of crisis and myth.

No word has been used more consistently to describe rural America than *crisis*. And a perpetual sense of crisis has driven our attempts to understand and address what is going on in rural places in study after study, report after report, and policy prescription after policy prescription for at least a century. The DNA of that crisis has also been remarkably unchanging. Economic and social decline—"backsliding"—twine around each other to create a sense that something has gone wrong, whether in the 1880s, the 1930s, the 1980s, or today.

In recent years, opioid addiction has been the symbol of that ceaseless sense of rural crisis, and opioids have indeed wreaked a grim toll disproportionately in rural America. I live and work in rural Ohio, which can stake a claim to being the epicenter of the scourge, and I've had students squabble with a kind of gallows humor over which of their towns truly deserves the title "heroin heartland." Overdoses too numerous for rural health systems to handle have gone hand in glove with suicides, as rural Americans now take their own lives at significantly higher rates than those in metropolitan parts of the nation.[2] Suicide is a complicated, enigmatic phenomenon, but it appears that some combination of the very things that rural people extoll about rural life—the isolation, the perceived self-reliance, and the easy availability of guns—is precisely what makes suicide more common in those places.

The opioid crisis eclipsed the crystal meth crisis of just a few years earlier (at least, in the public imagination), but that, too, was a preponderantly rural phenomenon. According to one journalist, meth appeals to a "rural constituency because it's cheap, easy to manufacture at home, and requires no special equipment or expertise." Not for nothing has crystal meth been called "hillbilly cocaine."[3] As the national media covered those deaths of despair, to use the words of the economists Anne Case and Angus Deaton, and the rural communities torn apart by them, those stories also exposed anew an economic crisis.[4]

Routinely we hear that rural places have been "left behind," cut off from the rest of society by the lack of something—most recently, high-speed internet or adequate transportation networks.[5] Without these, they fail to attract jobs in our postindustrial and postagricultural "creative-class" economy. Pundits and policymakers wring their hands, whether looking at rural Kentucky or South Dakota or Nebraska, wondering if a lack of good jobs drives the young and the talented away from rural and small-town America, or does a lack of young talent keep the jobs away. Either way, the result is clear in the data: rural areas are getting older; rural areas are getting less education; rural areas continue to lose population. During the pandemic, COVID-19 infections and deaths replaced heroin overdoses on the front pages, exposing, yet again, the crisis of rural health care. Local and even regional hospitals have been closing in rural areas for some years—sometimes merged with larger facilities and sometimes not— all in the name of pursuing health-care "efficiencies," which efficiently leave more and more rural residents without access to an ER.[6] As a result of all that, rural America grows angrier at the rest of us.

All this despair and neglect, the accumulated suffering and hopelessness, boiled over with the election of 2016, we're told. Donald Trump channeled the anger and the fears and the frustrations of rural voters, who propelled him into the White House. Whether or not that narrative really explains the election results is beside the point. Rural America seemed to have become the kingmaker, and now the rest of the country had to sit up and take notice.

The problems are all real enough—the overdoses and the aging population and the abandoned storefronts along Main Street in so many small towns. But the word *crisis* is not, I think, the right one to use to describe all this suffering and sorrow. *Crisis* means a period of intense difficulty or challenge, like the Cuban Missile Crisis or Suez Crisis. It interrupts the normal state of affairs, and, most important, a crisis comes to an end, for better or for worse.

In this sense, rural America isn't in crisis today. Its condition is, more accurately put, chronic. Its history sounds a consistent refrain: rural America is in crisis, and something must be done about it! You can find those laments in the 1880s and in the 1980s and 2010s and in almost every decade in between. People have described rural America as being in a crisis of one sort or another almost continuously for nearly a century and a half.

The first version of the refrain came shortly after the Civil War, when the original Populist movement grabbed the nation's attention. Farmers, angry at an economic system they felt had ruined their livelihoods, organized themselves into a potent political force, especially in the midsection of the country. That crisis, in turn, generated the first national study of rural problems and the first set of proposals designed to address the rural crisis. President Theodore Roosevelt created the Country Life Commission in 1908, and its chair, Liberty Hyde Bailey, described the goal of the country life movement as "the working out of the desire to make rural civilization as effective and satisfying as other civilizations."[7] Implicit in that statement, of course, is that by the early twentieth century, "rural civilization" had somehow already been left behind.

By the time the commission issued its report in 1911, conditions in many rural places had gotten much better. Urban growth, and especially economic demand during World War I, drove up commodity prices for everything from Kansas wheat and Mississippi cotton to Kentucky coal and Oklahoma lead. But even high prices couldn't keep the kids down on the farm, and the crisis morphed from an economic one to a social one. Many commentators expressed shock and concern at the data from the census of 1910, which revealed that a significant number of rural counties had lost population, and those people who stayed were growing older. In one of these counties in Missouri, schoolchildren constituted 31 percent of the population in

1890; by 1910, that had dropped to 26 percent. The population of Bosworth, Missouri, founded in 1888 in the north-central part of the state, peaked in 1910 and has been declining ever since.[8]

Meanwhile, labor violence in rural mining regions had become distressingly common as miners found themselves beleaguered and abused and tried to fight back against large mining companies. Some of the names are familiar, others perhaps are not. Lethal violence erupted in all of them: Lattimer, Pennsylvania (1897), Virden, Illinois (1898), Paint Creek, West Virginia (1912), Ludlow, Colorado (1914), Matewan, West Virginia (1920), Herrin, Illinois (1922). The Country Life Commission wasn't much interested in these corners of rural America, and even today we don't necessarily think of the almost continuous violence and repression in mining country as a rural "crisis," because striking miners have not carried much rural resonance for us. Indeed, part of the problem of seeing rural America clearly stems from the fact that we tend to equate *rural* with *farm*, thus ignoring other kinds of rural places.[9] But we ought to acknowledge those miners. They were rural people in rural places, and their lives were as desperate as that of any Populist farmer.

Back on the farm, high commodities prices didn't last much longer than the Populist movement did. They collapsed after World War I, and agricultural America found itself in crisis again. During the interwar decades, the mechanization and consolidation of agriculture started in earnest. (It did so in mining as well. Employment in the nation's coal mines topped out in the 1920s and has been declining ever since.)[10] These changes in farming—from small scale to ever bigger, and reliant more and more on industrial technology—contributed to the fact that by 1940, nearly half of all farms in the country were tenant farms, up from 35 percent forty years earlier.[11] Thomas Jefferson, champion of the landowning yeoman farmer, was rolling over in his grave.

The Great Depression forced many Americans to confront poverty to an extent that they had never done before, and the New Deal responded, at least in part, with a dizzying number of programs to ameliorate it. In fact, though, many New Dealers—and President Franklin Roosevelt most of all—were concerned primarily with rural poverty. In 1935, the Works Progress Administration's Division of Social Research identified six "problem areas" in rural America: (1) the Appalachian-Ozark Area, (2) the Lake States Cut-Over Area, (3) the Spring Wheat Area, (4) the Winter Wheat Area, (5) the Eastern Cotton Belt, and (6) the Western Cotton Belt. Though there were commonalities across these regions, the researchers acknowledged that "each of the areas presents a distinctive set of social and economic problems which must be taken into consideration in planning a program of rehabilitation."[12]

This New Deal conceptualization did not claim to be comprehensive. The geographic regions marked in 1935 didn't include any of the rural areas west of the Rockies, nor did it look at the grinding poverty found across much of rural New England. Still, this six-part taxonomy reveals an assumption as true then as it is now. We conceive of rural in relation to how the land gets used, to the resources produced by it. Four of these six name specific and predominant crops—cotton and wheat—while the other two denote areas that had been logged over, mined to death, or both. *Rural* carries with it the expectation that people live and work more directly with the land than the rest of us.

Except that the connection between rural work and rural land was already fraying in the 1930s, and the pace of that fraying accelerated after World War II. Between 1950 and 1970, the total number of farms continued to decline, this time by roughly 50 percent, while the average size of a farm nearly doubled, from 205 to 400 acres. No surprise that the number of people living on farms declined from about twenty million to fewer than ten million during those two decades.[13] Then came the farm crisis of the 1980s, from which rural America—certainly agricultural America—has arguably never fully recovered. Profitability has gone up and down in agriculture (and in mining too), but the number of people who make their livelihood that way has only gone down—a trend observers started noting early in the twentieth century.

The semantics here matter. Describing rural America as in "crisis" implies, as I've suggested, that there was a normal, healthy, and stable situation from which we have deviated and to which we ought to return. But that, needless to say, raises the question of just when rural America was "normal." When, exactly, was rural America great? When the writer Dan Shaults returned to the small towns of his Missouri youth, he found them "uniformly drab." He acknowledged that "life wasn't beautiful" when he was growing up, but now those towns had collapsed "into ugliness of soul and body." He took that trip in 1962 and was looking back on the 1930s.[14] Like those mythological turtles, in our stories of rural America it seems to be declension all the way down.[15]

One could conclude that not only was rural America never the heart or the backbone or whatever other piece of the national anatomy, it has not been the mainstream of our national life for nearly two centuries. Certainly, the agricultural economy has been out of sync with the national economy more often than not since the end of the Civil War. The journalist Charles Morrow Wilson noted this as long ago as 1940 when he lamented, "We are beginning to realize that the United States is now out of step with the deliberate saunter of rural life."[16] Notice the nifty inversion: it is the majority of the country that is out of step. The word *saunter* is a nice touch too, implying that rural life is lived at a relaxed, easygoing, almost Thoreauvian pace, not the hurried, desperate rush with which, say, so many farm families fled the Grain Belt during the Great Depression.

The farm crisis of the late nineteenth century happened as the urban industrial economy boomed; the collapse of farm prices after World War I happened during what F. Scott Fitzgerald characterized as "the greatest, gaudiest spree in history."[17] The Depression certainly had a leveling effect on both urban and rural areas, but in the cities, things went from good to bad; in rural America, they went from bad to worse. Nearly four in ten residents of South Dakota—one of the most rural states in the union—went on New Deal relief during the Great Depression, the highest percentage in the nation.[18]

World War II revived both industry and agriculture, but afterward the pattern resumed. Farm country in particular did not enjoy the postwar boom to the same extent that the rest of suburbanizing, white-collar America did. In 1967, to take one data point, a presidential commission found that fourteen million rural Americans lived in poverty. "Rural poverty is so widespread," the commission wrote, "and so acute as to be a national disgrace."[19] The commission titled its report *The People Left Behind*, a phrase—and a phenomenon—that has echoed over the decades.

Conversely, during the stagflation years of the 1970s, while many Americans struggled with inflation and unemployment, some farmers did pretty well. Farm prices reached 71 percent of parity—an aspirational price for each commodity set by the USDA based on a complicated formula[20]—by 1979, driven by export demand and access to easy money. Both dried up after 1980. But during Ronald Reagan's go-go 1980s, when Ivan Boesky told us that greed was good, the farm economy tanked even as farmers continued to cheer Reagan himself. After helping to reelect Reagan to a second term, farmers became charity cases in 1985. Inspired by the Live Aid music festival to benefit Ethiopian famine victims, Willie Nelson co-organized Farm Aid to raise money for families losing their farms. The next year, farm prices dropped to 51 percent of parity—a level not seen in farm country since the depths of the Great Depression.[21] The Farm Aid project continues to this day. And the current rural crisis unfolded amid the longest economic recovery the nation has ever experienced.[22]

Crisis, then, simply won't do. What rural America has experienced over the last century and a half is the norm, sad though that may be. Far from being "real America," therefore, we might conclude that rural American life has increasingly been the outlier since the mid-nineteenth century, despite how many of us continue to believe otherwise. That unacknowledged contradiction, that yearning for a good ol' days, I think, lies at the heart of the way we have talked about rural America, a discourse that has alternated for decades between angry nostalgia and aggrieved despair. It still does.

As a student in one of my classes wonderfully put it, "Nostalgia is a dangerous drug." The nature of that nostalgia is what has trapped us in the language of crisis and decline. For many people, that nostalgia may be fixed to some very specific, local experience—a family farm lost to creditors, or the high school of one's youth closed for lack of enrollment. But at a larger cultural level, that nostalgia is for an imagined time and place, a projection of cultural desires and expectations. Rural decline must be measured against the image of what we have, at various moments, thought rural America ought to be, as much as against what it actually has been. Rural crisis is thus inextricably linked to our agrarian myths and pastoral ideals.

In 1955, Richard Hofstadter elaborated on the agrarian myth in his Pulitzer Prize–winning *The Age of Reform*. The hero of the myth, as he described it, was the Jeffersonian yeoman, who was considered "the ideal man and the ideal citizen." Living in "close communion with the beneficent nature," Hofstadter went on, gave the yeoman "wholesomeness" and "integrity" that could not be found among city dwellers. More than a way of life, the agrarian myth posited a moral proposition: rural life was essentially religious, as the yeoman was seen to be the "central source of civic virtue."[23]

But where did the myth come from? Not the small farms it extolled. "In origin," Hofstadter wrote, "the agrarian myth was not a popular but a literary idea, a preoccupation of the upper classes, of those who enjoyed a classical education, read pastoral poetry, experimented with breeding stock, and owned plantations or country estates."[24] Which is a pretty deft description of Thomas Jefferson himself, a founding father of the agrarian ideal.

There is a country mile between our rural mythologizing and rural reality, though it hasn't seemed to have mattered much to our public discussions. American pioneers and homesteaders, far from being anchored to the land like they were supposed to be, were restless and expansive and mobile, perhaps even more so in the nineteenth century than in the twentieth. Nor did they offer a virtuous bulwark against the rising tide of commercialism said to be corrupting American cities. Rural people were market oriented, commercially driven, and financially savvy from the very outset of the Republic. As the historian Christopher Clark has observed, in the early nineteenth century, farming "underpinned commercial and financial techniques essential to the rise of American capitalism." Farmers mortgaged their land to fund their own expansion, and farm mortgages quickly "became significant in the portfolios of banks, insurance companies, and other institutions."[25] As early as the 1870s, what we now call "mortgage-backed securities" emerged with farmland as the backing, and during the 1880s, 30–40 percent of homestead farmers—who got that land for free from the federal government, their paeans to self-sufficiency notwithstanding—were mortgaging their farms to raise more capital. And if Jefferson believed that freedom and liberty and the success of the Republic depended on (white) men farming their own land and the self-sufficiency that that would ensure, farmers themselves in the nineteenth century didn't quite behave that way. Instead, as Jonathan Levy has summed it up, "many farmers observed their rising incomes and land values, and with access to new financial forms of economic security, they happily proclaimed themselves 'independent.'"[26]

By the time Hofstadter wrote, myth had been turned into something like an ideology. In 1940, the Department of Agriculture announced, in yet another restatement of the agrarian ideal, that "the welfare of agriculture and of the Nation will be promoted by . . . efficient family-size owner-operated farms." Further, the USDA pledged to support "the establishment and maintenance of such farms." That report projected a future set of goals but also summed up what the USDA had already been doing. The Yale scholar A. Whitney Griswold soon noted that the "rugged individualists" of yeoman lore had become "one of the principal beneficiaries of government support. [The farmer] asked and received economic aid on an unprecedented scale." He concluded: "The Jeffersonian ideal has been translated into policy."[27]

Griswold and Hofstadter were among those who began to question the rural myth just after the Second World War. Driving from

Atlantic City to Chicago in the early 1950s, the writer May Watts noted: "The farms that had been bought up and absorbed into the wide fields that fitted the new machinery had usually left something to tell of their existence. Sometimes the foundation of the farmhouse and barn were still showing. . . . Sometimes the new owner had left the pump standing, or the cement stairs that had led up to the front porch. We watched hard for as many of these evidences as we could find, knowing that soon the powerful tractors will rebel at going around relics, and turn it all under and smooth it over for corn or soy beans. A way of life is past." At about the same moment, the historian Lewis Atherton counted 2,205 abandoned towns in the state of Iowa. "Contrary to nostalgic memory," he wrote, "[small towns] have lacked the stability, the changelessness, and the sense of continuity which people ascribe to them." What's more, those towns had been abandoned by 1930. What Atherton saw in those empty places was "a process as old as the town frontier itself."[28]

And yet the myth has persisted tenaciously. What began as a "literary idea" in the eighteenth and nineteenth centuries morphed in the twentieth into a fixture of mass media and popular culture. Publications such as the *Saturday Evening Post* along with nationally syndicated radio and television programming consistently presented rural life as idyllic—a healthy, simple life lived close to the soil and nearer to god. Newspapers printed columnists "who extol the virtues of ruralism" to their largely nonrural readers. The media might have been different, pastoral poetry replaced by TV's *Green Acres*, but the essential message remained the same, as did its intended audience. "The romanticization of rural life in press and radio," wrote the sociologists Arthur Vidich and Joseph Bensman in 1958, "reflects the need of the urban dweller to conceive of rural life as simpler and freer from the complexities, tensions and anxieties which he faces in his own world. Rural life is thus conceived as a counter-image which highlights his own situation."[29] That description nicely captures the appeal of "country music," which in recent decades has grown to be the most popular music genre in the nation. Peddling a perceived authenticity, country songs often tell tales of rural life that play exactly to the nostalgia and yearning—no matter how unearned—felt by the millions who consume them.

That view of the rural world has always been entirely white, at least in the white American imagination. From Jefferson's Platonic yeomen to the all-white cast of *The Andy Griffith Show*, Black, brown, and Asian people have had little place in America's rural mythologies, which, after all, have been projected onto a screen absent of Indigenous people in the first place. Their problems—Black land dispossession, working conditions for Mexican labor, endemic poverty on reservations, violence visited upon nonwhite rural people—are not, therefore, included much in this discourse of "crisis." When crack cocaine ravaged American cities in the 1980s, it was understood to be a "Black" drug and thus lawmakers created draconian drug laws resulting in mass incarceration. When opioids wreaked similar havoc on rural white communities, people have pleaded for compassion and called for expanded access to rehab services. Country musicians love to croon about truckers and farmers, but no one writes country songs celebrating the hardworking slaughterhouse worker from Central America.

The distance between what rural America is and what many wish it were continues to shape the very language we use to talk about these places and the dynamics that shape them. Take the word *farm* itself, for starters. It is basic to our conception of the rural, but I think it elides as much as it describes. It is an old word; strictly speaking, it refers to a piece of land on which crops and animals are raised. More imaginatively—and certainly by the nineteenth century—*farm* denoted a more or less self-sufficient productive unit with a homestead at its center, a kitchen garden next to it, animals raised for family consumption in a barn, and crops grown for market. Yoked to Jeffersonian notions of freedom, virtue, and citizenship, the word *farm* became freighted with our mythic and ideological conceptions of rural life. An American farm was not merely a productive unit. It was a way of life—the best way of life, in fact—and it has been venerated almost religiously.

That kind of farming disappeared more than half a century ago, at least. As one Illinois farmer described it: "General farming belongs to our past. . . . When I was a child, of course we had pigs, and put down the pork in brine for the winter, and of course we had chickens, and cows. . . . Orchards [were] plowed under to make room for more beans. That's what we grow now, soy beans and corn."[30] That was in 1957. Since then, of course, farming has only become more specialized, more mechanized, more dependent on chemical inputs. And bigger—much, much bigger. Farming, as it is practiced in the United States today, is more aptly described as industrial calorie production. To call 1,500 acres of corn, genetically modified to withstand harsh chemical pesticides and intended for a high-fructose corn syrup factory, a "farm" is a bit like calling a highly automated GM factory a "workshop."

But along the way, rural people, too, began to believe in the myth, even if it crashed up against their own realities. "Don't just focus on your urban areas," one rural resident scolded to an interviewer. "Focus on your rural areas where you still have strong morals and values."[31] Here, to take another example, is the University of Nebraska agriculture professor Terence Centner, who grew up on a farm: "Farmers tend to be friendly, healthy, honest, and hardworking. Farming is the most basic of occupations: humble, necessary, and worthy of support. Agriculture is like 'motherhood and apple pie'—it is America."[32] Or loopy politician-turned-reality-TV-star-turned-politician Sarah Palin, during the 2008 presidential campaign: "We believe that the best of America is in these small towns . . . what I call the real America."[33] That quip led to a small firestorm of outrage and critique, all of it richly deserved. Yet how different, really, was that gaffe from the remarks made by the political pundit and *New York Times* columnist David Brooks in a March 2019 column? After he had parachuted into Nebraska for about a week, visiting a few small towns, he concluded: "I keep going to places with more moral coherence and social commitment than we have in booming urban areas."[34] "Moral coherence" is simply a fancier version of "real America" and yet another rehash of a long-running and tired trope: small towns are filled with virtuous people bound in

social obligation to one another; cities are filled with atomized individuals living without any sense of "community" but desperate for it,
their fancy coffee beverages and ethnic eats notwithstanding. No one
has ever accused Brooks of being a profound thinker, and one almost
feels bad for him that he remains trapped in the morally incoherent,
socially alienated (and quite posh) neighborhood he lives in today.
Yet as of this writing, I do not believe he has sold his house in the DC
metro area and relocated to McCook, Nebraska.

Given how much rural areas are overrepresented politically, and
given how much federal policy has been focused on reviving rural
places, statements like those reveal a remarkable myopia. But even
more, they fail to acknowledge fundamental aspects of what drives
rural life. As one scholar has noted, people in rural communities have
continued to evoke "frontier images of close-knit communities," even
as they promote "the very forces that led and continue to lead to
their demise—free enterprise and corporate capitalism."[35] Squaring
that circle has forced all manner of mental gymnastics. Farmers may
have received considerable federal aid during the Great Depression
through a variety of New Deal programs, but that certainly didn't accord with their own sense of self-sufficiency and independence. So in
the postwar period, they simply pretended it never happened. Or, as
David Danbom has put it, they repressed their memories altogether:
"They were so successful that it is difficult today to find anyone in
rural communities who will admit that people in his or her family received relief during the 1930s."[36] Few in rural America today, I suspect,
want to acknowledge just how much federal subsidy they receive.

As is his habit, Brooks borrowed the idea of "moral coherence"
from sociologists, and in this particular case, probably from Robert
Wuthnow, who in turn borrowed it from Émile Durkheim. Wuthnow
insists that in the sociological sense "moral" does not denote "right"
or "good." Instead, as he writes, a moral community is "a place to
which and in which people feel an obligation to one another and to
uphold the local ways of being that govern their expectations about
ordinary life and support their feelings of being at home and doing
the right things."[37]

Except, apparently, at auctions during times of economic distress.

The picture of "moral communities" or, if you prefer, "moral co-herence" is hard to square with what the anthropologist Kathryn Marie Dudley found in western Minnesota in the aftermath of the farm crisis of the 1980s: "There is a serious disconnection between what we know and what we want to believe about farming as a way of life." In a hypercapitalist, globalized economy, "farmers find them-selves in direct competition with their neighbors," and more so than most Americans. That disconnect between image and reality was laid most bare when a family in the community lost their farm, and everything—land, equipment, outbuildings, even appliances—had to be auctioned off. "A forced sale can feel like a public flogging," Dud-ley writes movingly. Not to mention a deep source of shame, as your morally coherent neighbors come to pick over your stuff and haggle you down on prices, murmuring among themselves that you prob-ably overextended yourself at the bank or didn't handle your money properly.[38]

Having said all that, I've come to believe that rural America really does reflect what the nation has become, just not in ways we want to acknowledge, much less celebrate at the state fair. Rather than engage with the usual debates about rural America that tend to oscillate be-tween explaining rural decline and discovering rural resilience—two sides of the same coin, really—I want to explore how the transforma-tive forces in all of American life have played out in the spaces of rural America. Look past the narcotic nostalgia and the political rhetoric, and it is easy enough to see that rural spaces reflect the work of most of the major forces that have shaped twentieth-century America, especially after World War II. Rural spaces—whether agricultural, extractive, or the more recently tourist oriented—have always been at the center of and central to the nation's political economy, driven by the same relationships to capital and the same drives to profit as anywhere else. So in fact, far from being "left behind" by the march of the twentieth century, rural America has often been at the front of the national procession. Hardly sauntering along, rural Americans have more often than not been early adopters and enthusiastic embracers

of the major trends that have shaped American life since at least the
end of the Civil War.

I have divided this book into four sections, each of which deals
with one of the major forces of American modernity I mentioned
earlier—militarization, industrialization, corporatization, and
suburbanization—and sketches how each has shaped rural space, al-
ternating between high-altitude views and more fine-grained local
studies. Looking at these four big forces reveals that rural America
has never been immune from, resistant to, or otherwise left behind
in the mainstream of American life, though that is often the claim
(or lament) made by commentators and rural residents themselves.
Instead, I want to see rural America as having been shaped just as profoundly by that which shaped the rest of the nation as well. This is not
to say that the consequences have been the same. The experience of
those forces has been different from place to place—no question that
the geography of winners and losers has proved uneven. Indeed, the
economies of rural areas dependent on resource extraction—mining
and timber especially—might be said to suffer from the "resource
curse" that afflicts certain parts of the developing world: they generate great wealth that does little to make life better locally.[39] But I have
been struck over and over by how enthusiastically rural Americans
embraced these big forces and how often they cheered to bring them
to their own neck of the woods. In fact, rural America has been on the
leading edge of some of these transformations.

In this sense, wherever you find yourself in rural America, chances
are you are looking at a landscape thoroughly modern, and indeed often
high modern—in the developmental, planning, and architectural sense of
the term. In his hugely influential study of developing countries, James
Scott describes how nation-states alter rural landscapes in profound
ways to make them "legible" and thus easier to control.[40] Scott's analysis
can be usefully applied to rural American spaces, I think, which have
been reshaped for the purposes of political and economic development.

Some of this reshaping came from the federal government, though it
was resisted in the nineteenth century by Native peoples. But some of
it has come from the "market" and has been driven at the state or local

level. Either way, rural Americans have been entirely enmeshed in the development of American industry and capitalism, in the expansion of the military, and in the suburbanization of the nation as a whole. Further, long before Le Corbusier offered his vision of a modernist city, rationalized and detached from the past, Americans had turned rural space into precisely such built environments: relentlessly geometrical, employing the latest technologies, and severed almost entirely from the existing ecologies. Rural America is just as militarized, industrialized, corporatized, and suburbanized as the rest of the county. We haven't seen that because many of us don't quite want it to be true.

My purpose is not to offer policy remedies for what ails rural America, nor to issue any call for political action. Back in 1975, John Fraser Hart, himself a child of rural America, complained that because 75 percent of Americans now lived in metropolitan areas, "for many of us today the countryside is a strange, exotic, perhaps even frightening place." He went on: "We seldom bother to look at it as we whiz through it, which is unfortunate, because we have interest, affection and concern only for things we understand and appreciate."[41]

He was right. Many of us see what we want to see when we bother to look at rural America. Those places have become blank screens onto which we project any number of our own fantasies—about "morally coherent" communities, about simpler living away from the stresses of the contemporary world, about what it means to be somehow more authentically American. Those fantasies tell us much more about those who project them than about rural places themselves.

There is something important at stake here. As the historian Kristin Hoganson has noted about rural mythmaking: "No matter what competing purpose [the myth] has served, it has achieved the same result: exacerbating the fundamental challenge of comprehending the world by insisting on fixity instead of flux, insularity instead of interdependence."[42] My hope is that by seeing these spaces more clearly, we can have more productive conversations about the future of rural America. Far from being some differently paced alternative to the national mainstream, rural America is a pure product of this country. We need to understand it as such.

The Cold War happened here.

PART I

MILITARIZED SPACE

You suddenly come upon a succession of trailer camps
and garish trailer sales lots on both sides of the road . . .
an incongruous sight in all this empty countryside . . . the
inevitable chopping up of the countryside around the site
of a war plant.

RICHARDSON WOOD, 1951

I'm standing in front of a padlocked chain-link gate on Todd Road,
off Ohio State Route 27, staring at one of the ruins the Cold War left
behind.

The chain link encloses roughly 150 acres, though it's hard to take
that in, since those acres are so overgrown with a tangle of weeds,
vines, and bushes. Unkempt as it is, the site sticks out amid the highly
manicured farm fields that surround it. Behind that fence and for just
over a decade between 1959 and 1970, this property hosted three Nike
Hercules missiles, buried in concrete silos—a macabre inversion of
the grain silos that rise in the tidy fields nearby.

The Nike missile program began toward the end of the Second
World War as a defense against a new generation of military jets that
flew too high and too fast for anti-aircraft weapons to shoot down.
By the late 1950s, when this site—officially, CD-78—came online, the
mission for Nike had changed. The job of the Hercules class was to
intercept incoming nuclear-armed intercontinental ballistic missiles.
CD-78 was part of the "Cincinnati Defense Area," designed to protect
that city from Soviet attack. CD-78 is roughly forty-five miles from

Cincinnati in rural southwest Ohio and, as it happens, about three and a half miles from my history department office. The Cold War in the cornfields.

CD-78 is a very small example of an astonishingly large, long-running, and ongoing phenomenon: the military transformation—occupation?—of large swaths of rural America. It is a truism of American history that the process of westward expansion was first and foremost a military conquest as federal troops (and state militias) cleared the land of its Indigenous people. From the very beginning of the nation, therefore, much of we now call rural America was a militarized space. At the turn of the twentieth century, with Indian removal accomplished, the American military transformed from a frontier force into a modern institution commensurate with our new global ambitions, and it did so in rural places. Long before the Cold War—indeed, from the very beginning of the nation itself—rural American space was shaped by the military in almost every conceivable way.

The US Army Corps of Engineers (USACE) is perhaps the single most enduring piece of the American military. Cavalry on horseback have come and gone, and so too has the Nike program, but the corps, founded as its own entity in 1802, keeps rolling along. And if, as the adage goes, water always seeks its level, then the corps has sought out its level through water in its work across the American continent. Canals, dams, and levees; straightening and dredging—there is hardly a watershed anywhere in the country that does not bear the imprint of the USACE.

The corps' history is so vast and so long, and the challenges of researching it sufficiently enormous, that it would take at least an entire volume to do it justice. Further, the effects of the corps' projects extend so far beyond the location of specific dams or sluiceways that attempting an account of their geographic and environmental impacts is similarly daunting.[1] But I have tried to give some sense of its immense influence in molding rural America by looking at a few specific episodes, including the Kinzua Dam project in remote northwestern Pennsylvania that flooded ten thousand acres of Seneca Nation land in New York.

The following two chapters are case studies of military bases and the impacts they have had on the rural locales into which they were dropped by the Department of Defense. They're useful to compare and contrast: One located in the South, the other in the North; one whose history is rooted in the Second World War, the other in the Cold War. One remains in operation; the other closed at the end of the twentieth century. Both have had profound effects on the rural communities that surround them.

Fort Hood started its life in the scrub country in the central part of the state preparing soldiers to fight in World War II. It has grown now into one of the two or three largest army bases in the country. Along the way, Fort Hood reshaped this rural corner of Texas profoundly. Put briefly, an agricultural area populated by Czech, German, and southern-descended farmers has become dependent on the military for jobs and economic growth. On the northern edge of the country, the air force opened Sawyer Base, part of the Strategic Air Command, in Michigan's Upper Peninsula and it is the subject of chapter 3. The air force used the UP to project Cold War power toward the Soviet Union, making this sparsely populated place a front line in that global struggle. When Sawyer arrived, it helped stimulate a region that once depended on logging and mining but which was in steep economic decline. Jobs, local purchasing contracts, people—all came to the area around Marquette along with the base. Then the Cold War ended and Sawyer was closed, leaving behind a set of facilities but taking away all of that economic activity. Those Yoopers, as the residents of the Upper Peninsula are sometimes called, who remained have struggled to reinvent a future absent of the air force.

Both bases also illustrate the extent to which the nation as a whole, but rural places in particular, have become addicted to the military. The money is the most obvious cause of it, as are the jobs that flow from it both directly and indirectly. While the footprint of the American military has spread over vast areas of the rural space, in recent decades that physical proximity has also conditioned who joins the military, who supports it, and the politics of rural people more broadly. But I am hard pressed to think of another country that still calls itself a democracy that has made as much of a fetish of its military as this one. In this sense, the military is a source of national identity, and that is particularly true in rural places.

Up on Todd Road, CD-78 sits as a small example of the military presence in rural America, but it is typical and simply one of roughly five thousand abandoned defense sites, most of them in rural areas.[2] In 1958, the Defense Department seized several tracts of land here, including those owned by Opal and Homer Tingle. They were paid in "fee simple" for their land. After the missiles were removed, the Defense Department leased about half the property to my employer, Miami University, which purchased it outright in 1999. That land was the "launcher" area of the 150 acres—including those three concrete missile silos. Those, in turn, have over the years filled up with two million gallons of water contaminated with vinyl chloride and trichloroethene. Nothing to worry about in the groundwater, officials have assured everyone, as long as the water stays in those silos. And so in 2004 the Army Corps of Engineers announced a cleanup plan it called "monitored natural attenuation." All for a price of nearly $1 million. The Cold War isn't entirely over in this corner of rural Ohio.[3]

CHAPTER 1

ENGINEERING
THE LANDSCAPE

On July 7, 1919, a convoy of eighty-one vehicles and nearly three hundred men left Washington, DC, on a great American road trip. More than three thousand grueling miles later, on September 7, the group arrived in San Francisco, having averaged just fifty-two miles per day in large part because the roads would not permit the vehicles to move any faster.

The road trip had an official name: the First Transcontinental Army Motor Transport Expedition. The vehicles included light and heavy trucks, two mobile machine shops, and one mobile blacksmith shop. The travelers were all army personnel—24 officers and 258 enlisted men. It set a distance record for an army convoy, smashing the previous one held by a group that had traveled from Chicago to New York. Those who took part had some sense that they had done something truly significant. The trip was "the first motor convoy to cross the American continent, comparable in its sphere, to the first ox-team prairie-schooner trek; the first steam railroad train, and the first airplane flight across the vast expanses of fertile valleys, rolling prairie, rugged mountains, and desolate wilderness that lie between the Atlantic and Pacific Oceans."[1]

After departing from Lafayette Square in the nation's capital, the convoy made it as far as Frederick, Maryland, on its first day—a trek of about forty-five miles. There it picked up another passenger, Lt. Col. Dwight Eisenhower, who had spent World War I training tank crews. Memories of the trip stuck with him, so the story goes, and seeded the idea of an interstate highway system in his imagination. As president, Eisenhower made the Federal Highway Act of 1956 his signature domestic accomplishment.

That story is probably true as far as it goes, but Eisenhower was certainly not alone in imagining a nation crisscrossed with new roads. The Lincoln Highway Association—what we might call today a lobbying organization—saw the convoy as the first official support it had received from the federal government, and the "Good Roads" movement of the 1920s made use of the convoy's travails to promote a national road-building agenda. George Kissel was among those who hoped the convoy would leave a trail of paved roads in its wake. "I think that every good roads association in every city, town, and village through which this truck train will pass," he pronounced, "should use the event as a big publicity feature, pointing out to the local people the urgent necessity of reconstructing their roads and building new ones."[2] That might have been a tad self-serving, since Kissel was president of the Kissel Motor Car Company and good roads surely meant bigger sales. Still, the urgency was real—that fifty-two-mile-per-day average reflected road conditions that oscillated between bad and worse, especially in the trans-Mississippi West. In fact, the convoy arrived in San Francisco six days behind schedule. The army also promoted good roads in its publicity for the trip. A War Department release announced that the convoy would "demonstrate to the nation the inestimable value of a system of national highways."[3]

But promoting asphalt was decidedly not the army's primary purpose when the convoy hit the road. The First Transcontinental Army Motor Transport Expedition was a military mission first and foremost. "The principal objectives of the expedition," according to the official report filed by Captain William Greany, "were to service-test the special-purpose vehicles developed for use in the first World War, not all of which were available in time for such use; and to determine by actual experience the possibility and problems involved in moving an army across the continent."[4] Those "vast expanses" in Iowa and Nebraska and Wyoming, in other words, were seen by the army as a great proving ground for its motorized military technologies.

The report makes the expedition sound a lot like a war-games exercise, downright chilling in its descriptions. The task, in the army's view, was to see how to move an army across the United States "assuming that railroad facilities, bridges, tunnels, etc. had been damaged or destroyed by agents of an Asiatic enemy." And indeed, "the expedition was assumed to be marching through enemy country and therefore had to be self-sustaining throughout."[5]

At the same time, the Transcontinental Army Motor Transport Expedition was an opportunity—with the First World War just concluded and with regrets about it already growing—for the military to make a great public show of itself. Three miles of military vehicles snaking their way single file across the continent would provide "a spectacle of military efficiency," according to the War Department, and would demonstrate to the public that "from a military standpoint the necessity of good ocean-to-ocean highways is incalculable."[6]

That the army could conceptualize much of the space between Washington and San Francisco as a military zone—"enemy country"—should not be altogether surprising. From the very outset, Euro-Americans saw what they considered the "frontier" as essentially militarized space. The trans-Appalachian West was "opened up" to settlement through the distribution of so-called military bounty lands. Congress designated these tracts of land as bonuses to veterans of the Revolutionary War. It went without saying that the Native peoples who lived there already would have to yield that land either by coercive treaty or by military conquest. Westward, the course of empire may have taken its way, but only after the frontier had been controlled and pacified by military force. Reminders of the nineteenth-century military presence dot the landscape still and shape the militarization of much of rural America. Fort Leavenworth was established in 1827, for example, at the intersection of the Santa Fe and Oregon Trails in order to protect settlers moving west.[7] By World War I, it stood as the largest army base in the country. In fact, many urban centers in the area between the Appalachians and the Sierras started as military installations—from Pittsburgh (Fort Pitt) to Minneapolis–St. Paul (Fort Snelling) to Laramie (Fort Laramie), Wyoming—all positioned to project American military power at and toward Native populations. In this sense, much of the United States has been viewed as "enemy country" by the federal government from the very beginning.

Yet even before the modern constellation of military bases had been created or even imagined, the army had already been hard at work reshaping the American continent in ways so profound that its work often hides from us in plain sight. Given the extent and scale of that work, "conquest" does not seem too much of an exaggeration, though the agents of that conquest weren't cavalry units or militias. They were engineers.

The United States Army Corps of Engineers proudly dates its own history to 1775, before there was a United States. More formally, the need to create an army engineering corps became the central rationale when Thomas Jefferson authorized the establishment of West Point in 1802. Sylvanus Thayer, the "father of West Point," didn't arrive until 1817, when President James Monroe appointed him superintendent. That appointment came after Thayer had spent two years in France studying French methods of military training, especially at the École Polytechnique. Much impressed, he brought back some French military men and French organizational ideas with him and refashioned West Point in a Parisian image—our own piece of Napoleonic bureaucracy on the banks of the Hudson.

Almost from the beginning, the corps took on civilian as well as military duties. And at the risk of hopelessly oversimplifying, here's a summary of the thrust of the corps civilian work: for roughly the first half of its history, the Army Corps of Engineers spent its energy trying to get America's water to flow more beneficially; for roughly the second half, it has worked to stop the water from flowing.

In 1824, seven years after Thayer took over at West Point, Congress authorized surveys to plot new roads and canals, and it passed an act to facilitate shipping on the Ohio and Mississippi Rivers by clearing out sandbars as well as trees growing in those rivers and other such impediments. Congress made the corps responsible for carrying out those tasks. As it fixed its gaze across the trans-Appalachian West, the corps saw that vast expanse as an endless set of engineering problems—natural barriers and limitations to be overcome in order to make remote places traversable and navigable. Plotting canals and clearing "snags" foreshadowed the much larger ship channel and river dredging project the corps would undertake in subsequent decades as it worked to turn the natural features of the landscape into rational handmaidens of water-based commerce. The Panama Canal, completed in 1914 under the supervision of the corps, stands as the most spectacular, arrogant example of that impulse, quite literally cutting North and South America apart. These projects undertaken during the long nineteenth century marked the beginning of the military-engineering complex.

Then, in 1927, the Mississippi River flooded, calamitously. As many as five hundred people were killed by the raging water; five hundred thousand wound up displaced. Memphis Minnie got the song "When the Levee Breaks" out of it in 1929 (and Led Zeppelin got an even bigger hit out of *that* decades later). Congress initiated what has become the Mississippi River and Tributaries Project in 1928 and made the corps responsible for constructing a vast system of outlets, levees, and floodways across the Mississippi River drainage area, a land mass approximately 40 percent of the continental United States. Congress then decided, in 1936, to make flood control a federal issue, and it put the Army Corps of Engineers in charge of making all of America's water behave.

The corps certainly continued to channel water, to straighten rivers, but as often as not "flood control" involved building dams. In fact, Congress put the corps in charge of supervising private dam construction as early as the 1890s. Two federal acts required the corps to approve any significant dam project lest it hinder navigation. In addition to controlling water flow, dams can also be used to generate electricity, and so the corps promoted its work as protecting property from angry water and providing cheap electricity at the same time. When Congress created the Tennessee Valley Authority in 1933, it relieved the USACE of flood-control responsibilities along the Tennessee River (though the corps was still responsible for the water of the Cumberland). Ten years later, even as World War II occupied the nation, the Roosevelt Administration created a vast project to control the Missouri River. Known as the Pick-Sloan Plan, and ironed out at a conference in Omaha in 1944, the project called for more than 100 dams, 1,500 miles of levees, nearly 5 million acres of irrigated land, and 1.6 million kilowatt-hours of electricity. The corps was put in charge of all that. As Bernard DeVoto described it, the corps "have converted the Missouri's bends into frictionless drawing-board curves, they have made the river an instrument to control itself and co-operate with the human race, they have just about drawn its fangs from Kansas City on." As of this writing, the corps owns and operates nearly 750 dams across the country and Army Corps dams generate one-quarter of the nation's hydropower, an amount equal to 4.4 percent of all electrical output.[8]

The USACE exists in a curious bureaucratic matrix. On the one hand, it has been part of the US Army since its founding and is directly under the army's supervision. On the other, because Congress has charged the corps with large domestic responsibilities and appropriates the money for those projects, the corps deals with Congress directly and regularly to a greater extent than most other military units. Perhaps as a consequence of this betwixt-and-between arrangement, the corps operates with remarkably little oversight, accountability, or regard for public opinion, at least according to its critics. It dammed, channeled, dredged, and diverted wherever it wanted, and money was never any object. Wisconsin Senator Gaylord Nelson quipped during a 1970 Senate hearing: "The Corps of Engineers is like that marvelous little creature the beaver, whose instinct tells him every fall to build a dam wherever he finds a trickle of water. But at least he has a purpose . . . at least he doesn't ask the taxpayer to foot the bill."[9]

The cost overruns have become so extravagant and so routine that they now amount to another cherished army tradition. A few examples suffice to make the point: Construction began on the massive Chief Joseph Dam across the Columbia River in 1949 with a congressional allocation of $104 million. By 1966, the cost had risen 39 percent, to $145 million, and the project would not be fully completed until 1979. The Bull Shoals Dam across the White River in Arkansas was in some ways a quintessential corps project. It promised flood control to a region plagued by flooding and hydroelectricity to an underdeveloped part of the country. Quintessential, too, in its costs. Congress appropriated $40 million for the dam in 1947; it wound up spending over $88 million on the project—122 percent more than the corps had initially promised. Flood control again was the primary impetus to build the Whitney Dam in Texas, south of Dallas–Fort Worth. Authorized originally in 1941, the project had to wait until after the war to get under way. The corps asked Congress for roughly $8.5 million in 1947 and spent $41 million by the time the ribbon was cut. That's an overrun of a staggering 391 percent. No wonder the *Nation* characterized the corps as "the oldest established permanent floating boondoggle in American politics."[10]

In addition to the budget-busting costs, there were also complaints about the imperious way the USACE simply marched into an area and did what it wanted with little regard for the locals. In a 1952 editorial in the thoroughly middlebrow, middle-of-the-road *Saturday Evening Post*, Elmer Peterson protested that the corps had overstepped its jurisdiction and expertise by building dams, and creating reservoirs, on smaller rivers and creeks, often displacing people and flooding farmland as a consequence. "Usurpation of civilian prerogatives," Peterson called it and railed that "the Corps is invading the creek-dam field."[11] *Invading* was a nice choice of word and may well have captured the sense some farmers felt as the Army Corps rolled into their area.

One of the projects Peterson listed as an example of this usurpation was found in northeast Kansas, where the USACE proposed to put a dam across Tuttle Creek; this would flood fifty-five thousand acres of Kansas farmland behind it and put an end to what Peterson cited as $6 million of agricultural production ($62 million in 2020 dollars) while displacing several hundred farm families. To be clear, farmers in the Blue Valley wanted some kind of water retention built, and the disastrous flooding of 1951 only amplified the urgency of those demands. But the corps arrived with its own plan, utterly indifferent to the desires or experiences of the local farmers. The locals, having been ignored, mobilized to fight the mighty corps and succeeded initially in delaying the start of construction for two years. In the midst of that fight, James Robinson, writing in a Kansas newspaper, reduced the whole issue to its plaintive essence: "Is it selfish for a man to love his home and seek to preserve it?"[12] After several years, the farmers lost and it was probably a foregone conclusion. The dam was built and water started backing up ten years later; with it, four small Kansas towns disappeared from the map. By 1965, the Army Corps acquired more than sixty thousand acres of land from more than 1,700 individual owners through purchase and condemnation.[13] The USACE does not make a habit of losing fights over who controls the water and the surrounding land.

For its part, the corps defended itself by insisting that it only did what Congress told it to do—overlooking, perhaps, the question of whether the engineers went looking for projects first and then pliant politicians to sponsor them second. By the 1960s, the criticism of the corps began to increase. In the spirit of that moment, people began to assail the corps for its high-handed, cavalier, and thoroughly undemocratic way of imposing its projects whether people wanted them or not, and for being largely indifferent to, or obtuse about, the environmental damage all those dams were causing. The thrust of this new critique was captured nicely in a 1971 history of the Corps of Engineers titled *Dams and Other Disasters*.

Arthur Morgan was ninety-three years old when he wrote that book, and he knew a thing or two about building dams. He was brought to Dayton, Ohio, after the 1913 flood that nearly wiped that city off the map to design a comprehensive flood-control system for the Great Miami River watershed. Roughly twenty years later, he was chosen by Franklin Roosevelt to be the inaugural chair of the board of the Tennessee Valley Authority. He spent many of the subsequent years thinking about small towns and utopian experiments and small-*d* democracy. Toward the end of his life his attention returned to dams.

Dams and Other Disasters is really an indictment presented as history and argued through a set of case studies across roughly 150 years of the corps' history. And Arthur Morgan was a hydrological engineer, not a journalist, so much of the book is spent discussing those sorts of details. But he was a humanist and a moralist of sorts too, so the corps' pattern of wastefulness and bad planning offended his professional expertise as well as his rectitude. Several times in the book, Morgan blames West Point itself for the corps' failings. Trained as army officers first and last, the corps was thus steeped in "the destructive process of war, rather than constructive process of peace."[14] As the single largest entity involved in civilian public works projects, the Army Corps of Engineers looked at the nation's waterways—indeed, whole watersheds—as hostile territory to be conquered and controlled.

No surprise, in Morgan's view, that the corps had neither the expertise nor, frankly, any interest in what he called "environmental values." The corps' "lack of vision and imagination," baked into it from its very founding, simply made it impossible for them to even consider "ecological balance in their many projects across the country." The corps might now find itself under more public pressure from an energized environmental movement, but Morgan was under no illusion that this would "suddenly dissipate the century-long insensitivity."[15]

And I think it is fair to say that with the possible exception of the Homestead Act, no other federal enterprise has transformed the landscape of the nation, and rural spaces in particular, more than the US Army Corps of Engineers. From the canals they plotted in the early nineteenth century to the dam projects they built in the second half of the twentieth, there are few watersheds anywhere in the country that have not been altered by the corps' work. Thanks to the corps, as Nathaniel Rich has written, the Mississippi River "in its current form is less river than a highly engineered shipping canal."[16] Theirs has been a vision of conquest and control as they have gazed across the continent, one in which nature could and would be bent to human desire. Only under such a gaze could one imagine a major shipping port in Tulsa, Oklahoma—but there it sits, in the middle of a dry and landlocked state, courtesy of the Army Corps of Engineers.

The full measure of that transformation is difficult to take, in part because the corps itself does not keep centralized records. But consider these examples to get some sense of the wholesale scope of environmental change: When the corps built the Chief Joseph Dam on the Columbia River (mentioned above), it created a "lake" (called Rufus Woods Lake) that extends a full fifty-one miles behind the dam. Likewise, the Whitney Dam in Texas backed up water that covers thirty-seven square miles. Indeed, there are "lakes"—artificial reservoirs—all across what John Wesley Powell called the semiarid regions of the country. The corps has fundamentally altered the natural and therefore social ecology all over the country.

The ecological transformations brought on by these projects have also brought social and economic transformations. Hydropower enabled industrial and residential development in certain corners of rural America that might otherwise have remained sparsely populated. Irrigation projects made deserts bloom. Tourists across the country flock to all those artificial lakes for varieties of recreation. Texas, by one estimate, had exactly one natural lake before the dam-building bonanza. Now lake fishing, boating, and lakefront property development are important parts of local Texas economies.[17]

The Michael J. Kirwan Dam and Reservoir in rural Portage County, Ohio, resulted from another Army Corps project in the mid-1960s when it dammed the West Branch of the Mahoning River. The corps marched to exactly the same drummer as it always had: land purchased; landowners evicted if they wouldn't sell; houses and farm buildings demolished. There doesn't seem to have been any particularly urgent flood-control imperative behind the project. Instead, as the writer Scott Sanders has described it, the reservoir has "provided owners of loud boats with another playground for racing and water-skiing." That playground submerged Sanders's childhood—a small valley with a modest river running through it and rich bottomland soil that was still being farmed by horses when Sanders played in it in the 1950s. As he paused to consider the loss of a childhood now "drowned," he noted that the corps, in order to prevent occasional flooding in the future, had created a permanent flooding over his memories.[18] The elegy he wrote about this tiny place in rural Ohio might well capture the feelings many have had about rural landscapes where the USACE has done its work.

It isn't just rural tourism and vacation houses, of course, that have benefited from the USACE's relentless controlling of American water. Any number of cities and towns exist in their present form only because flood-control projects built by the corps make those areas habitable. Likewise, American agriculture across much of the trans-Mississippi West is made possible only by irrigation using water made available through corps projects. Given how extensively the corps has reengineered American watersheds, one is hard pressed to find too many rural spaces that haven't, in the end, been altered by the Army Corps of Engineers.

The costs of all those projects, and not just their dollar figures, are harder to tally. The corps is quick to publicize the money it believes dam projects have saved in the form of flood damage avoided, but to call that math speculative is charitable. Like the land behind the dam walls, however, the costs of the environmental degradation and social dislocation that have often accompanied the dams remain submerged by the corps. As Sanders put it as he stared out at the reservoir, "No effort of mind could restore the river or drain the valley. I surrendered to what my eyes were telling me. Only then was I truly exiled."[19]

The Army Corps of Engineers insisted that it wanted to protect Pittsburgh from flooding when it proposed a dam across a stretch of the Upper Allegheny River, in a remote part of northwestern Pennsylvania. It began to move forward with that project in 1956. It was less forthcoming about the lake that would be created behind the

dam. That water would stretch up into New York and flood roughly
ten thousand acres owned by the Seneca Nation, forcing approximately six hundred people to move. That implicit land grab also violated a treaty George Washington had negotiated with the Seneca
Nation in 1794.

Among his case studies of the Army Corps' intransigence and in-
competence, Arthur Morgan took this one personally. Shortly after
the plan was announced publicly, Morgan got a phone call from Cor-
nelius Seneca, president of the Seneca Nation. He was looking for help
and hoped Morgan could give it to him. For his part, Morgan had not
heard about the dam project, nor did he "know of the existence of
the Seneca Nation."[20] But perhaps because the two men shared Quak-
erism in common, Morgan agreed to help. That Quaker connection
may also have helped convince the American Friends Service Committee in Philadelphia to turn the dam into a national cause. The Treaty
of 1794 Committee mobilized opposition to the project through the
newspapers, lobbying efforts, and a public vigil on the site. The committee's members came to include Bayard Rustin and A. J. Muste.[21]

As he dug into it, Morgan became convinced that the Kinzua Dam
was needlessly expensive and would not solve the problem it was intended to solve. In fact, he concluded, the dam offered "the prospect
of a waste of more than a hundred million dollars in the plans of the
Corps."[22] And then, having completed his study, he severed his ties
to the tribe. He wanted to fight the project as an independent agent
without being accused of acting only on the tribe's behalf. And he did
indeed design an alternative flood-control plan for this area of the
Upper Allegheny, one that he believed would be cheaper and more
effective.

Seneca leaders and their allies had hoped that the new US president, John Kennedy, would put a halt to the dam while alternative
ways of controlling the Upper Allegheny could be explored. Shortly
after Kennedy's inauguration—in fact, on Washington's birthday—the
new Seneca president, Basil Williams, sent an imploring letter to Kennedy reiterating the tribe's position that if there were no other viable

alternative to the Kinzua Dam, the tribe would "abandon [their] op-position," but insisting that Morgan's alternative had not been given fair consideration.[23] In June 1961, Eleanor Roosevelt wrote a column about the dam that ran in a number of newspapers and called the ab-rogation of the 1794 treaty "a shameful thing."[24] The *New York Times* chimed in with an editorial praising the Quakers for tweaking the conscience of the nation, supporting their request for an impartial body to evaluate the dam, and insisting that "Congress must, in all conscience, recognize the treaty rights of the Seneca Nation."[25]

The campaign to halt the dam even linked it to Kennedy's Cold War agenda. In an editorial on April 8, 1961, the *Washington Post* tried to chastise Kennedy for ignoring the Seneca by writing that he needed to make clear "that the United States will in the future treat its own mi-norities with the same scrupulous respect that it repeatedly urges on Mr. Khrushchev." The literary critic Edmund Wilson asked pointedly, "For whatever the difference in scale, is there any difference in prin-ciple between uprooting whole communities of well-to-do Russian farmers and shipping them off to the Urals, and depriving the Senecas of the use of their lands in such a way as to shatter the republican unit and telling this intelligent and capable people to go and find homes where they can?" Some politicians, such as Pennsylvania Senator Jo-seph Clark, were not amused.[26]

In the end, Morgan lost. As he presented his alternative plan to various players involved, he succeeded in stalling construction of the corps' project a little. But he was an engineer, not a politician, and outflanked by the corps in Congress. Though Morgan was promised an "impartial" comparison of the two projects, Congress never au-thorized it.[27] On August 9, 1961, Kennedy finally responded to Wil-liams, informing him "that it is not possible to halt construction of the Kinzua Dam currently underway." After all, Kennedy wrote, he had been assured by the Army Corps that it had vetted all possible alternatives, including Morgan's.[28] The dam was operational by 1965.

The Senecas, of course, lost more. They believed that the Treaty of Canandaigua, signed by President George Washington and ratified in

1794, protected their property rights. In 1959, a federal district court thought otherwise.[29] It was the era of Native Termination, after all, when official federal policy aimed to end Native nationhood altogether. With the dam almost complete, the Seneca negotiated for money to relocate the people whose homes were about to be submerged. As a final insult, the federal government insisted that the Seneca submit a plan for their own termination in order to receive the money.

Those six hundred people inhabited nine villages, all burned down once the people had been removed. Among them were fluent speakers of the Seneca language, older people who spoke the language at home with their children and grandchildren. The creation of the lake thus took a significant toll on the language and therefore on Seneca culture writ large. Stephen Gordon grew up in one of the villages eliminated by the project. He sees 1964 as a turning point where the Seneca Nation was forced to leave "our past behind."[30]

In fact, we might see the Army Corps of Engineers as an integral part of the Termination Era for Native Americans. The Kinzua Dam was by no means the only one the corps put up that resulted in the destruction of Native land and in displacement of Native people. Congress authorized the Garrison Dam on the Missouri River in North Dakota toward the end of World War II. The Three Affiliated Tribes, whose land the corps intended to flood, were informed of the project only in 1946. The corps broke ground the following year, and when the dam topped off, 155,000 acres of Native land now sat under water. Everyone living on those acres had to be relocated.

And relocating those affected by their projects was not something that interested the corps very much. North Dakota Congressman William Lemke found himself baffled and angry in testimony he submitted before the House in 1949. He had assumed, he said, that when the federal government took land from people, it would do fairly and offer "just compensation" for it. Disabused of that notion now, Lemke went on: "The real estate division of the Army Engineers Corps did not understand what was meant by just compensation. In place of decency and justice, I discovered that they used the bulldozing and threat methods."[31]

And nowhere were those bulldozers busier than across Indian Country. The Painted Rocks Reservoir, authorized in 1950 as part of the corps' larger plan for controlling the Colorado River Basin, necessitated flooding the Papago village of Sil Murk. A small place, to be sure—roughly twenty families, and they were not in a position to mount much opposition. Instead, in 1959 they struck an agreement that they would move into a new village constructed "at the expense of the Corps of Engineers, in accordance with construction plans submitted by the Engineers, which have been examined and approved by the residents of Sil Murk." Imagine the surprise, then, when the Papago learned that the corps had communicated directly to the Arizona congressional delegation that it had no authority to carry out the plan as it had promised. In a letter to the Papago, the corps called this bait and switch a "misunderstanding." Congress finally sorted out this mess through legislation in August 1964. By that time, the dam had already been completed, leaving the Papago homeless and floating in a Kafkaesque bureaucratic limbo.[32]

There is a grim symmetry in the story of the Kinzua Dam. The military assault on Native America, what turned "wilderness" into "rural" in the first place, began in earnest almost immediately after the creation of the United States, and it lasted for a century. In the twentieth century, the USACE replaced the army itself in taking land, violating treaties, and displacing Native people. In the case of the Seneca, what the US Army did not do to them in the nineteenth century, the US Army Corps of Engineers did in the twentieth. The corps' website boasts that the Kinzua Dam has saved $1.2 billion in flood damage averted. It makes no mention of the Seneca Nation at all.[33]

FROM RURAL COMMUNITY TO ARMY TOWN

It does not exaggerate too much to say that the transformation from "frontier" or "wilderness" to "rural" in the nineteenth century was, at its root, a military one. Certainly Lt. Col. Hunter Liggett saw it this way. With the exception of the Mexican and Civil Wars, he wrote in 1912, "the army for three quarters of a century found little reason for existence except in the Indian struggles that filled the period."[1] The Francis E. Warren Air Force Base, just west of Cheyenne, stakes a claim to be the oldest continuously operating military post in the country. It was established by Congress in 1862 when Congress authorized the transcontinental railroad. Its purpose was to provide military protection for railroad workers against "hostile Indians." Fort Russell, as it was originally named, opened in 1867.

As a consequence of this history, Liggett pointed out, army bases remained scattered through rural, often remote parts of the nation. "The army was thus mainly left in the most sparsely populated sections of the country," Liggett told readers of the *Independent*, "in the neighborhood of the towns that had become accustomed to the presence of troops, and liked them no doubt, for the life and color they helped provide, but also for the commercial benefit the troops meant to the community."[2] In a rapidly industrializing and urbanizing society, Liggett worried, this geographical legacy had created an army fundamentally alienated from the growing centers of American population and thus from the mainstream of American life, and he called for military bases to be relocated to major cities. That didn't happen (though naval yards, especially on the East Coast, were located in big cities such as Boston, Brooklyn, and Philadelphia). But Liggett did inadvertently predict a central fact of the twentieth century: as the American military grew in size, it had a disproportionate impact on rural places; those places, in turn, disproportionately depended on the military for their prosperity, and even for their identity.

Nowhere has this proved to be the case more than in the post–Civil War South. Federal troops occupied the defeated Confederacy, however briefly, in order to ensure an orderly postwar transition and to ensure the rights of newly freed African American citizens. The apartheid regime of Jim Crow emerged as those federal troops pulled back, and by the end of the nineteenth century, the New South had been built solidly on a racially segregated foundation.

Almost immediately, however, the army (and the marines and eventually the air force) came back to the South. As racial segregation hardened across the South, and as the military conquest of the West had been more or less completed, a new generation of army installations appeared around the country and particularly in the old Confederacy. Marines first landed at Parris Island, South Carolina, in 1891; twenty years later, it became the place where new recruits arrived to receive their training. Just over the South Carolina border, the army built Camp—later Fort—Gordon during the First World War. Fort Bragg, in North Carolina, began its life as a field artillery site founded just as the First World War came to an end. In a perverse "we beat them so now let's join them" gesture, Forts Bragg and Gordon are both named after Confederate generals. John Brown Gordon was a slave-holding plantation owner before the war who very likely became involved with Georgia's Ku Klux Klan afterward. Indeed, as

I write this, ten military installations, Forts Bragg and Hood among them, are still named after Confederate generals—yet another example of the rapid journey these men took from traitorous villains to venerated "heroes."[3] Just as the military found its primary raison d'être in the "Indian struggles" of the nineteenth century, so too the growth of the modern military was intertwined with Jim Crow.

If you had to pick one spot on the map where the South meets the West, you could do no better than Bell County, Texas. Roughly halfway between Dallas and Austin, Bell County sits on a climatological line that separates the east Texas cotton fields from the drier grain fields and cattle ranches to the west. When the county was officially organized in 1850, it was inhabited by six hundred white settlers and sixty enslaved Africans. Railroad development in the late nineteenth century connected Bell County agriculture with national markets, which, in turn, drew more migrants. Between 1880 and 1910, the population of the county roughly doubled, to nearly fifty thousand. During those thirty years, emigrants from the South had been joined by Czech and German immigrants. The vast majority of those people lived rural lives.

In 1945, the anthropologist Oscar Lewis spent eleven weeks in Bell County, delving into its history, totting up its statistics, and talking to its residents. He found a place "in a state of great flux." Most obviously, the population had dropped by roughly five thousand souls between 1930 and 1940, and the rural farm population had dropped to 50 percent of the whole by 1940. When Lewis visited after the war, 60 percent of the county's residents lived in the towns of Temple, Belton, and Killeen.[4] In other words, Lewis discovered that the forces at work across much of agricultural America—consolidation, mechanization, concentration, and the rest that drove farmers off the farm, into town, or out of the county altogether—had arrived in this corner of central Texas too.

Even if Lewis couldn't see the full extent of it, he glimpsed something that would transform the county more thoroughly than the shifts in agricultural production. In January 1942, just as the United

States entered World War II, the War Department selected 160,000 acres—some on the western side of Bell County, next to Killeen, and the rest in adjacent Coryell County—for a new training facility. Camp Hood opened in the fall of the same year.

Anyone glancing at this corner of Texas in 1942 would probably have seen it as largely empty. Gatesville, Coryell's county seat, was a metropolis of 3,200 in 1941, while Killeen was home to a mere 1,300. And empty was what the War Department required. Among Camp Hood's primary missions was to test and train tanks and antitank weaponry. The War Department wanted land that it could chew up and pulverize. Over and over again. In what became known within the camp as the "impact zone," the army turned farm- and ranchland into a pockmarked moonscape, rendered unusable for virtually any other purpose.

But those tens of thousands of acres had not been exactly empty. Nearly 1,200 landowners in Coryell County alone had their property taken from them in order that the army and its tanks could roll in. It all happened with dizzying speed. The public first heard about the land seizures on January 14, 1942, through an announcement in the local paper. Within weeks, the army had drawn the final boundary lines of the camp, paying little attention to what those lines might cross, bisect, or cut off. As Representative Bill Poage recalled years later about the army's mapmakers: "They'd cut a fellow's house in two . . . or they'd cut off his field. They'd take his water and those sorts of things. . . . [They] destroyed the usefulness of the rest of his land."[5] At the end of February, a group of forty-nine landowners met to discuss any recourse they might have. On March 9, James Stevenson, about to lose his farm, spent the day sitting on his front porch insisting to friends that he wasn't going to move. Then he killed himself—the first of several suicides among those who had their homes confiscated. By the end of April, people were moving out, though many had no real place to go.

The army told families forced to move that they should leave most everything behind, especially anything metal such as well pipe, casings, and fittings. That proved a larger hardship than it might sound, since wartime rationing meant that metal could not be replaced wherever those displaced people happened to wash up. They had to leave their houses too, of course, and the army used many of the abandoned buildings for target practice. In what must surely be one of the most perverse PR stunts ever undertaken, the army even invited former owners to watch as their houses were blown up by artillery. Altogether, between four hundred and five hundred farm families moved into town from the surrounding area during the war, and about two hundred of those had been displaced directly by the military.[6] In interviews conducted later, those who had been evicted reported varying degrees of anger, bitterness, and betrayal at the way they had been treated by the army. They also reported a fear of voicing those complaints at the time—the war was on, after all, and they were being asked to do their patriotic duty.[7]

Let Camp Hood stand in for any number of military installations as an example of how the military turned rural landscapes into militarized ones by brute force. Wherever the military chose to open a new facility, property owners were forced to vacate and were paid some version of market value for their land. Those who didn't own property—tenants, renters, laborers—had to leave too, but they got nothing. In either case, military officials seldom provided much by way of relocation assistance. So, for example, when the Atomic Energy Commission began to clear out land for its massive Savannah River plant, designed to refine material for use in nuclear weapons, one study found that "aged and indigent people were generally unable to bear the expense or arrange the details of locating to a new place. . . . State and county welfare agencies assisted in some cases brought to their attention but there was no systematic contact procedure, and the resources of these agencies for dealing with this problem were extremely limited."[8]

Using the power of Congress and the courts, the military displaced thousands of rural people in order to empty the space necessary to train troops, test weapons, and otherwise practice for war. The military transformation of rural space entailed radical changes to the social and economic ecology of those places, and equally dramatic changes to the land, water, and the rest of the natural ecosystem. Federal policy, and therefore federal money, lay at the root of all those changes both directly and indirectly, and especially in the South. The states that rebelled against the Union together received just over a third of all the bases built on the continent during the Second World War, and housed two-thirds of all army and navy bases. The South, it is probably fair to say, became the first region of the country to become dependent on federal money to such an extent, creating what the historian Bruce Schulman has cleverly called "the military-payroll complex." And as James Sparrow has persuasively argued, World War II also effectively created a "warfare state" that was not rolled back once the war was over.[9] That warfare state and its attendant payroll complex rooted deeply in rural soil.

In fact, there were two Camp Hoods established during the war—a north and a south. And in Temple, a town in Bell County outside the base compound, the army opened McCloskey Veterans Hospital: a four-thousand-bed facility that boasted the tragic distinction of being the largest hospital devoted to amputations in the world. This constellation of military facilities created an extraordinary if entirely unintentional and utterly haunting scene in this Texas scrub country. New recruits arrived for basic training to begin their war; wounded veterans returned to end theirs. "The infantry trainees look young," Morris Friedman wrote in the *New Republic* after visiting Camp Hood. "They wear their shirts closed to the top, ties on, sleeves down and buttoned according to rule." Over by McCloskey, however, he found "the boys with the crutches and empty trouser legs, with the awkward deliberate stop of an artificial limb, with flat, pinned-up sleeves. These men wear no ties. . . . They hobble around aimlessly, hang around corners and in drinking places [and] sit on the occasional benches scattered about the city. They don't salute." As Friedman put it succinctly: "The beginning of war and the end of war meet in Temple, Texas."[10]

What had been a wartime exigency in 1942 became permanent in 1948. The military had invaded Bell and Coryell Counties and occupied them, and the area would never be the same. Those war-time facilities would be joined by several other installations in the subsequent years, gobbling up more land in the area. Fifty years after the army moved in, Fort Hood—as it was all now collectively named, in homage to the Confederate general—sprawled over more than two hundred thousand acres, making it the largest active-duty base by size in the country.

Even in 1948, Oscar Lewis could see the changes already in motion in the county he came to investigate. He wrote somewhat dryly that "the impact of the war on Bell County farmers has been profound," and he saw that change primarily as eroding family farms and farm life, probably because that was what he had come to Bell County to study in the first place. But he went on to explain: "Large-scale enterprises, employing thousands of workers, have come into or near the county since the war. These establishments, together with minor ones in Temple and Belton, have created a great demand for labor and have drawn large numbers away from the farms." As a result, the tiny town of Rogers, "located on the Santa Fe Railroad and once a thriving cotton-gin center" but at the other end of the county from Camp Hood, "now [gave] the impression of a poor, dying town, kept alive only by the greater abundance of money since the war." Enrollments "at the White high schools"—this was segregated Texas, after all—dropped across the county, except in Killeen, where "more than half the students now attending Killeen High School [were] newcomers to Bell County," many of them presumably army children.[11]

Lewis's casual observation about the enrollments at "White high schools" stands as yet another reminder of just how cozy the US military had become with Jim Crow. But Lewis published his observation in an epochal year for Fort Hood and the rest of the military. When Camp Hood opened, it welcomed recruits into a still-segregated army. In this sense, racial oppression on the base mirrored racial oppression off it. On July 6, 1944, Lieutenant Jack Robinson—he would become better known as Jackie—boarded an army bus on the base and was ordered to the back. He refused, was arrested by military police, and found himself court-martialed (he was acquitted) and left a promising career in the military. (He settled for a career in baseball instead. The army made no mention of the episode in a book celebrating Fort Hood's fiftieth anniversary.)[12]

In 1948, President Harry Truman issued Executive Order 9981 desegregating the military. On paper, at least, that meant racial rules on military installations in the South would clash with the laws of the southern states that hosted those bases. One of those clashes, fittingly enough, came over the schools for children living on military bases. The federal government provided money for those schools but turned that money over to local educational authorities to administer. Needless to say, local authorities, committed as fiercely as ever to racially segregated civilian schools, wanted to run segregated schools on military bases too.

At a press conference shortly after he took office in 1953, President Dwight Eisenhower seemed surprised by this problem. Asked about it by a reporter from the Associated Negro Press—and the specific example she used came from Fort Belvoir, Virginia—Eisenhower promised he would look into it but reiterated his commitment to desegregate the military. Meanwhile, officials at Fort Hood were apparently preparing to lease land on the base to the local school district to establish a segregated school for base children in an attempt to skirt the clash between Texas law and Truman's order.[13]

Four years later, Fort Hood found itself on the front lines of another desegregation fight. As the Second Armored Division prepared to return to Fort Hood from a tour in Germany, Texas State Representative Joe Pool was apoplectic. Apparently, some number of African American members of the unit had married German women while stationed overseas, and these mixed-race couples intended to live in Texas! So he offered a resolution, calling on Eisenhower to bar the entry of such couples into the state at a special session of the Texas legislature. "Our sense of decency is shocked," Pool sputtered, "by this terrible revelation that the Army might allow such unnatural marriages to be

brought to Texas." Pool also joined with other segregationist legislators in calling on Governor Price Daniel to tighten Texas's Jim Crow
laws further in response to the army.[14]

Despite Pool's best efforts, however, the civil rights movement
came to Texas, and it came, at least in part, through military bases.
In the spring of 1961, Robert Curtis and Samuel Gillian Jr., Black soldiers stationed at Fort Hood, led a sit-in of a variety store lunch counter
in Killeen, along with a number of other African American soldiers.
They issued a statement urging their fellow soldiers on bases across
the South to join them.[15] The two were arrested and "tossed in the
brig" by a provost marshal. For its part, the army reiterated its policy
that soldiers stationed anywhere were expected to conform to local laws and customs. The Congress of Racial Equality took up the
case and responded in a message to President John Kennedy, "We in
CORE have always believed that local customs were subordinate to
the United States Constitution, that inferior officers were required to
obey their Commander-in-Chief."[16] Just three months after students sat
in at a lunch counter in Greensboro, North Carolina, African American soldiers had brought the civil rights movement to Bell County.

Five years after the sit-in, the nascent antiwar moment arrived in
central Texas too, also brought by soldiers stationed at Fort Hood.
James Johnson, David Samas, and Dennis Mora, privates all, refused
their deployment to Vietnam from Fort Hood in 1966. And they did so
publicly at a press conference on June 30. Calling the war in Vietnam
"immoral, illegal, and unjust," they deliberately identified themselves
as representative of American diversity: "We represent in our backgrounds a cross section of the army and of America. James Johnson
is a Negro, David Samas is of Lithuanian and Italian parents, Dennis
Mora is a Puerto Rican." Diverse as they were racially and ethnically,
the "Fort Hood Three" certainly did not represent the demographic
of surrounding rural Texas. They have the distinction of being the
first soldiers to be court-martialed during the Vietnam War. Here,
then, was one way the arrival of a large military installation could
convulse a rural area. Not only did large numbers of young men come

to and through this part of Texas, but those men represented, espe-cially during the Cold War/Vietnam–era draft, a more complete cross section of American society than would likely have made it to Killeen otherwise.[17]

Military bases thus became microcosmic flashpoints for conflicts going on around the nation that otherwise seemed far away from these rural settings. And in the South particularly, military bases highlighted a larger hypocrisy that played out over the role of the federal government. Southern states were perfectly happy to host US military installations with all the money and jobs that came with them. In fact, the spectacular rise of the Sun Belt during the Cold War should be seen as fueled by military spending, not just warmer temperatures. Along with the bases, of course, came the production plants, the research labs, the suppliers, and more. Once centered in the industrialized Northeast and Midwest, these places relocated to the rapidly militarizing South and Southwest. In 1952, nearly 60 percent of Pentagon contracts went to firms in the industrial Mid-west and mid-Atlantic; by 1984, that figure had dropped to 21 percent. Given the flow of military money from the Northeast to the South and West, the Sun Belt is better characterized as the "Gun Belt."[18] None other than William Faulkner in 1956 quipped about the South he knew so well: "Our economy is no longer agricultural. Our economy is the Federal Government."[19] Yet at the same time, southern leaders howled at having federal laws and policies about racial discrimination "imposed" on them.

BEFORE AND AFTER

The physical effects of the army's arrival in the region, so rapidly and on such a scale, could be seen as one walked the once-sleepy streets of Killeen. Located just two miles from Camp Hood, Killeen had transformed in just a few years into "an overcrowded boom town," according to Oscar Lewis.[20] Killeen held no particular geographic advantage—it was simply where the Santa Fe railroad put a stop on a spur line in 1882. There wasn't really much else to recommend the place. With that railroad depot, Killeen served as hub for the surrounding agricultural economy until 1942.

After living next door to the army base for a decade, Killeen had adjusted to some extent to being a military boomtown. Nevertheless, in May 1953, Killeen's chamber of commerce engaged the Bureau of Business Research at the University of Texas to do an economic survey of the town, with an eye toward developing economic opportunities beyond the military. Those who commissioned the study recognized that what the army had given by building a base next to Killeen, it could take away by leaving, and the town's business leaders wanted "to neutralize its elements of impermanency and to consolidate a firm basis for future development."[21]

The report, issued in January 1954, didn't offer much that was concrete. Economic predictions are devilishly hard to make, it hedged; Killeen didn't really have an economic past upon which an economic future might be built. But the authors were confident about one forecast: "Although Killeen developed until 1940 as an agricultural center, it is considered that agriculture will not be important in its economic future."[22] Killeen would be a farm center no more.

While some business leaders may have worried about impermanence, at virtually the same moment that UT students gathered their data on Killeen, the Defense Department was taking steps to make Fort Hood even more permanent. On June 24, 1953, the Senate Armed Services Committee held hearings to consider army acquisition project 54-A. That was the administrative label for the Defense Department's request to expand Fort Hood by more than fifty-four thousand acres. The reason the army needed to acquire this land, as Maj. Gen. L. L. Doan, commander at Fort Hood, fully and a bit pompously explained, was so that gunners could train on the new 120mm guns coming into the army's arsenal. "I consider it vitally urgent," General Doan told the senators, "for the same reason that airfields have had to expand their runways, because of new planes. We have to expand our ranges because of new armament."[23] Bigger guns need bigger spaces in which to fire them.

The hearing was short, friendly, and largely perfunctory. Not a single person who opposed the land acquisition was invited to testify. The lone civilian at the hearing served as perhaps the most enthusiastic cheerleader for the project. Roy J. Smith came to Washington as president of the National Bank of Killeen, and his role was to reassure senators that whatever opposition there might be to the base expansion, it was small, inconsequential, and probably the result of outsiders. "There is no centralized opposition to the acquisition of this land," Smith insisted, then went on: "There are still 1 or 2 people who reside in our State but do not reside on the land, who have opposed it."[24] As president of the local bank, Smith knew on which side his Texas toast was buttered. What was good for the army had been good for Killeen and for Killeen's bank. In a measure of just how quickly the Bell County city had embraced its new status as a military town, Smith also represented the Killeen Chamber of Commerce as chairman of its new military affairs committee.

Still, the expansion of Fort Hood required, again, the appropriation of farmland and the displacement of the people who lived on it. More specifically, the army proposed to acquire five hundred tracts of land, of which 350 were "improved." As Senator Francis Case clarified, this meant dislocating 350 farm families, and the committee entered into the record a letter from one of them. Elizabeth McCorcle's "home place" was located near the southwest corner of the proposed expansion. The homestead had been in her family "for almost 100 years, and my aged mother (87) is living on the place now." She pleaded: "I am sure you can readily see how it will affect her, if and when we are compelled to move." Even here, Roy Smith was ready to calm the waters, telling senators that "a number of those people [who would be displaced] are customers of our bank. They have taken options on other land." The only real issue that remained was to negotiate a price.[25] The project went ahead, needless to say, and Fort Hood grew even larger.

David Boroff was one of those tens of thousands who started his World War II at Camp Hood. Twenty years, give or take, after his basic training and now living in New York, he returned to Texas for a visit. Anyone looking back from a distance of two decades and at perhaps the formative moment of his young adulthood is bound to experience some vertigo. Change was to be expected, and change Boroff found. When he was a recruit, Camp Hood seemed as far away from his America as it could be, and he found Camp Hood so awful—especially its unrelenting summer heat—that "when an officer revealed that most of us would go overseas right after basic training . . . we felt almost relieved. Anything seemed like an improvement over Camp Hood." Life off base held no allure either. As Boroff remembered it, "The small towns near the camp—Killeen and Belton and Gatesville and even Waco—offered little relief. The men on pass simply milled about the streets." This corner of Texas, Boroff and his army buddies concluded, "was the cloaca of the U.S., except that we phrased it differently."[26]

Driving into Killeen twenty years later—this time on paved roads!—Boroff noted, "Killeen had grown," and then added, "grotesquely." *Grown* might not quite have been the right word. Killeen was no longer a small town for sure, but to read Boroff describe it, the town had metastasized: "In an obscene parody of urbanism, the main street . . . housed a neon stretch of loan companies, used-car lots, and pizza places."[27] Killeen—never mind the concerns expressed by the business schoolboys from the University of Texas—had well and truly become an army town.

Things on base looked quite different. "There has been much building at Fort Hood," Boroff found during his visit. More remarkably, in addition to the old barracks of his youth, Boroff discovered "real villages . . . where married enlisted men and officers, separately to be sure, live in trim ranch houses." (He seems not to have noticed that housing for Black soldiers was not quite as neat and tidy as it was for white soldiers—that had been one of the charges leveled by Gillian and Curtis in their sit-in statement.) No used-car lots on base, nor loan companies, but "churches, schools and bowling alleys," instead—a "public-spirited community" with road signs telling people to drive carefully and a base newspaper running announcements of Cub Scout meetings. In short, Boroff returned to the hellscape of his basic training and found it "a bizarre blend of Sparta and suburbia."[28]

In the two decades since the army first arrived, this rural part of Texas had been thoroughly militarized. In the process, the base itself and the areas of Bell and Coryell Counties that surrounded it had morphed into an extreme version of the postwar American landscape. At Fort Hood itself, single-family ranch homes, with the army acting as a kind of homeowners' association to guarantee that the grass was always cut, the gravel walkways remained "immaculate," and the rules of order were observed. Next door in Killeen, a strip-mall townscape of lowest-common-denominator retail catered to the tens of thousands of men, most of them under thirty, who cycled in and out of the base, a khaki-green version of the restless mobility of the postwar population. Sparta had indeed become suburbanized in a pattern that repeated itself at other once-rural, now-militarized places around the country. In fact, the area attached almost umbilically to Fort Hood isn't even considered rural anymore; the Census Department has classed it as part of the Killeen-Temple Metropolitan Statistical Area.

CHAPTER 3

THE COLD WAR COMES TO THE U.P.

Military bases and installations (the Department of Defense draws a distinction between the two, but I will not) dot the American map. They are located in every state and the District of Columbia. Some of them are tiny, and others sprawl over enormous amounts of land. Just how many there are, however, is a trickier question than one might imagine. Since the early twentieth century, bases have opened, and they have been closed; they have been transferred from one branch of the military to the other, and they have been "realigned." The last comprehensive directory I have been able to locate lists more than 1,100 American military bases worldwide, though the vast majority of them are in the United States. That was published in 1995 and almost poignantly does not list any American bases in Iraq or Afghanistan. In 2019, the journalist Samuel Stebbins counted "over 1000" bases across the country occupying more than 25 million acres, an area roughly the size of Kentucky, and approximately 2.5 percent of the land mass of the continental United States. The White Sands Missile Range alone covers 3.5 million acres of New Mexico.[1] And this, thirty years after the end of the Cold War.

If coming up with a simple number is hard, then tracking the growth of the military's physical footprint on the nation is equally difficult. A study done as part of the Air Force History and Museum Program examined where air force bases have been located and created a periodization of the process. The first period ran from 1907, when the army first began incorporating airplanes into the military, until 1947, just after World War II and the almost simultaneous start of the Cold War. The second, from 1947 to 1960, represented the rapid, Cold War–driven proliferation of facilities. By 1960, according to the study, "the time of rapid force expansion and new bases was over." The years between 1961 and 1987 constituted a period of "retrenchment, consolidation, and stabilization" as the Cold War wound down. Finally, the remainder of the twentieth century saw major reorganization as a result of the base realignment and closure process created by Congress in 1988.[2]

To be sure, this chronology is specific only to the air force, the last of the Pentagon's branches to be created. Still, I think it serves as a rough-and-ready guide to understanding the growth and development of the American military presence more broadly. At the turn of the twentieth century, with the Indian wars concluded and imperial aspirations percolating, the navy modernized and the army took on a more professional, twentieth-century cast as well. Two world wars provided the impetus for further expansion in all sorts of ways, and the Cold War only led to yet more growth—especially for the air force, split from the army in 1947—and made it all more or less permanent. After the Cold War ended, the military footprint on the landscape shrank in some places as bases were closed—though, frankly, not nearly to the extent that might have been expected. In other places, it actually grew.

The military has had its own set of reasons for choosing base locations that all have to do with the logic of military readiness and calculations about political expedience. In 1963, the air force produced a report for Secretary of Defense Robert McNamara detailing what constituted an "ideal" base. The somewhat unimaginatively named

Ideal Base Study focused largely on geophysical questions: flat terrain, soil stability, prevailing winds, and the like. So while it is difficult to quantify with any precision how many military installations are located in rural areas, to say that "many" are isn't to say all that much. As David Sorenson notes, "Rural America offered more room to maneuver, to fly, to make noise, to conduct secret operations—to do all the things that need both space and privacy." And in an age when the constant threat of intercontinental ballistic missiles loomed over the nation like a mushroom cloud, locating important military installations away from population centers made even more sense. That would avoid what the 1963 report called, in a grim bit of Pentagonese, "bonus effects," should the enemy target military sites with nuclear weapons.[3]

There has been more than convenient space that has drawn the military to rural America, however. Rural America has been seen to have a formative (normative?) connection to the very sense of military identity. As Sorenson puts it, "For the professional military, there was something corrupt about the civilian world that soldiers and sailors were best kept away from. The civilian world was too undisciplined, too filled with temptation that ran counter to military professionalism and sacrifice. . . . But if the military had to be near civilians, better that those civilians hold the small-town values of Manhattan, Kansas or Moses Lake, Washington, rather than Manhattan or Seattle."[4] Only by training and housing our military personnel in rural places can we produce virtuous, yeoman soldiers. Call it the Jeffersonian myth, military edition.

There is another side to this coin, of course: if the military got its sense of identity from those "small-town values," then reciprocally, large parts of rural America had their identity shaped by the presence of the military as well. Looking back on his own experience in the European theater during World War II, John Brinckerhoff Jackson realized that "armies do more than destroy, they create order of their own."[5] In the United States—invaded or occupied by its own military if not destroyed by it—that order has been imposed overwhelmingly on rural spaces.

THE AIR FORCE LANDS IN THE UPPER PENINSULA

R. L. Polk's *Marquette City and County Directory* appeared in 1895 and stands as a testament to local pride and prosperity. In 1895, Marquette County, sitting more or less in the middle of Michigan's Upper Peninsula (the UP) with shoreline along Lake Superior, had roughly forty thousand residents. The *Directory* ran to over 550 pages.

Marquette city and county exist at all because of mining and, more to the point, iron mining. It doesn't take too much sleuthing through Polk's *Directory* to figure that out. The list of mines runs a full six, tightly spaced pages, from the Ada Mine to the York Iron Company. By my rough count, the *Directory* lists more than five thousand people with the occupation "miner."[6]

White settlers first noticed iron outcroppings in the Upper Peninsula in the 1840s; the region seemed so promising that Marquette's daily newspaper, founded in 1841, was named the *Mining Journal*. It publishes to this day. The Jackson Iron Company, founded in 1845, holds the distinction of being the first organized mining venture in the region. Other mines, forges, and blast furnaces followed. Those furnaces smelted iron with charcoal, which created a demand for timber. That demand, in turn, led to the denuding of much of the local forest.[7]

Iron matters primarily as the necessary ingredient for making steel. Steel, in turn, framed the new skyscrapers of New York and Chicago; it formed the tracks of the nation's railroads that by the First World War constituted a network of roughly 250,000 miles. Iron was the indispensable raw material of America's industrial age. All that growth and the demand for steel that lasted through two world wars, however, created the inevitable problem for an economy and society dependent on resource extraction. Demand for iron created jobs and brought money to the Upper Peninsula, but it also depleted the finite supply of "high-grade" iron ore in the first place. As the *New York Times* noted in 1956: "The tremendous forest and mining reserves were exploited by early entrepreneurs," and by then there wasn't much left of either. In the 1950s, American steel companies had begun to import iron from other countries.[8]

After the war, Yoopers had to reckon with the looming decline of the mining industry and what that might mean for the region. The numbers looked chilling. Between 1920 and 1957, the population of the UP had dropped by about thirty-five thousand, even while the population of the rest of the state doubled. In 1954, a group of local boosters organized a four-day tour of the Peninsula for real estate agents, industrial development specialists, and state and federal economic policy types to show off the region but also, in essence, to ask for help. Three years later, Michigan Senator Pat McNamara came to Marquette to hold a one-day hearing to address the economic problems of the area.[9]

Help arrived at just about this moment, though, and it came from the recently created US Air Force (USAF). Folks in the UP had heard rumors early in 1954 that the air force might put a base on the peninsula. The American Legion Post 444 in Baraga took out an ad in local papers urging people to write to the Michigan congressional delegation asking for a base to be located nearby. "This would greatly help our critical economic situation," the Legionnaires implored. At the end of July, Michigan Senator Homer Ferguson announced his expectation that $20 million would be appropriated for air force base construction throughout the state.[10] The following year, the air force announced that it wanted to lease the Marquette County airport, named after Kenneth Sawyer, the local commissioner who had championed the project during the 1940s, and turn it into an air force base. (Baraga County sits just to the west of Marquette, but one suspects that Post 444 wasn't too disappointed with the decision.) As discussions percolated, some locals grumbled about the air force's plan. At a public hearing to discuss the details of the lease, Marquette Mayor L. W. Brumm stood up impatiently to insist, "We should accept the Air Force's terms without any more bickering, before we lose the base entirely." You can almost hear the desperation in his voice when he complained, "Many of these objections [raised at the public meeting] are penny ante in comparison to what we'd lose if we didn't get the air base."[11] The air force got its terms, and the base was "activated" in 1956. Three years later, the first runway capable of handling the air force's big planes opened and the K. I. Sawyer Air Force Base took its place as part of the nation's vast Cold War military infrastructure.

No branch of the military was more responsible for changing rural space in the Cold War decades than the air force. In an age of intercontinental ballistic missiles and long-range nuclear-armed bombers constantly in the air, the air force stood at the vanguard of America's Cold War posture, and the USAF postured from rural places—from the Loring base carved out of the Maine woods in the early 1950s, to the Edwards base at the southern end of California's Central Valley. Colorado Springs, the town the air force chose for its officer training academy, has seen its population increase by a factor of ten since the academy opened in 1954, from forty-five thousand inhabitants in 1950 to nearly half a million today. Hill Air Force Base in Utah had grown by 1956 to be the largest employer in the entire state.[12]

Military bases sit aboveground. This makes them visible and thus vulnerable. So when the Pentagon's nuclear Mephistos developed nuclear-armed intercontinental ballistic missiles (ICBMs), they decided to bury them underground across an enormous swath of the Great Plains. The Pentagon began its ICBM program when it developed the Minuteman missile in 1958. Between 1961 and 1967, under control of the air force, the Defense Department deployed one thousand missiles in underground silos primarily in the Dakotas, Montana, Wyoming, and Missouri. By 1962, for example, 150 Minuteman silos lay buried and scattered across South Dakota.[13] Sunk three stories deep, the silos required only roughly two acres on the surface. But they had to be spaced at least three miles apart, so in the end, the entire array of Minuteman missiles covered tens of thousands of square miles. Underneath the cattle ranches and grain fields—so evocative of the nation's pioneering, homesteading mythologies—lay some of the most sophisticated technology on the planet and certainly the most destructive. Each missile could deliver its 1.2 megaton warhead to a target inside the Soviet Union in roughly thirty minutes. Of course, while those silos couldn't be seen, Kremlin warmakers knew exactly where they were and targeted their own ICBMs at them. Considered in both directions, the air force created an invisible landscape of Armageddon across the rural Great Plains, or what one scholar has called "the largest peacetime militarized zone on earth."[14]

In the Upper Peninsula, nuclear weapons weren't buried in the ground. They came and went on planes instead. Initially, the planes stationed at Sawyer served as part of the Air Defense Command—jets there would intercept incoming Soviet planes in the event of an attack, what Assistant Air Force Secretary Roger Lewis called "a perimeter defense around the border of the United States" when he came to sell the project to local residents in 1954. Lewis gave the crowd the Cold War hard sell underscoring the urgency of building the base by reminding them: "We know that the Red giant across the roof of the world is developing the power and ability which would enable him, if unopposed, to strike at our industrial and military strength."[15] A few years later, the base became part of the Strategic Air Command, and after a new runway two feet thick was poured, heavy planes started arriving, including the B-52 "Stratofortress." The K. I. Sawyer Air Force Base turned this remote corner of northern Michigan not only into a piece of our defensive "perimeter" but also into a center of the nation's projection of military power. And like the missiles underneath the ranches and farms of the Great Plains, Sawyer turned this played-out mining area into a centerpiece of the Cold War and those who lived nearby into inadvertent Cold Warriors.

Air Force officials regularly insisted that dispersing the nation's nuclear arsenal across the widest area offered the best way to protect from a Soviet attack. In essence, the air force scanned rural America looking for places to hide. Inadvertently, perhaps, but no less significantly, putting facilities out in the country also meant that the places from which a war against the Soviets would be launched and the technologies used to deter that conflict stayed largely out of the way and out of sight for most Americans. And so, out of sight

and on the northern edge of the nation, the K. I. Sawyer Air Force
Base quietly carried out its mission—or as quietly as it could, with all
those planes taking off and landing. During the 1950s, Sawyer flew
largely below the national radar, grabbing attention only when one of
its planes crashed, as happened a few times across the decades. "K. I.
Siberia" they called it, referring both to the climate of the UP and its
sense of remote isolation.

Quietly, perhaps, but in just over a decade of operation, K. I. Sawyer had grown to be the fourth largest city in the Upper Peninsula,
with a base population roughly the size of Marquette City itself—
and there is no question that it altered the local economic dynamics profoundly. In 1960, no employer in Marquette had more than
450 employees, and only four had staff of more than two hundred.
Sawyer, on the other hand, already hosted three thousand active-duty
personnel by 1960, making it the largest employer in the county. And
while some in this conservative community initially greeted the base
with a certain skepticism or with the suspicion that often characterizes the small-town reaction toward strangers and change, by the
early 1970s there was no escaping how much money the base brought
to town. An extensive economic impact study released in 1973 concluded that the base pumped $45 million (roughly $250 million in
2020 dollars) into the Upper Peninsula each year. By 1979, Sawyer
had grown to rank as the UP's third largest "town."[16]

Events happening in the rest of the nation could not be kept entirely at bay, of course, and the presence of the base brought social
conflicts to the Upper Peninsula as well, mirroring what happened
in central Texas. Almost a year after students at North Carolina A&T
in Greensboro staged their sit-in at a segregated lunch counter, an
estimated one hundred "Negro airmen" marched into Negaunee,
Michigan, a small town near the air base. (The reliably right-wing *Chicago Tribune* wrote that they "invaded this iron mining community.")
Earlier in the day, in fact, a group of six airmen had been attacked by
a group of white locals. "Trouble between Negroes and Negaunee
residents," the *Tribune* reported, "most of whom are miners or

lumberjacks of largely Finnish origin, has been building all summer
with numerous unpleasant incidents." In the end, "two Negro airmen
and one white man were jailed on disorderly conduct charges."[17]

Several years later, eighty of the roughly six hundred Black airmen stationed at Sawyer presented a list of grievances and demands
to newly appointed base commander Col. Nathaniel Gallagher. The
complaints largely concerned matters internal to the base, and most
were not new. The preamble to the list of demands, however, read,
"We, the black members [stationed at Sawyer] are totally dissatisfied
with the way we are forced to exist both at K. I. Sawyer and in the
Marquette City."[18] That last phrase reminds us that however much
race relations in the military may or may not have changed by the
time these demands were issued in 1974, Black men still faced a hostile civilian world in the small cities outside their bases. Many of the
personnel who rotated through the base may have referred to it as
K. I. Siberia, but for the Black airmen, the racial climate in the region
proved as frigid as the weather.

Life could be just as alienating for Black airmen attached to the two
air force bases in North Dakota. A grand total of 257 Black people lived
in the entire state, according to the 1950 census, with exactly one living
in Grand Forks. During that decade, the air force opened bases near
that town and next to Minot. As a consequence, by 1960, the Black
population had more than doubled, to 777. Without enough housing
on base, Black airmen were sometimes forced to look for apartments to
rent in those two towns. They found themselves routinely denied, and
if they wanted to drown their sorrows in Grand Forks, they discovered
that about half the bars in town simply refused to serve Black people.
"We never, never expected this here," said the wife of one of these Black
airmen. "We've been treated better some places in the south."[19]

Racial conflicts were not the only things to intrude on the life of
the base and its surroundings. In 1979, the Sawyer base found itself
involved in what might have been an accidental apocalypse. On November 9, ten F-101 and F-106 interceptor jets took off from three
bases, including Sawyer, in response to an incoming Soviet attack.

The scramble resulted from a computer error "when a test tape was loaded into . . . a computer as part of a computer test," the Pentagon reassuringly explained. "The tape simulated a missile attack against North America."[20] In fact, such false alarms were alarmingly common during the Cold War, but for six minutes in November 1979, air force pilots taking off from Sawyer thought the Cold War might go thermonuclear.

Events like those, among other concerns, helped stoke the antinuclear movement that began in the late 1970s and grew in the early 1980s and which made its way to the Sawyer base in 1982. On Good Friday that year, demonstrations took place at military bases around the country and included veteran peace activists Daniel Ellsberg and Daniel Berrigan. In the Upper Peninsula, a group of about forty protesters calling themselves the Lenten Peace Community held a prayer vigil at the installation's gates. Eight of them—four clergy members and four laypeople—carried a cross onto the base and were arrested. Peace demonstrators arrived again in August of the following year, and, again, some were arrested. "Their crime included kneeling and praying," a local columnist, Jim Fitzpatrick, wrote sarcastically. He then warned: "But 3 of them were quickly released and, at this very moment, are free to wantonly kneel and pray in unsuspecting communities anywhere."[21]

As the Cold War waned, K. I. Sawyer also emerged as part of public discussions when the Defense Department considered closing and shifting military installations. During the Cold War, closing military bases became notoriously difficult and entirely political. Pentagon officials had little trouble persuading members of Congress and officials from across administrations of the absolute necessity of their requests to build more and bigger; they had a harder time convincing those same people of the utility of closing bases that were no longer necessary. In part, those difficulties were the perfectly predictable consequences of the Pentagon's own strategy to spread defense dollars across as many congressional districts as possible. If virtually all members of the House—and absolutely every member of the Senate—had constituents who depended on military money, then congresspeople found that the best way to protect those dollars was to promise to protect the money of their fellow members. Still, the Department of Defense pushed ahead periodically to adjust its footprint on the nation to reflect changing missions, changing technologies, and different geopolitical realities. Most remarkably, perhaps, Secretary of Defense Robert McNamara managed to close ninety-five bases in 1964 as the initial Cold War building boom came to an end. Likewise, as the Vietnam tragedy concluded, military planners looked to close bases down.

Sawyer hung on during those years and even found itself the beneficiary of some of the Pentagon's realignments. Sawyer's fleet of B-52s grew a bit larger in 1975 with the addition of two from another base. The base added almost 130 new jobs in 1975 as well.[22] In 1977, the air force announced the closing of three bases, including another base in the Upper Peninsula. Several of the B-52H bombers stationed at the Kincheloe base were reassigned to Sawyer, about 150 miles to the west. The Carter administration identified the Sawyer base as integral to the ELF, a network of underground/underwater antennae designed to facilitate submarine communication. President Jimmy Carter had earmarked $13 million for the project early in 1979 and pushed the project inside his administration. Yoopers, however, were not enthusiastic about this piece of the nation's global military infrastructure, especially after the National Academy of Sciences warned that someone dragging an aluminum canoe across the cables buried in wet soil might risk electrocution. The symbolism of canoers enjoying the remote waters of the UP being zapped by the military's high-voltage cables is almost too perfect. Ten counties in the UP put the program up for referendum votes, and ELF lost all ten times.[23]

By 1979, however, economic conditions had become even more precarious. Tourism provided a certain number of jobs, but only seasonally, and the season isn't very long that far north. One copper mine remained open in 1979, and a global slump in iron prices meant that the UP's iron industry, already drastically reduced as a source of employment, stagnated. Over 13 percent of the labor force sat unemployed—more than 5 points higher than in the rest of Michigan—and 7.5 percent of the peninsula's residents lived on some form of public assistance. Local officials echoed what one observer had said twenty-five years earlier: "Government money is truly the foundation of the peninsula's economy."[24] Sawyer was welcomed as an economic savior when it opened in 1956; by the late 1970s, the local economy relied on it to an extent few probably foresaw and fewer would probably acknowledge as a dependence on Big Government.

At that point, however, Sawyer and its symbiotic relationship with the local community seemed safe. The desire of individual congresspeople to protect jobs in their own districts dovetailed nicely with Ronald Reagan's vast military buildup. Between 1980 and 1985, no military bases were closed, and the Pentagon itself gave up trying.[25] Like any addict, Congress decided it could not control itself when it came to base closures, and so in 1988 and again in 1990 it created a process to remove itself entirely from the decision-making. They called it the Independent Commission on Base Realignment and Closure, BRAC for short.

The process works like this: As the Pentagon evaluates bases for closure or realignment—whether for budgetary reasons or military exigencies or both—each branch submits a list of facilities to be considered by the secretary of defense. The secretary reviews the list, adds to and subtracts from it, and sends the revised list to the commission. The commission holds hearings, collects information of various kinds, and then makes a final determination about which bases should be closed. It then sends the list on to the president, who either accepts the list in whole or rejects it entirely. The results have proved extraordinary—at least, from the Pentagon's point of view. Through the BRAC process, by 1995, roughly one hundred major bases and an additional two hundred smaller facilities had been slated for closure; 173 would be realigned.[26]

Congress created BRAC because, given its own track record in the previous years, it needed to outsource these politically difficult decisions to an independent body. But between the two actions taken by Congress to create BRAC, the Berlin Wall came down. With dizzying speed came the end of the Soviet bloc, and when the Soviet Union itself ceased to exist by 1991, the Cold War evaporated altogether. In other words, BRAC arrived amid the most significant changes in the geopolitical map since World War II, though no one predicted that when the commission first took shape in Congress. Without a Cold War to "fight," how to justify the sprawling network of bases—air force installations perhaps disproportionately among them—built for that purpose?

That was the question that faced the K. I. Sawyer base, and the answer seemed obvious. In that sense, no one should have been surprised in 1993 when the commission recommended that thirty-one bases be closed around the country and that Sawyer be among them. But the news hit Marquette County and the whole peninsula like a gut punch. "If the base goes, we're done for," a local resident told the reporter John Flesher. "Ask anybody in town and you'll get the same answer."[27] By that time, the Sawyer base was the single largest employer on the peninsula. All told, five thousand people relied on the base for their paychecks. Three thousand air force personnel and one thousand civilians worked on the base itself, and it generated roughly a thousand more jobs in the region. According to an air force study, the base generated 20 percent of the total economic output within a fifty-mile radius. No wonder, then, that Representative Bart Stupak vowed to get a stay of execution for the base: "We continue to fight and we continue to fight like hell."[28] That fight, however valiant, failed to keep Sawyer alive. One thousand people attended the twenty-sixth annual K. I. Sawyer–Marquette Area Chamber of Commerce barbeque at the end of August 1994. Those would be the last chickens thrown on the grill at Sawyer.[29] It closed roughly a year later.

There are two ways to describe the economic impact that K. I. Sawyer had on the Upper Peninsula. The figures I just cited reflect just how central Sawyer had become to the economic viability of the surrounding area, and they reflect just how little had changed in the nonmilitary economy since boosters had tried to generate new development after World War II. Even with the base, unemployment in the UP ran higher than the rest of Michigan, and certainly higher than the national figures. Without it, things could get grim pretty quickly. David Littmann, an economist at Comerica Bank in Detroit, predicted that closing Sawyer could "hasten the exodus of population" from the UP.[30] The announcement in July that the local utility company was closing a 17-megawatt power plant in anticipation of declining demand only seemed to confirm the dire predictions being made by local boosters about what the loss of the base would mean.[31]

Analysts at the time agreed that the effect of base closings on state economies would likely be minimal. Local economies might prove a different matter, however, and rating agency Standard and Poor's warned that the disappearance of military money from the economies of small communities might hurt the credit rating of those places. "The larger and more diverse an economy, the less chance it will suffer any lasting impact from military facility shutdowns or employment scalebacks [sic]," explained Claire Cohen of Fitch Investor Service, offering the kind of deep insight we've grown to depend on from finance people.[32] Needless to say, the Upper Peninsula did not have a large or a diverse economy, nor did many of the rural communities that have seen military base closures. When Congress created BRAC in 1990, the "economic impact on communities" sat as item 6 on the commission's list of criteria to evaluate base closings. Sixth for the commission, perhaps, but first for those communities and the politicians who represented them. Those politicians demanded studies that predicted what would happen if a base would close, and then they followed carefully what happened after a base had been shuttered. In truth, economic cause and effect is harder to pinpoint than many economists would have us believe. There is no way to run the experiment twice to determine the economic results had a base stayed open. One 2012 study, thick with data worked over with sophisticated statistical techniques, managed the somewhat underwhelming conclusion "that changes in military base employment do indeed have a statistically significant impact on local non-base employment."[33]

Nevertheless, while politicians may have been removed from the base-closure process through BRAC, they had a vested interest in trumpeting any good economic news that resulted from base redevelopment. Though the creation of BRAC preceded the Clinton administration, most of the base closing took place under President Bill Clinton. Late in Clinton's term, the White House issued a lengthy and thoroughly upbeat statement about economic redevelopment at former military installations. Nearly half of the civilian jobs lost at the bases closed after 1988 had been replaced. "Clos[ed] military bases," the White House asserted, "are becoming engines of local economic renewal all across the country." In testimony given before the House Subcommittee on Government Efficiency, Financial Management, and Intergovernmental Relations, Barry Holman reassured House members in 2001 that "while some communities surrounding closed bases are faring better than others, most are recovering from the initial economic impact of base closures" as measured by employment and other figures.[34]

Even those who brought the optimistic news conceded that things in rural communities such as in the Upper Peninsula might not be going quite so well. When Holman testified before Congress, he reported that rural counties constituted half—ten out of twenty—of those that lost income after a base closure.[35] In 1993, in anticipation of a new round of closures, Congress enabled local municipalities to purchase or lease military properties at below-market rates. But in an acknowledgment of the depressed economic conditions in rural America, and in another example of the federal subsidies extended to rural places, rural communities could get those properties for free. In fact, the air force began offering its buildings at K. I Sawyer to the local conversion authority rent free in 1995, even before the base was completely shut.

In the Upper Peninsula, an initial burst of enthusiasm about a postbase future yielded inexorably to a grimmer economic and social reality. Michigan Senator Carl Levin jumped on some good employment news in 1998, issuing a statement that the number of new jobs created at the defunct Sawyer base (818) had surpassed the number of civilian jobs (788) on the base when it was closed, a feat "once thought by skeptics to be almost impossible to reach." Representative Stupak crowed: "We have an opportunity to showcase for the entire nation that small business can find a friendly home in northern Michigan." The White House statement the following year picked up on Levin's happy news and noted that the Potato Growers' Association of Michigan had repurposed the base's central heating plant into a potato processing center.[36]

Troubling numbers appeared amid the good news. A 1995 estimate revealed that Marquette County posted the second largest population decline in the state, down 7.7 percent. Even worse was Iosco County, home to another closed air force base (Wirtsmith, decommissioned in 1993), with a 9.5 percent loss. In both cases, demographers pointed to the closure of military bases as the reason people left.[37] A decade after that, things looked even more dire: population across the entire Upper Peninsula dropped in the first decade of the twenty-first century. But perhaps the best way to measure the health of a community's ecosystem is to look at its schools. Jobs may have been created at the Sawyer base, but children, apparently, were not. Enrollment in Marquette County's schools never recovered from the loss of Sawyer and in 2011 stood 25 percent smaller than in the early 1990s. Nearly $3 million had to be cut from the budget in that year alone.[38] By that time, the Sawyer base had not become an engine of local economic renewal. Instead, it had become blighted and acknowledged officially as such. With nearly half a million dollars from Michigan's Blight Elimination Program, demolition of thirty-six abandoned buildings on the Sawyer site began in June 2013. Officials announced "no immediate plan for how the site will be used."[39]

For many, the phrase *rural blight* rings as an oxymoron. But in the case of Sawyer, the term fits, whatever the dissonance. In addition to the larger empty buildings officials hoped would attract new businesses, the county took possession of 1,500 residential units on the

base that had housed air force personnel. By the time Blight Elimination came to Sawyer, 35 percent of those housing units had been
abandoned. Roughly three thousand souls occupied the rest, 25 percent of whom had no employment and nearly 50 percent of whom
lived in poverty. As a result of all that, Sawyer acquired the nickname
Little Detroit.[40]

A comparison to Detroit. The word *blight* modified by *rural*. These
phrases point to the ongoing problem we have talking about rural
poverty. *Blight*, without a qualifier, is understood to be urban; Detroit
is the metaphor we use for economic collapse. Both have a color in the
American imagination: Black. Likewise, when many white Americans talk about "welfare" and "government dependency," they see the
same color. Nonetheless, the people of Marquette County, like those
in all rural areas with a large military installation, depended on federal money, and its withdrawal has only amplified the poverty there.
The challenge we have facing rural poverty squarely is exacerbated
first by our racialized conception of poverty, by our lazy conception
that poverty is urban, and by our enduring notion that rural people
are rugged, self-sufficient individualists not dependent on government money. That last represents a neat trick—convincing people that
Pentagon spending is not somehow Big Government spending. Many
Americans—not just rural ones, to be sure—have decided military
spending isn't government spending at all.

When the air force came to Marquette County, it did so for its
own reasons, and those did not include the economic redevelopment
of an already struggling rural area. When the mental health professional William Birch described the base closing as "like losing a close
member of the family," one suspects the air force did not feel quite
the same way.[41]

The local economy isn't the only casualty of a base closure. The
military does not do a good job cleaning up its messes when it shuts
down a facility, and people in the surrounding communities have
been shocked to discover that the mess is often highly toxic. It is
probably not an exaggeration to claim that the American military has

been the single largest source of toxic pollution in the country since the end of World War II. It is certainly the most common name on the Environmental Protection Agency's Superfund National Priorities List. Three of the twelve such sites listed in Maine, for example, are military installations, as are five out of six in the state of Alaska.[42] K. I. Sawyer isn't on that list, but the air force neglected to clean up after itself there when it shuttered the base. In 2014, the Michigan Department of Environment, Great Lakes, and Energy received word from the USAF that there might be toxics in as many as fifteen places around the facility. Officials worried that the chemicals might have seeped into local drinking water. Investigations ensued, water tests conducted, and as I write this the situation remains . . . ongoing.[43]

For old-timers such as Eleanor Vercoe, who had spent her whole life in the small town of Gwinn, it was déjà vu all over again. She grew up when the Cleveland Cliffs Iron Company dominated the area. In fact, Gwinn itself was built by Cleveland Cliffs in 1908 as a model company town, and Vercoe's father worked as one of the company's miners. "It was wonderful," she recalled, "people had gardens and the company was wonderful." Then Cleveland Cliffs shut down, unable to weather the Great Depression. When the air force landed, "the town came alive again. The churches filled up with new people. Our schools filled up with kids. People started new businesses."[44] It was 1993 when she chatted with friends at the community center and they recognized that Gwinn was facing another Great Depression. Gwinn was a town of 3,500 people as she reminisced; by 2000, it had shrunk by almost 45 percent.

In the end, the K. I. Sawyer Air Force Base had pumped money and people into Marquette County for forty years. Then it was gone. Like the base personnel who came and went, the base itself proved only to be a transient resident of the UP. In this sense, Sawyer, in its decay, stands as the latest and perhaps last "boom" in a region whipsawed by boom-and-bust economic cycles for well over a century. Iron. Copper. Timber. B-52s.

ADDICTED TO THE MILITARY

Fort Hood and Sawyer Air Force Base represent two sides of a coin. Located on the rural edges of the nation, both bases transformed the immediate area where they grew economically and socially. One no longer functions—another name on the long list of abandoned military installations that dot rural America—while the other remains open, vital to both the Pentagon and to that part of east-central Texas. Both also represent the extent to which large parts of rural America have become addicted to the military and highlight the price of that addiction.

In many corners of rural America, the Pentagon is the only economic game in town. As one study put it in 2017, "Military installations and contract spending of the Department of Defense" are "important economic drivers in many rural locations." That report was written by none other than the Department of Agriculture. Further, in a nice bit of bureaucratic understatement, it noted, "Rural manufacturing facilities and vendors are buoyed by the Department [of Defense], providing goods and services for our nation's military forces."[1] When a military base grows and roots itself permanently, it alters the surrounding area

almost completely. When a military installation closes in a rural lo-
cale, the economic hit can be severe and exceedingly difficult to recover from. Either way, the military has had, and continues to have, a
profound impact on the economies of those rural spaces in which it
operates—whether fueling a boom in towns like Killeen, or in leaving
a void like in the Upper Peninsula—and on the shape of the land itself.

If many rural places rely on the military for their viability, the ob-
verse has become increasingly true as well: the military relies on rural
places and rural people. The location of military bases turns out to have
a profound effect on who volunteers for the military. The Vietnam War
raised questions about racial and class equity in the military. At least initially, Black soldiers did a disproportionate amount of the dying in Vietnam. They also left the military with less-than-honorable discharges
at higher rates during that war. In fact, working-class kids, Black and
white, unable to take advantage of deferments that favored the middle
class and wealthy, wound up as the bulk of Vietnam's draftees.[2]

Since the Vietnam draft, however, and discounting the brief surge in
voluntary enlistment immediately after September 11, military recruits
have come increasingly from families of military members and from
the counties adjacent to military bases. Insofar as military bases have
left more densely populated urban areas—there are hardly any left now
in the Northeast, and not surprisingly, there are 20 percent fewer recruits from that region than one would expect based on population—it
means that the makeup of military personnel has trended rural (and
small-town) since the draft ended in 1973.[3] In 2019, 79 percent of army
recruits reported having a family member in the military, and this in
a population where less than 1 percent serve. In that same year, Fayetteville, North Carolina, an army town that has grown alongside Fort
Bragg, produced more than twice as many new recruits as Manhattan,
though Manhattan is eight times as large. In total, according to a 2015
survey, more than 40 percent of active-duty military personnel came
from rural areas—a vastly disproportionate figure.[4]

Likewise, if proximity to a military base draws new recruits in,
then the areas around those bases also serve as places where retired

military people return. Veterans are overrepresented in rural places by 20 percent, according to that 2017 study.[5] Think of it as a cycle: Children raised next to a military base (and perhaps by military parents) are far more likely to join up. After they complete their service, they settle near a base to raise their own children, or to live out their retirement taking advantage of base amenities and supported by their military benefits. This familial aspect of the military is something the army in particular has worked hard to cultivate. As the historian Jennifer Mittelstadt has explained, the post-Vietnam, all-volunteer army sold itself to potential recruits as a family that "took care of its own," in the words of one of its slogans. Taking care of its own in the post-Vietnam era meant being taken care of through the most expansive social welfare program the nation has ever created. As the military became more rural after the draft ended, therefore, that welfare system benefited rural families even as the notion of taking care of one's own reinforced the idea of tight-knit self-sufficiency. The military welfare system that expanded in the late twentieth century shrank dramatically at the turn of the twenty-first century. Much of what remained had been outsourced to private contractors.[6] The military "family" had been betrayed by the nation, many in the military doubtless felt. That sense of being cheated out of what they deserved from our country may well have contributed to rural anger at Washington and politics more broadly.

This symbiotic relationship between the military and the rural has caused consternation in some observers. Participants at a roundtable discussion sponsored by the Center for Strategic and International Studies in 2017 worried that "past BRAC rounds had led to a concentration of major military bases in certain regions of the country while drawing down the military's presence from major population and economic corridors in other regions. This participant feared that regional concentration of military installations was creating greater alienation between the American people and their military." Two years later, acting Under Secretary of Defense Anthony Kurta fretted: "A widening military-civilian divide increasingly impacts our ability to effectively recruit and sustain the force."[7] Lt. Col. Hunter Liggett worried about exactly this problem in 1912.

While rural bases have been closed through the BRAC process, large military installations have all but disappeared from bigger urban centers and from the more densely populated northeast. The Philadelphia Navy Yard also closed in 1995, the same year as Sawyer, and that closure ended more than two hundred years of the navy's presence in the city. Further north, the storied naval shipyards in Brooklyn and Boston had already been closed, in 1966 and 1974, respectively. In this sense, the physical presence of the military has run counter to the drift of the American economy and population over the last century. As Americans themselves have become more and more urbanized, the American military has located more firmly in rural areas.

In turn, rural areas have become more and more politically conservative since the 1960s. This represents a significant political shift. Rural people once eyed the growth of the military with considerable suspicion and saw, more clearly than many other Americans, that opposition to "big government" meant opposition to an ever-expanding military. Oklahoma saw perhaps a higher percentage of draft evasion than any other state during World War I, and South Dakotans elected the antiwar champion George McGovern to the Senate in the 1960s.[8] The militarization of rural America, therefore, has played a central role in the creation of what the historian Catherine McNicol Stock has aptly called "the Rural New Right."[9]

Dependent now on Defense Department money and the economic effects it has on otherwise struggling places, rural Americans who live within the Pentagon's vast archipelago of military installations vote consistently for whichever candidate promises to spend even more on the military. But it isn't just about the money. That commitment to the military altogether shapes conservative attitudes in all sorts of other ways too—about religion, race, gender, and sexuality, and about the meaning of citizenship and patriotism. As Stock notes astutely, while we have focused on Kevin Phillips and Richard Nixon and their southern strategy of race-baiting to explain the rise of the New Right, the militarization of rural America is at least as important in explaining the rightward lurch of American politics in the last decades of the twentieth century.[10]

Here, then, is perhaps the prime example to illustrate my point that rural America has not been "left behind," in the phrase used too often, but has been exemplary of how the nation has changed. After all, the United States as a whole has become an enormously militarized society measured in almost any way you choose: from the military budget, which Eisenhower told us represented a theft from other priorities, to the video games our children (and many adults too) play obsessively, to the military surplus that enables our police forces to turn city streets into battlefields. "We all live in an Army camp," writes Catherine Lutz in her study of Fayetteville, North Carolina, home to the army's Fort Bragg, whether we want to acknowledge that fact or not.[11]

Still, rural people live in proximity with the military, are familiar with it, and depend on it for their livelihoods to an extent that isn't true for most of the rest of us. And they have had to live with its worst consequences more than the rest of us too. According to a report early in 2007 by the Associated Press, roughly half of the Americans killed in Iraq came from towns of under 25,000 people, 20 percent from towns smaller than 5,000. These are small-town kids, many of them poor—almost 75 percent of those killed to that point came from towns with per capita incomes below the national average. Rural states—the Dakotas, Nebraska, Wyoming, Montana—suffered the highest death rates in Iraq. If Vietnam was a working-class war, Iraq and Afghanistan have been small-town wars. By 2013, as those wars failed and were forgotten, nearly 40 percent of the veterans of the Iraq and Afghanistan wars who returned home resided in rural areas, according to one study.[12]

At the outset, urban and rural attitudes differed sharply about those feckless military fiascos. When George W. Bush launched the invasion of Iraq, 73 percent of rural Americans supported it; only 43 percent of urban Americans did. By 2007, when the cheap triumphalism of

"Mission Accomplished" had dissolved into a chaotic occupation and a vicious civil war, those attitudes had drifted remarkably close. Urban support for the war had dropped to 30 percent, while rural support had plummeted to 39 percent. Yet substantial numbers of rural Americans remained personally invested in the war—through sons and daughters, nieces and nephews, neighbors and coworkers—to an extent that simply has not been true for most metropolitans. The familial relationship rural people have with the military, often literally and certainly metaphorically, has meant that the realities of our most recent wars have made rural opposition to them far more complicated than for those outside the family.[13]

Maybe *contradictory* is a better word than *complicated*. On the one hand, rural families have suffered loss and grief as a result of the "war on terror" much more than the rest of us. At the same time, they want—they need—to support the military unflaggingly, not merely for the jobs but because the military gives them their sense of American identity and their system of values and, in a very real way, their sense of family. So I'll end with a speculation: when rural Americans turned out in 2016 to vote overwhelmingly for Donald Trump, they found a candidate who embodied that contradiction.

Trump channeled the anger of those inside the military family and directed it at those who launched two wars whose burdens they have borne far more than the rest of us. He denounced military leadership— always popular with the grunts—while he simultaneously promised an even bigger military, though to what end, given his promise of a neo-isolationist foreign policy, he never clarified. Some of those rural voters may have genuinely believed Trump's empty economic promises; many of them responded no doubt to his venomous xenophobia and his virulent white nationalist rhetoric. But I suspect many of them were embittered toward an establishment that sent their children off to be blown up for no good reason and without any positive result. In a poll of voters in the three states that gave Trump his Electoral College victory—Wisconsin, Michigan, and Pennsylvania—Francis Shen and Douglas Kriner found that "even controlling . . . for many other alternatives, we find there is a significant and meaningful relationship between a community's rate of military sacrifice and its support for Trump."[14]

Yet at the same time, they did not want the institution of the military to be criticized or in any way threatened. Trump served as a megaphone for the fury of those who had sacrificed that they had been lied to about the war, and he demanded yet more military spending, wanted big, Soviet-style military parades, and casually talked about going to war with North Korea and Iran. Rural voters inside the military family cheered him for both positions.

Agriculture has always been industrial.

PART II

INDUSTRIAL SPACES

A national rural development program must encourage
industries to locate their plants in rural areas.

SENATOR HENRY BELLMON, R-OK, 1972

On its face, the phrase *rural industrialization* might strike some as
oxymoronic, but the machines have always been in the American
garden.

Leo Marx was surely right that nothing embodied the conflict between nature and industry for writers and artists in the nineteenth
century more than the vertiginous growth of railroads. Nothing came
to symbolize more the incursion of the urban into the rural than the
sound of a train whistle heard in the forest.

In fact, though, American industry was born in the rural hinterlands at least as much as it was in the city. In the eighteenth century,
the first iron forges, for example, operated next to iron mines and
depended on ample supplies of wood from nearby forests, turned into
charcoal, to smelt the metal. Mills of all sorts, too, initially located
near water sources necessary to provide their power. The first paper
mill in the country was established in the late seventeenth century
roughly seven miles from the center of Philadelphia, which at that
moment was far away indeed.

The railroads that so vexed writers such as Henry David Thoreau did
intrude on the American rural, but they also facilitated the centralization

of American industry in American cities especially after the Civil War. By the turn of the twentieth century, the vast majority of the nation's industrial production took place in urban places while the contrast between the rural bucolic and the urban infernal became fixed in the national imagination.

This created something of a paradox with which Americans have struggled ever since. On the one hand, that contrast satisfied the almost moral conviction that many Americans hold that cities are dirty and polluted while the countryside remains clean and pure. On the other, it was clear by the turn of the twentieth century that the farm economy did not yield the same kind of economic prosperity as the industrial economy did. Hence, the rural exodus of young people, many of them taking the train, from their farms and small towns to urban centers that was already clear in the census data before World War I. The solution to this conundrum seemed straightforward: move industry out into the country, where it would bring economic opportunity while, somehow, instilling factory operations with rural virtues.

Industrial decentralization—the term used widely by its enthusiasts— percolated as a topic among planners, critics, and some politicians in the 1920s. It became a policy goal during the New Deal. Chapter 4 tracks the federal debates over decentralization starting in the 1930s and then examines how efforts to move industry out of urban areas accelerated during and following World War II.

This drive to use industry to revitalize struggling rural areas transcended administrations and parties—a measure of just how widely shared the idea was. What Franklin Roosevelt initiated, Eisenhower pursued further. So did Lyndon Johnson, and Richard Nixon as well. By 1987, the Department of Agriculture could write in one of its bulletins: "In recent decades, the rural economy has shifted from heavy dependence on natural resource-based industries to more reliance on manufacturing and service industries."[1] That the USDA could publish that in 1987 marks the success of several decades of federal policies.

Those policies came with subsidies. While federal subsidies to agriculture have been much discussed and debated, the federal government has also offered a variety of incentives to get industry to locate, or relocate, to the country, and those efforts have received much less public attention. Those programs often combined with state and local goodies—mostly in the form of tax breaks of one sort or another—to draw manufacturing into rural locales.

Chapter 5 offers two case studies of this rural industrialization, both from the auto industry. Decentralizers in the 1930s believed that electrification in the countryside would enable industry to move out of the cities. The interstate highway system (and the general expansion and improvement of road infrastructure) proved much more effective. The automobile industry—second perhaps only to meatpacking in its concerted move from urban into rural space—stands as both cause and symbol of industrial decentralization.

My two case studies come from rural Ohio. Before GM announced the closing of its assembly plant in Lordstown, making it yet another emblem in the national press of Rust Belt deindustrialization and the failure of Donald Trump to deliver on his bloviations, it had been among the very first examples of the auto industry's move into the countryside when it opened in 1964. Cheap land plus good access to that new interstate system made Lordstown an appealing location for GM's rural experiment. New roads also meant that the plant could draw from a wide catchment for its labor force. But regardless of how far those workers drove to work, they remained members of the United Auto Workers (UAW) and GM brought its union problems with it when it opened.

Honda became the first Japanese car company to open manufacturing plants in the United States, and it did so in rural Ohio. Pursued aggressively by state officials and attracted, too, by cheap, easily acquired farmland, Honda did not have UAW baggage to carry when it arrived. It got cheap land, cheap transportation, and nonunionized labor when it started making cars in Ohio.

The efforts to industrialize the countryside have yielded mixed results. That 1987 USDA report acknowledged that "much of [the industrial development is] in low-wage, low-skill jobs." Now GM is leaving

Lordstown, and in this sense it can also serve as a reminder that rural areas no less than urban ones have suffered from the effects of deindustrialization. In fact, the effects of deindustrialization may be more painful in rural America precisely because that plant is virtually the only major employer around and there is very little left upon which to rebuild the local economy once it leaves for still-greener, even more heavily subsidized pastures. Even so, much of rural America has been industrialized—from the factories that have popped up in the farm fields, to the workers who commute to those factories from equally rural places, to the networks of suppliers and distributors that have come to form an industrial web across rural space.

CHAPTER 4

FACTORIES INSTEAD OF FARMS

By any definition, West Virginia has always been among the most rural places in the country. Despite the fact that the state's population, like the nation's in microcosm, is urbanizing, in 1990 two-thirds of West Virginians were classed as rural, and Charleston—West Virginia's largest city—still has fewer than fifty thousand residents.[1] And that number is down from the 2010 census.

West Virginia is also perhaps the first, best example of the apparent paradox of rural industrialization. By the turn of the twentieth century, in a state without a major city and only a handful of minor ones, West Virginia's economy and its hills and hollers were among the most heavily industrialized spaces in the country. That industrialization can be summed up, of course, in a single word: coal.

After the Civil War, coal mining—mining altogether—was at the vanguard of American industrialization at two levels. First, and perhaps most obviously, coal fueled the steel furnaces and railroad locomotives and transoceanic ships that we associate with late nineteenth-century industrial growth. It would remain the essential form of carbon for our industrial ambitions until oil began to displace it by the mid-twentieth century. Likewise, iron mined in the ranges of northern Michigan and Minnesota provided the raw material for Pittsburgh steel mills, and copper from Montana made the revolution of electric technology possible. Without belaboring the obvious, mining is dependent on where the resource happens to lie underground, and those resources—from Montana copper to Texas oil, from Nevada silver to Pennsylvania coal—mostly lay underground in places that had not been urbanized.

Just as important, the way coal (or copper or iron) gets removed from the ground was, and is, itself an industrial operation. Individual prospectors might eke out a living panning for gold, but coal was valuable only in volume, and digging it out of the ground in sufficient amounts required enormous investments in technology and the mobilization of huge numbers of workers. And most important, perhaps, it required vast amounts of capital. That capital bought up the mining rights (and often the state and local politicians who facilitated those land grabs in the first place), it paid for machinery, it structured the managerial organization of the coal companies, and then almost as an afterthought it paid for the miners themselves, as exploited an industrial proletariat as Karl Marx ever imagined. Not even our Jeffersonian myths about the rural, powerful though they have been, ever conjured the image of the independent, yeoman coal miner. In all sorts of ways, then, greater West Virginia—that arc of coal country that reaches west into Kentucky and Ohio, and north into Pennsylvania—stands as probably the first heavily industrialized rural section of the country, and the region still bears the scars that large-scale industrial capitalism has left on the land.

If we don't immediately think of West Virginia's coal mines as part of our rural imaginary, it's doubtless because we think of "factory" as the antithesis of "farm." Yet that dichotomy is a false one altogether—certainly in the United States, and certainly since the Civil War. From that point to the present, American agriculture has industrialized relentlessly in ways quite similar to any other industrial production, though the process has perhaps moved a bit more slowly. The technologies of agricultural mass production came first to wheat and rice by the turn of the twentieth century. And if the agricultural sector had not yet "modernized" by the outbreak of World War I, industrial technology, managerial rationalization, and investment capital, aided by a phalanx of specially trained agricultural engineers and economists, arrived with a vengeance after the war was over. Farmers became, or were forced to become, businessmen, and the ones who failed to adjust often found themselves out of business. "Every Farm a Factory," read the ad slogan for International Harvester in the 1920s, expressing the new ethos of modern, industrial agriculture and linking it neatly with the latest IH equipment.[2]

Just as agricultural production became increasingly industrialized, so too did agricultural processing. In his 1922 survey of rural Michigan, the writer Lew Allen Chase devoted an entire chapter to "rural manufactures." These included food processing plants and a handful of local farm equipment manufacturers of the sort already being squeezed out of the market by the likes of John Deere and International Harvester. Of course, John Deere—the man—invented the steel plow in 1837 in Grand Detour, Illinois, a speck of a place on the Rock River about halfway between Chicago and the Mississippi River. American agriculture grew up hand in glove with American industry.

An economy that moved on the rails concentrated things, including food processing. Fort Worth, Texas, exists at all because the army wanted an outpost on the bluff overlooking the Trinity River, a part of militarizing the American continent we discussed earlier. But Fort Worth owes its growth to the longhorn cattle business collecting steer from far-flung Texas ranches. Minneapolis–St. Paul milled the wheat that poured out of the upper Great Plains. And a nearly five hundred acres area south of Chicago's Loop served as the holding pen for millions of animals before they were slaughtered in the city's abattoirs.

An economy that packed more and more into trucks, however, as became increasingly the case across the twentieth century, enabled large-scale agricultural processing to move out to the country. After the Second World War, it did—both grain mills and animal slaughterhouses. What is now the nation's second largest grain elevator opened

in 1961 in the south-central Kansas town of Hutchinson (pop. 40,000).
On September 18, 2019, dignitaries from the agribusiness colossus
Archer Daniels Midland cut the ribbon on the largest flour mill ever
built on the continent—located in Mendota, Illinois (pop. 7,000), a
little more than thirty miles south of Grand Detour. These facilities
are as technologically sophisticated as any other kind of industrial
plant, and they achieve the same economies of scale. For better or
for worse, everything about American agriculture is "modern" and
up-to-date, and it always has been.

Often for worse. That America's taste for meat is satisfied by rurally
located processing plants, staffed usually by low-wage, often female
and/or immigrant workers, has been a recurring story for some time.
These constitute nodes in a web that connects our appetite for cheap,
fast food to university food labs to the migration of labor from Mexico,
and to the indifferent protection that workers now receive from state
and federal government. At the center of that web sit distant, enormous corporations whose appetite for profits can apparently never
be sated. America's chicken-processing plants and its factory-scale
pig farms do not look much like the mills of Manchester or the steel
plants of Pittsburgh. Indeed, these buildings make very little statement at all from the outside. Bland and anonymous, they have an
almost transient, temporary quality to them. These low-slung boxes
almost make one nostalgic for the magisterial industrial buildings of
the early twentieth century. But those anodyne, flimsy-looking buildings are no less dark or satanic to the people who work inside them in
grueling, dangerous jobs for pittance wages.

If Upton Sinclair were to descend to earth and rewrite *The Jungle*,
his classic exposé of industrial brutality in food processing, today, he
very well might set it in Gainesville, Georgia, rather than Chicago.
The large chicken-processing plant in that town is part of a rural archipelago of such facilities in the state and part of what has made
Georgia the nation's largest producer of chicken. Those plants turn
out a staggering thirty million pounds of chicken every day. Much of
the weight comes from Gainesville. Chicken plants number six out of
the ten largest employers in the city of forty thousand, and Gainesville

stakes a claim to being the poultry capital of the world. Foundation Food Group's slaughterhouse in Gainesville doesn't belch coal smoke into the sky the way those old factories once did. But on January 28, 2021, a pipe carrying liquid nitrogen ruptured and killed six workers in a freezing fog of the gas.

Initial reports included eleven others injured by the gas leak, but that number is surely low. The plant, like all the others in Gainesville, relies on immigrant laborers, many of them undocumented. The city itself, between Atlanta and the Tennessee line, is now 40 percent Latino even as Gainesville—politically in a deeply red part of Georgia—has taken an aggressive position against immigrants. As a consequence, many workers will not visit any medical facility for fear of being swept up by ICE and deported. Some number of the injured on January 28 simply took their nitrogen-damaged bodies home and hoped for the best.[3] Some of the nation's worst industrial accidents once took place in New York and Chicago. That isn't true anymore; now they take place in small towns surrounded by farm fields, whose bucolic settings belie the brutality of the work.

All of which is to say, large parts of agricultural America are industrialized spaces and have been for a long time. That industrialization hasn't only been the result of convenience or proximity but because of a desire to use factories to replace farms as the source of rural prosperity.

THE DECENTRALIZING NEW DEAL

The desire to decentralize American industry from cities and out into more rural areas grew almost in tandem with urban industrial concentration in the first place. Early in the twentieth century, even as the big industrial cities grew bigger and bigger, plenty of people—journalists, critics, moralists, and others—lamented urban growth and the centralization of the nation's heavy industries that accompanied it and hoped it could be reversed. "Under such beguiling titles as 'Industry on the Move,' and 'War [World War I] the Great Decentralizer,'" the geographer Alfred J. Wright archly observed, decentralizers "sought to discern a trend away from the industrial concentrations toward non-manufacturing areas."[4] But discern it they could not.

The country life movement, an outgrowth of Theodore Roosevelt's Country Life Commission, saw the industrialization of agriculture as a way of improving the quality of life for the nation's "backward" farmers. Industrialization didn't simply involve the technologies of agricultural production and distribution. For movement enthusiasts, industrialization meant a broad program of modernization—it would bring about better schools, modern infrastructure, even reinvigorated churches. The country life movement was also, as those who have studied it have pointed out, largely an urban phenomenon that projected its own fantasies about country life onto a rural canvas.[5]

These yearnings and laments about American urbanism constituted part of what I have called the "anti-urban impulse" in American life. I won't review that tradition here. Suffice it to say that in the first third of the twentieth century, decentralization existed as a small and inchoate movement. It lay behind the drive for regional planning, especially in New York, in the years surrounding the First World War. But for the first three decades of the century, the movement to decentralize America's cities and their industries had little to show by way of success. Cities continued to grow bigger, and their share of the nation's industrial capacity grew right alongside them.

Until 1933. The Great Depression not only brought a painful, dramatic contraction of American industry, and along with that a (temporary) slowdown in urban growth; it also brought to the White House a president wholly sympathetic with the goals of the decentralists and one with a mandate urgent enough to create programs and policies to make decentralization happen.

Rexford Tugwell called Franklin Roosevelt a "child of the country," and a 1940 biography of FDR is titled *Country Squire in the White House*. In his bones, Roosevelt disliked American cities; he "recoiled instinctively" from them, according to Tugwell.[6] But Roosevelt's anti-urbanism was more than merely visceral. As governor of New York, and just before he ran for president, Roosevelt had lunch with Clarence Stein, among the leading planning advocates for decentralization. In that same year—1931—Roosevelt traveled to the University of Virginia to attend a conference of the Regional Planning Association of America (RPAA), where decentralization was much on the agenda. The trip was a family outing to Charlottesville too, since Eleanor Roosevelt served on the RPAA board.

As he geared up for his run at the Democratic nomination, Roosevelt put regionalism, decentralization, and his concern that the nation's population and economy had become "over-balanced" at the center of a speech he gave in August 1931. "Too many people, in very large cities, too few in smaller communities," as he summed it up. And in case anyone wondered whether this was mere electioneering, Roosevelt came back to the same theme in his first inaugural address when he insisted that the nation "must frankly recognize the overbalance of population in our industrial centers, and by engaging on a national scale in a redistribution, endeavor to provide a better use of the land for those fitted for the land." As one commentator put it after the speech, "For the first time, centralization was officially acknowledged as a national problem."[7]

Roosevelt's New Deal looks to us now as a many-splendored thing, a hodgepodge of initiatives thrown against a wall to see which might stick. In that sense, generalizations about the ideological nature or even coherence of the New Deal have been notoriously tricky to make. Still, I think it is fair to say that Roosevelt saw the New Deal as a way to rescue and revive rural America—he simply cared more about rural places than he did about the fate of the nation's cities. Surveying the country in 1938, Roosevelt believed that its no. 1 economic problem was also its most rural region: the South. In the White House, Roosevelt surrounded himself with "agrarian intellectuals" who pushed a vision of rural America that was modern and decidedly not urban.[8] Many of the most sweeping, widest-reaching New Deal experiments targeted rural America—from the Agricultural Adjustment Act to the Civilian Conservation Corps to the Greenbelt Towns program—or were designed to decentralize the cities.

Perhaps the two most significant programs designed with decentralization as their goal were the subsistence homestead program and the various hydroelectric dams built across the country, those associated with the Tennessee Valley Authority (TVA) chief among them. Roosevelt himself called the TVA the "widest experiment ever undertaken by a government," and it is worth taking him at his word. At its most ambitious, the TVA proposed to transform the entire middle portion of the South from an underdeveloped, poor, and largely rural region into something modern, fully developed, and yet still predominately rural. Dams and other flood-control measures would tame the waters, making living in the region less perilous and unpredictable; domesticating the water would increase opportunities for navigation, connecting often remote corners with national networks and markets; dams would generate electricity, bringing the power of the future to an area largely bypassed by the energy revolution of the late nineteenth century. Multifaceted though this all was, the goal, as summarized by Harcourt Morgan, one of the TVA's first directors, was simple: "Electric power, navigation, and flood control cannot be detached in national planning from decentralization of industry."[9]

Or, to take another example: the initial money appropriated for the subsistence homestead program was buried deep in the National Industrial Recovery Act, the legislation designed ostensibly to revive the nation's manufacturing economy, and by extension the cities where it languished. In it, Congress set aside $25 million to fund back-to-the-farm initiatives. The money was administered through the newly created Division of Subsistence Homesteads.

This was thoroughly Rooseveltian. Unlike the homesteading of the late nineteenth century, this version was targeted at unemployed industrial workers in an attempt to lure them out of the city and onto small farms. Looking back on it, Tugwell wrote that Roosevelt "saw no reason why millions of [city] families might not have subsistence farms."[10] Roosevelt's vision, however, was nostalgia updated. He understood full well that if city people were going to head out to the country, rural life needed to be made more attractive. This goal certainly underlay the Rural Electrification Administration's efforts to bring electric light to dark rural corners. Only 11 percent of rural residents received "central station electrical service" in 1935 when the program was launched; by 1960, that figure stood at a stunning 97 percent.[11]

But Roosevelt also recognized that the world of self-sufficient, family-based farming had passed. Instead, homestead farming, 1930s-style, could act as a sort of safety valve for industrial workers during periods of economic downturn, or as a balance between wage work and farm income. As Tugwell recalled it, Roosevelt "persisted even in contending that urban workers could succeed in part-time farming, thus relieving city congestion."[12] In this sense, Roosevelt understood, even if he did not quite articulate it fully, that the future of rural America could no longer be synonymous with nineteenth-century-style homestead farming. Rural America needed to industrialize. That might mean that rural homesteads would serve as the home for industrial workers who farmed on the side, or it might mean moving factories out into farm fields. Either way, the future of rural places would include industry.

In the end, New Deal efforts to move industry and people out of the city and into the countryside, like so much of the New Deal altogether, constituted a start, not a finish. Even FDR's government was not prepared to force these relocations, but, as Ralph Woods put it in 1939, "these various government activities [were] valuable chiefly because they [led] the way for private enterprise by tilling the social and economic soil for future industrial transplantations."[13] As the nation approached World War II, decentralization had become part of the national agenda.

WHAT THE NEW DEAL STARTED,
THE WAR ACCELERATED

World War II certainly expanded the nation's industrial capacity. Even before the official declaration of war, the lend-lease program initiated an investment in new production to meet wartime demand from the Allies. During the war, the federal government invested roughly $33 billion ($475 billion in 2020 dollars) to build new plant facilities: $20 billion of that went to build industrial plants, while the remaining $13 billion "went into facilities designated by the War Production Board as military."[14]

In the end, the war did reorient the geography of American industry, though hardly in the ways regional planners had imagined during the interwar years. On one hand, it concentrated manufacturing even further in the Great Lakes region, turning the Motor City into the "Arsenal of Democracy," for example. But it also put "a great deal of industrial capacity" in the West and South, especially Texas and California.[15] The war did not decentralize American industry in an intentional, planned way, but it did rearrange it considerably. As *Challenge* magazine put it in 1954: "Undeniably, the features of the occupational geography of the United States have been vastly altered."[16]

Even as the war raged—and perhaps recognizing an opportunity to be more deliberate about this "occupational geography"—the Senate established a special committee late in 1943 "to investigate the effects of the centralization of heavy industry" on the nation's economy. The committee's charge revealed its assumptions. Authorized to make a "full and complete investigation" of interstate commerce, the committee wanted to pay particular attention to "whether such centralization inhibits or deters adequate use and development of natural resources or hampers the full and free flow of commerce." That stirred some consternation. The committee chose the steel industry as its first case study, which prompted the nation's "steel men" to react. In response to an idea (and it was only that) floated by the committee that federal funds be appropriated to establish steel plants in states without any, steelmakers began to assemble data both economic and historic to justify why steelmaking resided just where it did.[17] In any event, they never got the chance to argue their case before the committee, because it was dissolved late in 1944.

Shortly after that, however, the Senate resurrected the idea, this time in the form of a subcommittee of the Committee on Interstate

Commerce to investigate the decentralization of heavy industry. Chairman Brien McMahon (D-CT) held the group's first hearing on October 9, 1945, less than two months after the end of the war, and two more in the spring of 1946.

Nevada's Democratic Senator Pat McCarran was the chief force behind these Senate committees and served as the primary cheerleader for decentralizing the country's factories. He had to walk a fine line. In his October 9 testimony, he acknowledged that he was promoting his own regional interests. "It is certainly my hope," he told the subcommittee, "to encourage industrial expansion in the South and West." But he immediately insisted that he had no intention of "limiting industrial growth in the Northeastern States." McCarran did not advocate sectionalism, he intoned, and clarified that "what I am advocating, and have been advocating, is that we put an end to sectional discrimination."[18] Whatever that meant.

McCarran nodded toward the objections his cheerleading had already provoked. Voices from New England in particular had "damned the committee black on the strength of a press release, and have continued their opposition with Emersonian consistency." And McCarran acknowledged that New England had "unhappy memories. She [remembered] the transfer of textile plants from Chicopee and New Bedford and Springfield and Taunton and Providence." But, the senator continued, "that was decentralization by removal," and not what he was talking about at all. Instead, he wanted to direct future industrial expansion into nonindustrialized areas and believed, therefore, that as far as industrial employment went, cake could be eaten and had too. A few years later, *Challenge* magazine largely agreed. The industrial decentralization already taking place had been "more the result of absolute industrial expansion than of shifting relocation." A more evenly spread industrial capacity would create "a broader distribution of the national wealth."[19]

As one of the few Democrats to oppose the New Deal and as a supporter of Francisco Franco's takeover of Spain in the 1930s, McCarran hardly needed to defend his antisocialist bona fides. Still, he made sure everyone understood that he did not approve of a

"Government-planned economy" to achieve industrial decentralization. Not at all. Free enterprise—what "made this country the greatest
industrial nation in the world"—would do the trick, provided the government would "adopt a policy which [would] give industry the free
hand it [needed]." But here's where things got murkier, almost con-
spiratorial, for McCarran. He told the Senate subcommittee that the
current industrial landscape resulted from "an economy planned in
shortsightedness, for the benefit of special interests, and perpetuated
by restrictions and artificial barriers in the creation and continuance
of which the Government [had] too often been a skillfully used tool."[20]
That statement echoes faintly the complaints of the Populists half a
century earlier, evoking a shadowy cabal manipulating the people's
government, only this time about industry rather than agriculture.

What McCarran tried to articulate, however vaguely, was a notion that industry should be spread evenly across the then forty-eight
states—a kind of geographic balance that would enable a better, more
efficient exploitation of the country's natural resources and spread
economic growth to the places it had not reached. "It is just plain
common sense," McCarran told the room, "that half this country, or
a third of this country, cannot be soundly prosperous if the rest of the
country is existing on a marginal economy."[21] That third was the industrialized, urbanized Northeast and Midwest; the rest was largely rural.

Most proximately, McCarran and his allies in Congress worried
that wartime plants, which had been established widely across the
country, would be closed. McCarran seemed oblivious to the irony
that free enterprise had played no part in this incipient industrialization of the South and West that he now wanted to preserve and
expand. The stakes were not small. Most wartime plants were sold off
to the private sector for pennies on the dollar amounting to, as one
historian has observed, "perhaps the largest one-time capitalization
of private industry in American history."[22]

Nonetheless, McCarran wrestled with a genuine conundrum:
plenty of people in Washington wanted to decentralize urban America by developing industry in underdeveloped rural areas, but there

wasn't an obvious way to do that without some sort of heavy-handed federal intervention. For his part, the *New York Times*'s Kenneth Austin was having none of it. He editorialized that if Congress was going to insist that steel be made in every state, it might as well dictate that cotton and lemons be grown in every state too. "This probably could be accomplished," he wrote caustically, "if costs, to say nothing of profits, could be ignored. The lemons could be grown in Minnesota hot-houses reproducing the necessary actinic, temperature and humidity conditions."[23] Sarcasm to one side, Austin pointed to a basic problem: How, exactly, could industrial decentralization be accomplished in a country that had little appetite for central planning or industrial policy altogether? After all, as the economist Alexander Melamid pointed out, a desire to spread industrial production evenly across the map "accords also with communist ideology, being considered part of the principle of economic equality."[24]

McCarran and his committee fizzled ultimately, but the call to industrialize the countryside continued. Some members of the House tried again to bring Congress to bear on the issue in 1951. In July, the House fiercely debated an amendment to a defense production bill that would have made "dispersal" a "yardstick" in any government built or financed defense plant. Opponents cried socialism, while proponents, now invoking the Cold War, insisted that moving production out of the crowded Northeast and Great Lakes regions and into empty rural places like Wyoming would make the nation's plants safer from Soviet attack. In the end, the amendment was defeated 134–79—not along ideological lines, but entirely along sectional ones. The industrialized states of the Northeast and Great Lakes still had that much legislative clout.[25]

The prospect that Soviet nuclear missiles could wipe out America's industrial capacity certainly fueled an urgency for decentralization during the Cold War. The Office of Defense Mobilization, for example, asked Congress to form another committee to look at the question, this time through the lens of Soviet nuclear capabilities. In August 1951, President Harry Truman announced a national goal of industrial dispersal to keep productive capacity safe from Soviet missiles. As part of that executive initiative, the Department of Commerce published and distributed several booklets promoting decentralized industrial planning, including the wonderfully titled *Is Your Plant a Target?* Even the imperatives of the Cold War, however, could not overcome the aversion most Americans had to planning and control from Washington. The Commerce Department's publication *Industrial Dispersion Guidebook for Communities* offered a template for how to apply "national dispersion standards" to locales but insisted that the whole project of industrial dispersal "can best be carried out by communities themselves"[26]—a DIY approach to decentralizing in effect.

While the rationale might be different—the fear of intercontinental ballistic missiles rather than achieving a geographic balance—the goal remained to move industries out of the big cities and relocate them to rural areas. The *Wall Street Journal* was more than a little skeptical. The editorial board didn't believe there really was any way to achieve "'effective' defense of the economy through industrial dispersal," short of a massive expenditure of money and wholesale dislocation of people. "Some of the suggested attempts in this direction," the *Journal's* writers concluded, "could have worse results than an attack itself."[27] Businesses, for their part, did not seem to heed the nuclear warnings coming from Washington and elsewhere. When the Conference Board, a research organization for business founded in 1916, studied plant locations and expansions between 1946 and 1951, it discovered that national security concerns "had little effect" on how and where companies chose to build. In fact, of the 138 companies that returned the board's survey, only seven listed security as the primary reason for where they put a new plant. But lest the decentralists in Washington be too discouraged, the board also reported that national security would play a part in their siting decisions in the future.

The fate of wartime manufacturing plants, and whether or not they would be decentralized to more rural parts of the nation, worried the International Association of Machinists sufficiently that the union passed a resolution in 1949 opposing such moves. At the end of that year, the six-hundred-thousand-member union—two-thirds of whom worked in defense plants—had "laid the groundwork" for what it called "an all-out fight" in Congress "against the dispersal of war plants from coastal areas." Anticipating what the *Wall Street Journal*'s editors would write in 1955 (and this might be one of the precious few times the nation's unionized machinists found common cause with the *WSJ*'s editorial board), union head Al Hayes insisted that the disruptions and costs of moving military production into rural places in the interior of the country would outweigh any military advantage gained. "The cure may be worse than the disease," he told the press. Hayes already saw ominous signs on the horizon. He pointed out that the air force had awarded a contract to Boeing for the new B-47 bomber on the condition that the work be done in Kansas, not at Boeing's main facility in Seattle. Likewise, the Pentagon had encouraged the Chance Vought aircraft company to move its facilities from Connecticut to Texas. According to Hayes, Chance Vought took three thousand employees with it.[28]

The signals coming from Congress about the direction of postwar manufacturing—especially as Congress considered the fate of all those newly established, newly expanded wartime plants—may not have resulted in much by way of legislation. But congressional mandates, or the lack thereof, hardly seem to have mattered. A 1948 report from the Census Bureau found that the wartime exodus of Americans out of the middle of the country and to the West Coast continued apace. As the *New York Times* reported: "Unlike the conditions of earlier times, the shift westward is not for land and the open spaces." This time, people flocked to areas "in which new industries sprang up during the war." Three years later, these industries were "holding or adding to the gains." Census Bureau analysts saw "a vast industrial and economic decentralization."[29] Young men and women still headed west (and south), this time to factories, not farms.

THE RURAL LOGIC OF DECENTRALIZATION

———————————

Manufacturing companies had a variety of reasons for moving to proverbially greener pastures when they built new factories. In choosing

new sites, companies balanced proximity to their existing plants and
workforce, accessibility of transportation networks and markets,
proximity to natural resources, the labor supply available locally, as
well as other variables. And not all the movement out of the Northeast and Great Lakes regions landed in rural areas. The growth of
manufacturing in the Los Angeles area, which began during the war,
accelerated the growth of an already urbanized area, for example.

But three factors loomed large as firms expanded into the southern
and midwestern countryside—the three Ls: land, labor, lifestyle.

It is only to state the obvious that land in rural areas came at a cheaper
price than it did in metropolitan areas. But the lower price per acre was
only part of the attraction of rural land. Companies could build on those
sites without having to pay much attention to existing physical fabric.
No neighbors to relocate, no complaints from abutting landowners, no
restrictive street grids. Roads could be built, widened, or rerouted more
easily than railroad lines—and more cheaply too, if federal, state, or local government paid for the improvements. Likewise, new plants could
be built to whatever dimensions designers wanted, unconstrained by
other considerations. "The new plants," *U.S. News & World Report* told
its readers, "are low-slung buildings, designed for efficient operation."
In addition, these new plants had "ample parking" and were often "adjacent to freeways or interstate highways."[30] Cornfields amounted to
locational blank slates for plant designers.

Out of those cornfields sprouted structures "sleek and modern."
Over and over again, those words described the new facilities companies put up in the postwar period on rural land. *Modern* meant
new, rather than old: new kinds of heating, cooling, and ventilation
systems; new kinds of lighting; new ways of arranging work space.
Sleek served as a virtual synonym for *horizontal*. It meant one story,
low to the ground, and trimmed with clean, unadorned lines that
signaled efficiency. If skyscrapers done in the international modern
style consisted of glass and steel rising dozens of floors without frills
or ornamentation, then these "sleek" new factories were their industrial, horizontal analogs.

The war played a significant role here too. In addition to rearranging the geography of production, wartime exigencies changed the shape of manufacturing plants themselves. Albert Kahn, perhaps the nation's preeminent designer of industrial buildings in the middle decades of the twentieth century, reminded an audience of this in a speech about wartime manufacturing. "Never in history," he told them, "has so staggering a program been undertaken . . . nor . . . as much accomplished." He went on to talk about buildings more specifically: "For manufacturing buildings there has been developed a certain type . . . the one-story structure of incombustible materials, with enormous uninterrupted floor spaces under one roof."[31] In this way, rural land allowed industrial companies to reimagine manufacturing altogether, transforming those processes in profound ways.

These single-story sheds also cost less to build and maintain than the older, more vertically arranged production spaces; modern, therefore, also meant cheaper. But more than that, they allowed factory planners complete freedom to design the "proper 'flow sheet' arrangement of equipment" and thereby achieve maximum production efficiency. As H. K. Ferguson, president of the H. K. Ferguson Co., added: "Improved possibilities for transportation, supervision, and inspection, in single-story buildings, with clear floor space, are also very helpful."[32] By the 1950s, it had become plain to efficiency experts and others who planned manufacturing plants that moving material up and down in multistory buildings was more expensive than moving that material horizontally in single-story facilities.[33] Cheaper, then, several times over—the cost of the land itself, the cost of construction and maintenance, and reduced costs of operation.

Rural land appealed for another, perhaps less measurable reason: urban industry had become synonymous with urban pollution—with smog and soot and fouled water and bad smells. Moving a factory out into the country, and building on what have become known as "greenfield" sites, made them and what they did seem more "natural." Opening a plant in a cornfield allowed executives to escape the bad environmental reputation their urban plants had earned.[34] That bit of PR-through-new-construction became particularly appealing by the late 1960s, when urban pollution became a central focus of new environmental activists. Manufacturing plants could be rebranded bucolically as "industrial parks," of which there were more than two thousand by 1970, set in surroundings that seemed practically pastoral.[35] That these new plants opened in places with lax or nonexistent environmental regulations was another bonus.

The labor to be found in rural areas also drew firms to the countryside. Nationally, the Conference Board's survey revealed that labor-supply questions affected only 12 percent of the firms surveyed. Regionally, however, the figures varied widely. For those companies choosing to operate in the South and in the "North Central" parts of the country, labor factored in nearly one-third and in more than 50 percent of those decisions, respectively. In both areas, changes to the agricultural economy meant a surplus of farmworkers. Those underemployed farmworkers could, therefore, be turned into factory workers pretty readily. According the Conference Board, the North Central region had "untapped sources of labor on which to draw," and the South offered "almost limitless supplies of labor."[36] It went without saying that this limitless supply came at a cheaper price than it would back in the central city—a notion that resonated with one of the goals of industrial decentralization articulated in Washington since the 1930s. Plants would provide jobs for unemployed or underemployed locals for whom farming and related agricultural work no longer provided a full-time livelihood. Those rural workers might earn less in a rural plant than an urban one, but they still often made more money than they would have in the faltering local economy.

The expectation was that these workers would not be union members. This could not quite be said out loud and also went without saying. And without unions, workers turned out to be more pliant and less trouble out in the country than they were back in the city. As the historian Steven High has put it: "Corporate executives readily conceded that the search for pleasant surroundings and cheap labor tended to be one and the same." A nonunion workforce might also have been a whiter workforce as well. During the postwar period, rural southern Black residents continued to move into urban areas, often hoping for jobs in industrial plants that were now closing and relocating in the countryside. A study done in the early 1950s on the impact of a new plant in rural Charlotte County, Virginia, found that between 1950 and 1954, "the decline in Negro population continued" despite the new jobs available; meanwhile, "there was an increase in the white population."[37] Though the evidence is certainly tentative, it suggests that rearranging the geography of American manufacturing might well have rearranged the racial composition of rural communities where those plants located.

Those two Ls—cheap land and cheap labor—could easily be totted up by the corporate accountants and shown to shareholders for their approval. Underneath that financial rationality, however, commentators repeatedly invoked rural places as simply better—better to live in, a more wholesome place to raise children, more "American" altogether than urban environments. Robert Leak explained in 1969 that "rural areas are naturally free from the complex problems surrounding the urban crush, with congestion, pollution and labor turmoil ordinarily virtually unknown." That might have been a tad self-serving, since Leak served as an administrator in North Carolina's division of Commerce and Industry, charged with helping plants set up shop in the rural parts of the state. Still, he expressed the hackneyed but still common belief that country living was ipso facto a vast improvement on life in the city. Rural places sold their "general livability" as they tried to lure new plants. As another observer put it: "With our teeming cities beset by crime and contamination . . . it is in the countryside that we can find the clean air, clear water, living space and tranquility for tomorrow's people."[38] These sentiments rewrote the agrarian myth by stripping it of its landowner independence and its aversion to industry. Rural industrialization meant that people could work for wages in a plant—a clean, modern one, not some smoke-belching inferno—while retaining the moral virtues of the countryside. Without actually farming it.

Leak's essay for *Nation's Business* ran right after an article titled "Cities Fight Back" that reported on efforts cities were making to remain economically competitive as the problems of American cities seemed intractable. Whether the editors juxtaposed these two deliberately, I can't say. But the pairing serves as an important reminder that urban deindustrialization occurred as rural industrialization accelerated. That doesn't mean that every factory closed in Detroit was replaced by one in some rural hinterland. The dynamics of the manufacturing economy are surely more complicated than that, though in the industrial production of meat we can see an almost one-to-one correspondence. Since the 1950s, beef disassembly plants have closed in Kansas City and Wichita and opened in rural counties in the southwest corner of Kansas. Likewise, in Nebraska, plants closed in Lincoln and Omaha while they opened in rural Norfolk and Lexington.[39] Urban deindustrialization and rural industrialization need to be seen as two sides of the same coin.

DECENTRALIZING FROM FDR TO NIXON

President Dwight Eisenhower took a valedictory lap on January 12, 1961. He stood before Congress to deliver his last State of the Union address and took the opportunity to itemize all the things he believed he had accomplished in eight years. Not surprisingly, "agriculture" came only after "foreign policy," "national defense," and "the economy," but in that section Eisenhower told the nation: "The problems of low-income farm families received systematic attention for the first time in the Rural Development Program." The program had already started in thirty-nine states, Eisenhower went on, "yielding higher income and a better living for rural people in need."[40]

That program had been created in 1955, and the fact that Eisenhower included it in his swan-song State of the Union, brief though the mention was, gives some indication of the importance he attached to it. Eisenhower was, after all, the last president to have been born in the nineteenth century, and he grew up in Kansas surrounded by farms and farm families. At one level, Eisenhower paid homage to that childhood through his Rural Development Program (RDP).

At another level, Eisenhower glossed over some of the contradictions and confusions not simply about his program but about rural development that January night in 1961. Whatever his nostalgia for the lost world of nineteenth-century Kansas, Eisenhower knew full well where the arrows were pointing down on the farm. The total number of farms continued to decline across the 1950s, and along with them the total number of farmers and farm families, as farming consolidated and farming operations grew ever larger. That process, as we have already noted, began several decades earlier. In fact, the primary goal of Eisenhower's agricultural policy was to reduce the amount of government support for it in order to let a more laissez-faire market take over, even as no one believed small family farms could survive in a world increasingly dominated by expensive technology and economies of scale.[41]

The Rural Development Program reflected that truth. Shaped by Secretary of Agriculture Ezra Taft Benson, a hard-right, high-ranking Mormon, the program wanted to promote rural development in total, rather than simply agricultural development. Working primarily through existing networks of extension agents, the RDP proposed to use minimal federal investment to stimulate greater state and local activity to improve the quality of life for poor rural residents. In fact, the places where the program first took root lay outside the Farm Belt of the Midwest and Great Plains and included perpetually poor areas such as the Ozarks, Appalachia, and the Southern Piedmont.

The RDP had two broad goals: to improve the quality of rural life—better infrastructure, more accessible health care, and the like—and economic development. And while the program did propose to help some farmers "modernize" their operations, attracting and developing new industries—mining, forestry, even tourism—seemed a more promising route to rural prosperity. Eisenhower wanted the federal government's role in agriculture to be reduced, but the goals he hoped to achieve through the RDP sounded much the same as Franklin Roosevelt's twenty years earlier. Expanded vocational training meant "that off the farm opportunities could be utilized on a part-time basis" while new factory jobs in rural areas, in turn, would allow "small farmers . . . to farm on a part-time basis."[42] Industrial development was peppered throughout the RDP's initiatives. It provided guidelines to local committees to help them think about how to recruit manufacturers; extension agents went to work gathering data, conducting surveys, and writing reports that were then used to lure new industries.

The Rural Development Program surely helped some rural communities imagine an economic future different from their past, but those successes depended on a whole range of variables, some of which could be altered, some of which couldn't. Local boosterism might be catalyzed, but access to transportation or power or even developing a work force ready to take industrial jobs often lay beyond the capacity of local leaders. Still, the creation of the Rural Development Program signaled a widespread consensus that rural America's future depended on industrial development, even if Eisenhower insisted it would all be in the service of preserving family farming.[43]

However tricky it might be to measure the success of Eisenhower's RDP, it helped set the stage for further federal initiatives during the Kennedy and Johnson administrations. Such initiatives to promote industry in rural areas found their way into the Economic Opportunity Act of 1964, the Public Works and Economic Development Act of 1965, and the Appalachian Regional Development Act, also passed in 1965. The 1970 Federal-Aid Highway Act included $100 million appropriated specifically to facilitate rural industrialization by building roads to connect sparsely populated areas with job opportunities, presumably in larger industrial areas. As Transportation Secretary John Volpe explained, "We hope this demonstration program will . . . help in checking or slowing down the present migration of people to larger and more congested areas."[44] Throughout the decade, Congress made it clear that it wanted industrial development outside large metropolitan areas, in keeping with the ethos of decentralization discussed above, and it did what it could to hurry that along. From 1960 to 1970, manufacturing employment in metropolitan regions had grown 4 percent; in rural areas, it grew 22 percent. Those percentages reflect different baselines, to be sure, since manufacturing was already concentrated in metro areas and growth over a much higher starting point would necessarily be smaller in percentage terms. Still, that 22 percent represents the success of "policy goals of federal legislation."[45] "Drive across the countryside almost anywhere in the United States," *U.S. News & World Report* told its readers, "and this is what you'll see—sleek, modern factories, office buildings, and research laboratories are springing up right in the middle of farmland. Often these plants are surrounded by fields that still yield corn and wheat."[46] And in a remarkable development, the Agricultural Act of 1970 committed the government to developing rural industry by providing financing for infrastructure projects of the sort required to attract manufacturers. The dream to decentralize American industry by moving it into the country that began in the 1920s and '30s seemed finally, as the 1960s rolled into the 1970s, to be coming true.

And yet . . .

Whatever success these initiatives might claim, they appeared to have done little to stem what many saw as a deepening rural crisis. Certainly, the flight of rural people to metropolitan areas continued apace. "In the past 25 years," Georgia Democratic Senator Herman Talmadge told readers of *Nation's Business* in 1972, "some 30 million people have left our villages, small towns and small cities." Another writer sounded almost hysterical in 1970 when he cried: "Rural America is an economic, social, and educational disaster area!"[47]

This was certainly the view of President Richard Nixon's White House. Rural development, as a White House task force wrote in 1970, mattered because it would alleviate the urban crisis that, more than commodities prices and farm consolidation, kept Nixon up at night. In prose remarkably purple for a government publication, the task force saw cities that had "become huge, ungainly, and unkempt organisms that in noisy and unsightly paroxysms regurgitate their wastes upon themselves." The task force estimated that it would cost $100 billion every year for ten years for the "corrective surgery" necessary to fix American cities. Meanwhile, many rural towns were "yawning shells" of their former selves. The solution to this, therefore, was to encourage the decentralization of people and jobs from those ugly cities and out into the depopulated country. "Rural America and metropolitan America," the task force insisted, "are in partnership together. What helps one also helps the other."[48]

Nation's Business was the house organ for the US Chamber of Commerce and at one point was one of the most influential business magazines in the country. Senator Talmadge was particularly keen to speak to this readership. Talmadge had been the political force behind the Rural Development Act of 1972, and he wanted to extoll its virtues to America's business leaders. He no doubt hoped that they would take it up on its several offers to develop businesses in rural places. He called it nothing less than "a strategy for survival of the countryside."[49]

A month before he wrote for the US Chamber, Talmadge testified before his own colleagues to explain the legislation. Given the sprawling reach of the bill, the summary Talmadge offered was a model of rhetorical efficiency. There was a certain amount of predictable boilerplate, to be sure, as when Talmadge assured other senators, "Our purpose is to encourage and speed up economic growth in rural areas, to provide jobs and income required to support better community facilities and services, to improve the quality of rural life, and to do so on a self-earned, self-sustaining basis."[50] Or when he harkened back nearly thirty years to Senator Pat McCarran by reassuring everyone that rural development was not a competitive, zero-sum game: "Rural development cannot succeed unless it results in a major net addition to the jobs and business opportunities in the national economy. It cannot succeed merely by shifting jobs and business activity around from one part of the country to another."[51]

There was also a bit of federal coercion tucked into the proposal. Talmadge noted that federal law already required the executive branch to locate installations or offices "insofar as practicable" in areas of "lower population density." There was too much wiggle room in that language, Talmadge insisted, and very few new facilities were actually sited in rural areas as a result. So his 1972 revision to that language "require[d] that first priority in the location of offices and other installations shall be given to rural areas as defined in the act."[52]

But the meat of the bill, as Talmadge described it, reflected a vision for a rural America not wholly tethered to agriculture and farming, perhaps for the first time. It took the accumulated wisdom from three decades about how to encourage industrial development in rural areas and packaged it into a single document. Loans for the infrastructure often lacking in rural places but which companies would not build on their own—"the essential community facilities," as Talmadge put it, "water supplies, and other industrial prerequisites and an attractive environmental and economic climate that encourages and facilitates the development of new and expanding rural industry and business." Loans for rural housing would "make it possible for the schoolteachers, doctors, dentists, industrial managers, and other relatively higher income people whose services are so vital to successful rural development and a higher quality of life in rural America to obtain [credit] to acquire or build adequate homes for their families." In all, Talmadge could tally ten new "major farm and rural development loan programs and nine new programs of Federal cost sharing for specific types or rural development projects and purposes ranging from rural industrial parks to scientific research, rural fire protection, and credit for young farmers." Loans for industrial development came without any predetermined caps, and, because the bill expanded the definition of *rural* altogether, they were available to places as big as fifty thousand people. This latter reflected a growing consensus that rural decentralization would probably be more successful if it could take advantage of the infrastructures even small cities had to offer.[53]

That focus on loan programs addressed a financial asymmetry. According to one study, during the 1960s, the capital that flowed out of the rural parts of the Upper Midwest, primarily to banks in the Twin Cities, was not matched by loans made out to those areas. Likewise, in Central Appalachia in 1967 alone, "the region had a $109 million gross capital outflow." In addition, that study found that rural bankers were risk-averse and that "the portfolios of rural unit banks are nearly all tied to agriculture. Because they are less diversified than urban banks, it is rational for them to have a smaller proportion of total assets in loans." Niles Hansen, the author of this study, concluded: "Finally, it must be emphasized that among the greatest barriers to the provision of adequate rural development financing are the attitudes of many bankers in rural areas. . . . Bankers are simply not growth minded. Instead of vigorous competition in the marketplace for new economic activity, there is too often only conservative, personal inter-mediation, serving only to confirm and reinforce the local power structure and economic stagnation."[54] Main Street bankers—at least, in Hansen's estimation—still lived in a world remarkably like the Main Street of Sinclair Lewis's 1920 novel. Structurally and temperamentally, therefore, rural banks were not likely to finance rural industrial development. The federal government would step in to fill that void.

Sure, there were sops in the bill intended to foster farming and agriculture—kids could even apply for loans to develop business ideas through their participation in 4-H and similar kinds of clubs—but Talmadge made clear in his testimony that industry could revive rural places, and his bill was designed to foster industrial development. "Its primary thrust," Talmadge said, "is toward providing jobs and increased business income in rural America through encouragement of rural industrialization and increased business activity and income."[55]

The Rural Development Act of 1972, therefore, stands as a culmination of sorts. For roughly forty years, Washington had looked at ways to move industry out of metropolitan regions and into the countryside. That meant facilitating the necessary enticements, inducements, and finances to persuade industry to do that. The act provided all those. As Talmadge put it, "In this bill we put all the major components of rural development together in the same piece of legislation."

Likewise, the bill encapsulated forty years' worth of debate about industrial and geographic "balance." During the Great Depression, industrial decentralization promised to solve the problem of the urban unemployed; it promised to solve the problems of the "urban crisis" during the 1960s. Talmadge told readers of *Nation's Business* as much when he answered his own question about where those thirty million rural migrants had gone: "They flocked into the cities, turned them into overloaded pressure cookers and precipitated the terrible urban crisis that confronts us today." Rural development, in this sense, was a solution to urban problems as well—a geographical win-win. "Take New York," Talmadge offered. "It's ungovernable and unlivable, and a big reason for this is the large influx of unproductive people. . . . We can stop such influxes, if we really try, and hopefully can draw back some of those already in cities."[56] Federal support for rural development was sold as a tonic for urban ailments, though Talmadge failed to recognize that New York and other older cities were losing population, not gaining it, and his casual characterization of New York makes one wonder whether he thought cities could, or should, really be salvaged at all.

Given all this, Talmadge crowed that the Rural Development Act of 1972 stood as the "single most significant rural development legislation ever considered by Congress."[57]

NEW INDUSTRIES, SAME PROBLEMS?

By the middle of the 1970s, Congress had been trying to facilitate the industrial development of rural America for over a quarter century. As one report put it in 1973, the most significant thrust of federal rural policy during the 1960s had been "to create new jobs through the establishment of factories . . . in rural areas."[58] Those efforts attracted the attention of a group of sociologists, led by Gene Summers of the University of Wisconsin, to study the phenomenon. They titled their report *Industrial Invasion of Nonmetropolitan America*. That loaded word signaled not just the scale of what they found but also a warning: "We hope that our use of the word 'invasion' will arouse the reader's senses to be alert to potential dangers as well as desirable outcomes," they wrote.[59]

In fact, the researchers engaged in an enormous task of collation. They did not head out from Madison to study individual communities but rather collected as many case studies and reports as they could find—nearly two hundred in all. Taken together, those documents ranged across nearly 250 locations in thirty-four states and examined over 725 manufacturing plants. Sifting through all of this, the authors tried to draw some conclusions about the "invasion." They came up with a list of thirty-one "generalizations."

Some were not exactly earthshaking and were presented in the bloodless prose that characterizes so much social science: "In a clear majority of plant locations, the host community experiences population growth" (no. 1); "The rate of population growth clearly is a function of the size of the industrial firm" (no. 3). Others were a bit more interesting: "Many local residents express positive feelings about one or another aspect of industrial invasion; for example, population growth, economic diversification, improved local shopping [among others]; worker dissatisfactions with wage work in industry are offset by higher standards of living, job security, shorter hours, easier work [shorter and easier, presumably, than full-time farming], and greater chances of advancement" (no. 20). A number were cautionary: "There is virtually no evidence that industrial development increases the level of educational attainment in the host community" (no. 14); "those not perceiving personal benefits are heavily concentrated among the old, the ethnic and racial minorities, the unemployed, and farmers" (no. 26).[60]

Those last two must have chastened the enthusiasts of industrial decentralization. They had promised for decades that moving factories into the farm fields would solve the problem of rural un- and underemployment and raise the overall quality of life for rural communities. Summer's survey did not back that up. Educational levels went up in places that attracted more educated employees from elsewhere; income went up, but not for the already struggling residents of a community. And for those who kept the ledgers at the town hall or at the county seat, Summer had more discouraging news: many of these factories had been lured by "inducements" of one sort or another, but the costs of these were "outweighed by increased costs of providing services to the new industry and the community."[61] In fact, those findings were anticipated by Arthur Morgan twenty years earlier. We met Morgan as a staunch critic of the Army Corps of Engineers in chapter 1, but he was also perhaps the most thoughtful advocate for small communities of the mid-twentieth century. He noticed the problem of recruiting new industry to revive rural places almost at the same moment that governments at all levels began promoting the idea. "Frequently," he wrote in his 1953 book *Industries for Small Communities*, "such incentives are provided as free location, remittance of local taxes for five or ten years, or the purchase of a block of stock." And, in his estimation, "hundreds, perhaps thousands, of American small towns have records of securing industries by such enticements."[62] Even so, some number, after some amount of time, left for greener, cheaper pastures anyway, leaving those towns no better off and in some ways worse. For Morgan, the answer for small communities was to look inward, rather than outward—to cultivate local talent, to give it the space and encouragement to grow. If small places didn't do this, he reasoned, the young and talented would simply continue to move to the cities and small towns would never solve their own problems.

But clearly in his view, and in the view of subsequent analysts, bringing a new factory to a rural community was not a cure-all to the problems that ailed rural areas. It might not even cure much. How, then, to assess the postwar push to move industry out of the cities and into the countryside? At one level, it worked—rural-located manufacturing proliferated across almost all parts of America and especially in the South. During the 1960s, the South saw an increase of nearly 1.5 million manufacturing jobs, and more than half of those were located in nonmetropolitan areas. Across the 1970s, factory jobs rose at an average rate of 1.3 percent in rural areas. By the 1990s, 20 percent of all American factory jobs were located in the countryside.[63] The nonfarm population of rural places grew from thirty-one million to forty-four million in the two decades between 1950 and 1970, even as the farming population plummeted from 23 million to 9.7 million. Industrial development did open economic options for some rural people.

At the same time, Niles Hansen, in his study of rural banking, found that "manufacturing employment had declined from 34 percent of the nonagricultural total to 26 per cent" across the 1950s and '60s. Hansen didn't attempt a thorough explanation of this, but noted, "Until non-metropolitan areas, particularly those not proximate to SMSA's [Standard Metropolitan Statistical Areas], are able to capture firms earlier in the life cycles of their industries, they will continue, in too many cases, to run along the treadmill of trading dying industries for mature, low-skill, low-wage industries."[64] Congress and others might have thought industrial decentralization would save rural America; American industry did not necessarily see that as their problem to solve.

Meanwhile, the concentration of the nation's population in metropolitan regions, which these efforts had hoped to staunch, continued more or less uninterrupted. Summer's work underscored that some of those factory jobs—particularly the highly skilled and even managerial positions—were filled not by local people but by migrants who might stay but might also move on as other opportunities presented themselves. Nor could anyone seriously argue in the mid-1970s that industrial decentralization had delivered on its promise to alleviate the problems that plague American cities, not as many of those cities spiraled into their own fiscal and social crises.

As Herman Talmadge tooted his own legislative horn in 1972, he reiterated a central tenet of all federal action to encourage rural development: it would be voluntary. Writing in *Nation's Business*, Talmadge insisted: "This bill is by no means an effort to relocate people involuntarily. There is no thought of that. It also is not by any means a plan to 'keep 'em down on the farm' nor is it a 'back-to-the-farm' concept."[65] How could it be otherwise in a nation with such an aversion to central planning and a commitment to market forces? But note that the language here, even in 1972, conjured up an agrarian ideal.

Others, however, came to a different conclusion. The agricultural economist Marion Clawson believed that "in the case of nonmetropolitan America . . . something more fundamental than 'propping up' is required. I think that a basic restructuring of the pattern of human settlement on the land is required." The National Planning Association agreed. In a 1973 policy paper on rural development, the planners concluded that "because population continues to decline in rural areas and continues to concentrate in metro areas, causing social and economic problems for both . . . the United States needs to establish a population location and distribution policy."[66] At that moment, the American public might have had an appetite for that. In a 1968 Gallup survey, 52 percent of Americans thought the federal government ought to put the brakes on the growth of large metropolitan areas—somehow—and 58 percent of them thought the government ought to induce people and industry to move to small towns. Doing so would allow the 56 percent who wanted to fulfill their yearning to live in a small town and who would do so "if jobs were available."[67]

The trains that rattled past Thoreau's cabin at Walden Pond every day represented an incursion of industrial technology into his natural world and a threat to a life lived at a walker's pace. In truth, however, industry has always been part of the American pastoral, even if we have chosen not to see it. Those trains, riding along steel rails and fired by coal, were themselves the product of rural industrialization. Industry has never been foreign to the American rural, nor have rural people always been hostile to it—indeed they, and the politicians they have elected, have often worked hard to attract industry as a way of reviving their ailing communities. But industrialized rural areas find themselves enmeshed in a web of much larger economic forces over which they have little control. In this, they are no different than industrialized areas anywhere in the country.

CHAPTER 5

CARS IN THE CORNFIELDS

New Deal decentralizers believed cheap, widely available electricity would stimulate the move of industry (and people) out of the cities and into the countryside. The war intervened to rearrange the geography of American manufacturing before the results of those New Deal initiatives could really be measured. After it was over, cars and trucks became the instruments of decentralization. Cars and trucks required new roads, and the federal government obliged when President Dwight Eisenhower signed the Federal Highway Act of 1956. Plenty of states and localities undertook their own road-building projects too. Those roads made it possible for plants to locate almost anywhere with good highway access, they decentralized supply chain networks, and they enabled workers to commute from a much wider geographic area. While the Highway Act had many authors and satisfied many interests, it also accelerated the decentralization that the New Deal started—an asphalt version of the TVA on a genuinely national scale.

It should come as no surprise that the auto industry itself took advantage of those roads to reimagine the geography of its own manufacturing. In most cases, American automakers moved into rural areas intraregionally, though as we will see, regions could now be defined by interstate numbers rather than the usual criteria. When Japanese automakers, who had a history of centralized manufacturing, arrived in the United States, they created their own geographies of rurally located manufacturing. This chapter examines two generations of building cars in the cornfields.

All the huffing and puffing in Washington after the war about decentralizing American industry did not worry just New England and Great Lakes states politicians. Organized labor was listening to the congressional talk too and did not like what it was hearing. The United Auto Workers grumbled to such an extent that the Ford Motor Company felt the need to reassure its own workers by publishing *The Decentralization Story* in 1952. Responding to "a lot of loose talk" and "those scare headlines in a local Union publication," Ford's PR people insisted that decentralization "is NOT 'runaway shops.' It is NOT 'runaway jobs.' It is NOT a scheme to make a ghost town of the Rouge [Ford's huge—indeed, iconic—Dearborn plant]. And it is certainly NOT a means for our company to build new plants with taxpayer money, as some misinformed people seem to think." The use of the ALL CAPS underscores that this is exactly what workers thought decentralization really meant. Ford, the company acknowledged, had in fact embarked on a major decentralization plan, but it had nothing to do with moving plants or laying off UAW members. As the booklet went on to explain, Ford's decentralization involved devolving its management structure, to create more autonomous divisions, and a "broader delegation of authority and responsibility all down the line."[1]

That was all true, as far as it went, and we should take Ford's managers at their word. After all, by World War II, Ford had become such a managerial disaster that some in Washington discussed nationalizing the company.[2] But even as Ford was rearranging its managerial seating chart, its postwar expansion plans looked a lot like the other kind of decentralization. The year 1955 brought the news that a new 1.5-million-square-foot metal-stamping plant would be built in Chicago Heights, Illinois, hard by the Indiana border and at that point not yet swallowed up into sprawling "Chicagoland." A new glass plant outside Nashville was also announced in 1955; a new aluminum plant in the little town of Sheffield, Alabama. Ford's movement out of the Detroit area worried UAW Local 600 officials to such an extent that they launched a "Save Our Jobs" movement in 1957 and pleaded with the UAW International for help. Local 600 claimed that Ford was building forty-two new plants in states other than Michigan: "This means the loss of 5,000 to 10,000 jobs in the next two years." Ford officials denied any such job losses, but as the *Detroit Times* somewhat dryly noted reporting this story, "Ford, like other major automobile firms, [was] engaged in a move toward decentralization."[3]

In fact, these two conceptions of decentralization—managerial and centrifugal—could work hand in hand. A decentralized management structure could well make it easier, and create the decision-making flexibility, for a manufacturing firm to decentralize the location of its operations. That's what the Conference Board found in a report issued in 1952 from a survey of more than a hundred manufacturing companies. Seventy percent of the respondents told the board that "they practice[d] decentralization of manufacturing activities in varying degrees." Two factors loomed large in these decisions: a desire to locate plants closer to markets and a search for "improved labor relations."[4] Conversely, and not altogether surprisingly, centralized companies were more likely to expand their existing, centralized facilities. The economist Neil Hurley came to that conclusion in the study of auto plant locations he did at the end of the decade. He recognized that managerial decentralization and physical decentralization were "not completely unrelated," and that as the Big Three automakers adopted the former, the latter was likely to follow. Divisional managers with more and more autonomy over their vehicular fiefdoms were empowered "to seek out sites outside of Detroit and away from the traditionally congested loci of auto production." The rosy picture Hurley painted of this went as follows: "A moderate-sized community plant within an autonomous divisional unit can be placed in a semi-rural area, enabling an employee to ride from his bungalow type home to a spacious parking lot near the plant, free from all the inconveniences of commuting."[5]

If automobiles, and all the new roads built to accommodate them, made industrial decentralization feasible after World War II to an extent never before possible, then the automobile industry, perhaps more than any other, led the way in decentralizing its manufacturing operations. The UAW was not wrong to worry about the centrifugal shift of jobs away from the industry's historical center and out in the rural hinterlands. And even while Ford tried to calm its restive workers, General Motors was planning to build an assembly plant out in the cornfields of northeast Ohio.

General Motors' history in Lordstown dates back to September 29, 1964, "when ground was broken for an assembly plant, in what was formerly a cornfield in this rural community, just outside of Youngstown."[6] That's how General Motors officials looked back on its own foray into rural decentralization from the vantage of the late 1980s. When GM bought 1,100 acres for its assembly plant, Lordstown was a town of fewer than five thousand souls, and while it is located about fifteen miles west-northwest of Youngstown—and therefore on the edge of America's steel-producing heartland, which once arced from Cleveland to Pittsburgh—it was indeed surrounded by cornfields. Eighteen months after GM broke ground, on April 28, 1966, the first car rolled off the line, destined for nearby Martin Chevrolet for purchase by Helen Hart Hurlbert, the owner of the *Warren Tribune Chronicle*.[7]

Happy as that groundbreaking day surely was, GM's involvement in Lordstown actually stretched back nearly a decade before those ceremonial shovels went in the ground. In February 1956, Thomas Keating, general manager of GM's Chevrolet division, announced that the car behemoth would build its largest plant ever in Lordstown. The *Youngstown Vindicator* blared that this would be the largest auto assembly plant in the world in a correspondingly enormous headline.[8] Keating predicted a fall 1957 opening and a total of eight thousand employees.

Almost immediately, GM had to pump the brakes on the project. A year after General Motors announced the new plant, officials came back to town to placate an anxious community. Standing in front of a group of Lordstown's civic leaders on February 14, 1957, General Manufacturing manager E. H. Kelley acknowledged that promises had been made in 1956 and "now, a full year later, not a spadeful [*sic*] of soil [had] been turned toward the plant's construction." What followed was a minor masterpiece of obfuscating corporate-speak. GM remained committed to its expansion and modernization plans—"vast sums have been spent." GM had not seen "the magnitude of the problems ahead" in building in Lordstown. "Other studies were initiated." "The Lordstown plant was considered in connection with all these factors." "I assure you, gentlemen, you don't arrive at answers quickly when you're considering a 1,000,000 square-foot plant." And on and on. In a report, GM's PR flak Andrew O'Keefe, who had attended the luncheon, crowed: "Mr. Kelley's talk was excellent. As you know, it said very little. The favorable impact on the audience was made by his very sincere delivery."[9]

The Lordstown assembly plant did, in the end, get built, though by the time it opened, it had hired 4,800 workers rather than the 8,000 initially touted. When Semon Knudsen, head of the Chevrolet Division, delivered his groundbreaking-day speech, he took the opportunity not only to engage in the usual sorts of celebratory back-patting but also to comment on the relationship between the automobile and industrial decentralization into places like Lordstown. In a quick gloss on the history of America's industrial development, Knudsen told the crowd that railroads had "brought about concentration of homes, shops and manufacturing plants," but now "the automobile reversed the trend, set in motion more and more scattering."[10]

Whatever else those acres of Lordstown cornfields had going for them from GM's point of view, the plant sat less than five miles from the newly opened Ohio Turnpike (designated also as I-76, I-80, and I-90). The vast expansion of the nation's road network both drove and was driven by the country's huge and ever-growing appetite for cars. Knudsen understood that symbiosis full well, pointing out that cars created a centrifugal force that resulted in the "wholesale relocation of schools, churches, hospitals, shopping centers; and this in turn made people more dependent than ever upon the car." Not just schools and shopping centers, Knudsen pointed out, but factories too: "As people discovered they could live 15 or 20 miles from work—at the city's fringe, in a suburb, or in open country—industrialists discovered they could locate plants wherever they wished."[11] In the end, what was good for General Motors was good for industrial decentralization, and vice versa.

A confluence of factors surely contributed to the move of American industry away from its historical urban centers into suburban and rural locales. Firms wanted cheap land and the space to build low-slung manufacturing plants; many also wanted cheaper, more pliant labor; the federal government provided certain inducements through the tax code, but more than anything else, it created the interstate highway system, which made decentralization logistically possible.

Underneath these, however, remained a desire, an almost aesthetic plea, that urban and rural Americas had somehow gone out of balance and that the most promising way to fix that was to industrialize the countryside. More to the point, industry seemed the best, most effective way to save rural America from its perceived decline. Standing before the Economic Club of Detroit late in 1965, W. B. Murphy, president of Campbell's Soup, echoed Senator Pat McCarran and Franklin Roosevelt before him. "Had industry expanded by decentralization to a far greater extent," he told the businessmen, "rural citizens who could not make a living on their farms could have found jobs in local industry."[12]

By 1965, the tenor of concern had changed. If Roosevelt had hoped to alleviate urban concentration by moving people and jobs out into the country, Murphy explained that decentralization would keep rural people from moving into the cities in search of jobs and thus "the over-crowding of big city areas would be far less." Murphy was no economist, but he was convinced that the continued concentration of manufacturing plants in large metro areas wouldn't "solve the unemployment problems of the uneducated, . . . it [would] cause millions more from the rural counties to drift to the big cities to look for jobs." The view that urban unemployment, even in the midst of economic prosperity, resulted from the shift of poor rural people to the nation's cities became pervasive and persuasive across the 1960s. New Mexico Governor Bruce King certainly believed this when he told Congress in 1970, "Each time Albuquerque has announced the location of a new industry the unemployment rate has gone up. Much of this increase is the result of rural residents seeking those new jobs in the city." He went on to make the pitch for industrial decentralization in exactly the same terms that so many others had: "The solution to the rural problem is not more people on the farm, since there is no livelihood for them there. It is rather to keep the small towns, those from 1,000–30,000, alive and growing."[13]

Murphy spoke with a sense of urgency. Rural America seemed in desperate straits, and urban America fared not much better. He told the crowd in Detroit that in the two decades before 1962, rural industrial employment had increased by a scant 450,000, bringing the total number of industrial jobs in rural counties to 1.1 million. That seemed small to Murphy when compared to the 8.5 million manufacturing jobs in metropolitan areas. Still, one wonders whether some of those Detroit businessmen were surprised that there were already so many country people working in factories. Lordstown wasn't just a modern plant—it augured the future of American manufacturing.

NEW PLANT, NEW PROBLEMS

In the late winter of 1972, before the corn had been planted in the surrounding fields, the anger and frustration of workers at the Lordstown plant came to a boil. They went on strike on March 4 and stayed out for three weeks. The friction, everyone acknowledged, was not over pay or benefits but, rather, over working conditions in the plant. And it could be summed up in one word: Vega.

The Chevy Vega was GM's almost desperate response to the arrival of compact, low-cost, high-mileage Japanese cars on the American market, and the Lordstown plant was the place they were made. In order to bring the cost down so as to compete with those Japanese cars, GM retooled the plant to be among the most automated in the country. From GM's point of view, that meant the plant required fewer line workers. From the United Auto Workers' point of view, layoffs were bad enough, but the work now being asked of its members had been speeded up and made so routinized as to be soul crushing. As one striker, a thirty-two-year-old Marine Corps veteran, told a reporter: "If I had a choice between an eight-hour day in a Marine Corps boot camp and working inside Lordstown, I'd take boot camp any day." The automated assembly line turned workers into robots, many complained, and turned their dream jobs out in the cornfields into a nightmare, as one newspaper headline blared.[14]

Strikes were not uncommon in the early 1970s, and in fact, GM endured the longest strike in its history across 1969 and 1970. But the Lordstown labor action caught the nation's attention, morphing into something that sounded almost like a disease: the Lordstown syndrome. Its symptoms included absenteeism, high worker turnover, and even examples of vandalism and sabotage within the plant. The cause, according to observers, was the monotony of the work in the highly automated plant and the unyielding pressure put on workers by management. Younger workers—many of them just returned from Vietnam and now sporting long hair, mustaches, and bell-bottom jeans—seemed particularly susceptible to the malaise. By the end of 1972, newspapers across North America were reporting on these "blue-collar blues." "The 'Lordstown Syndrome' is not only real," warned the Rochester, New York, columnist Clayton Fritchey, "but spreading, in Europe as well as the United States."[15]

The Lordstown syndrome—old-fashioned worker alienation by a catchier name—turned out to be a short-lived phenomenon. By 1974, according to one editorialist, even workers back in Lordstown were more worried about the state of the economy generally and about their own job security more specifically. "Look," said one worker, "I got a house now, a house and a mortgage and a baby," prompting the writer to conclude that the very notion of the Lordstown syndrome had probably just been invented by eggheaded academics in the first place, and to dismiss the whole matter by saying: "A whiff of recession appears to have cured the blue-collar blues."[16]

Whether or not GM's Lordstown workers had had their alienation replaced with the gnawing fear of losing their jobs altogether, GM officials took a lesson from the strike: they started to move south. During the 1970s, GM built or planned no fewer than fourteen new facilities, almost all of them in the rural South. Lordstown had enabled GM to build on cheap, abundant rural land, but the UAW came along with those acres. Moving south meant that GM could have cheaper, maybe nonunionized labor along with cheap land. The UAW pointed out that several of these new operations made components also made in northern, unionized shops, thus insulating GM from strikes in any of those places. GM denied that there was anything sinister or even deliberate about their move south, but the UAW referred to these new southern plants as GM's "southern strategy."[17]

Ohio politicians also took a lesson from Lordstown. If they wanted to keep the auto industry in the state—and Ohio ranked second behind Michigan in the number of auto-related jobs—then they had to sell the state's rural land as locations for new plants and figure out how to keep unions out of them. They did so by aggressively courting Japanese automakers as they looked to move their manufacturing into the United States. Nissan executive Mitsuya Goto recalled meeting Ohio officials in 1980 and being told that Nissan should use the "cornfield approach" to plant location. By this, according to Goto, Ohio's representative meant "go into an area with no other large industries and be a community leader." He went on, "They told us we could get a lot of young workers and if these workers got a Christmas bonus . . . they would be very happy and would never want to join a union."[18]

In the end, Nissan did not settle in any of Ohio's cornfields. Nissan chose Smyrna, Tennessee, on the rural edge of Nashville. But the "cornfield approach" that Ohio pitched was exactly what Honda was already doing.

HONDA'S RURAL STRATEGY

News item from Anna, Ohio: "Mrs. S. A. Steely, Anna, Ohio, reports that she began Jan. 1, 1894, with 58 hens, and gathered 615 dozens of eggs up to Dec. 31, 1895, and in the meantime, raised over 100 chickens."[19]

Anna is a tiny speck of a place in Shelby County, Western Ohio. First settled by Euro-Americans in the 1830s, exactly at the moment Indigenous groups were being removed from the region, it platted itself right after the Civil War and formally incorporated in 1877. Probably the most exciting thing that Anna experienced during its first century and a half happened in early March 1937. Just as people had started their workday, an earthquake estimated at 5.4 on the Richter scale rumbled the town, knocking down chimneys and toppling some headstones in the local cemetery. Otherwise, the news out of Anna amounted mostly to items like Steely and her prodigious poultry production.

Even today, only 1,500 people call Anna home, making it, under Ohio law, a village rather than a town. The center of the village sits at the intersection of Main Street and Pike Street, otherwise known as Route 25, running north and south, and Route 119, running east and west. Those roads, however, are probably not the way most people get to town. The eastern edge of the jurisdiction abuts Interstate 75— exit 99 off I-75 will take you straight into Anna. Turn left and head south on Pike Street, past the fire department, and in just over two miles you'll see the Honda plant down Meranda Road on your right. You can't miss it—it is Honda's largest engine plant anywhere in the world.

The origins of the Honda of America Engine Plant in Anna date indirectly to the late 1970s. At that time, company head Soichiro Honda
decided it might be wise to open production facilities in the United
States as a way of staving off the backlash, often racist and ugly, against
Japanese imports. At the same time, Ohio Governor James Rhodes
(the same governor who sent the Ohio National Guard to Kent State
University in 1970) was keen to revive the state's ailing auto industry. Rhodes was not alone—nearly half of the fifty states made some
kind of pitch to Japanese automakers to open plants in the United
States. By 1977, Honda had zeroed in on Ohio and the small town of
Marysville, northwest of Columbus, in Union County. As anticipation
built, Honda managing director Hideo Sugiura confirmed that the
company had set its sights on Ohio, saying Honda hoped to achieve
"co-existence and co-prosperity" with the midwestern state.[20] The
deal became official on October 11, when Honda leaders and state officials held a news conference to announce the decision: Honda was
coming to Marysville. "'Ohio' in Japanese means 'Good Morning,'"
the *Marysville Journal-Tribune* told its readers, "and that's what it was
for residents of Union County and central Ohio."[21]

Though Japanese auto companies had staggered Detroit's Big Three
in the 1970s with their small, low-cost, energy-efficient cars, Honda
waded onto American shores cautiously. The Marysville plant would
produce motorcycles first—a dress rehearsal of sorts for bigger things.
Car production would follow, Honda promised, provided the motorcycle plant did well. "If the motorcycle assembly operation meets
our expectations," Honda vice president Kihachiro Kawashima told
reporters, "it is our present intention to start manufacturing automobiles by expanding the plant site."[22]

Motorcycles (a motocross model, as it happened) started rolling off the line in Marysville in 1979, and things did go well, indeed.
So well, in fact, that the following year, Honda announced it would
build a car assembly plant next door to the motorcycle facility—a one-
million-square-foot behemoth on several hundred empty acres. The
first American-made Honda Accord made its debut on November 1,
1982. Less than six years later, the plant had produced a million cars.

The decision to expand in Ohio sent Honda officials on another site-seeing tour, this time in search of a place to build a new engine plant. And again, Honda announced the plant would make motorcycle engines as a preparatory step before it began making car engines in the US. Much to the surprise of the locals, Honda announced in July 1984 that it would locate its new engine plant in Anna. Anna didn't have much to do with recruiting Honda, Mayor Stanley Egbert admitted, and he acknowledged that they "could go about anywhere they wanted to." In all his years living in Anna, he said, "I can't really say when the first new venture came in that meant anything more than about three employees. . . . We're hoping this will maybe draw some interest into town—maybe boost the area, maybe the entire county."[23]

Honda's decision to locate the engine plant on several hundred acres of Anna's farmland was not made by throwing a dart at a map. Honda, and the Japanese automakers that followed it, already knew they would build plants in rural America because, as the auto analyst James Rubenstein notes, they did not want to deal with unions, plain and simple. Rural places "would offer better prospects of finding anti-union workers than an inner city."[24] As Anna resident Roger Lentz figures it, five things made Anna an attractive location: easy access to I-75; railroad access as well; a strong school system; a good local workforce—as Lentz puts it, "Anna is filled with people with a strong work ethic who are used to working hard"; and finally, proximity to the Marysville plant.[25] Item 4 on Lentz's list is surely a bit of small-town boosterism. It might have been code that workers wouldn't want to join unions—and Honda's shops in the United States remain union free to this day.[26] It might have been an anti-urban refrain altogether, part of the enduring rural myth that insists that the virtue of hard work is only found in the country. Whatever the case, the idea that small-town folks work better and harder than people in the big city was a common sentiment held by almost everyone in the postwar period who tried to promote rural industrialization.

There may well have been a racial valence to that refrain too, though Honda's people knew much better than to utter it out loud. Plants might seek rural locations as a way of finding workers who wouldn't want to unionize, and those locations almost guaranteed an over-whelmingly white work force as well—certainly in rural Ohio, at any rate. Gerald Johnson grew up as one of the very few Black people in Sidney, Ohio, just down the road from the Anna Honda plant. He called the town "one of the most racist and oppressive cities in the state of Ohio," and described the population, much of which was connected to the plant directly or indirectly, as "a lot of Appalachian people from Kentucky and West Virginia" who had migrated to Sidney looking for work and "bringing with them their small minded belief systems."[27]

The last item on Lentz's list, however, was perhaps most important. As Honda began producing in the United States it imagined creating a solar system of suppliers and subsidiary manufacturers that would orbit around its central assembly plant in Marysville. Ohio Department of Development spokesperson Catherine Ferrari explained it this way in 1984: there was "a kind of a whole Japanese economic development of clustering supplies" around the Marysville operation.[28] In an astonishing five-week period in the spring of 1984, three Honda suppliers announced plans for new facilities within an eighty-mile radius of Marysville. Anna is a bit more than fifty miles away.

With Marysville at the center, the arc described by that eighty-mile radius sweeps almost entirely through small towns and farm fields. When Honda opened a third plant in Ohio in 1989, it built the 2.1-million-square-foot facility in East Liberty. East Liberty sits almost exactly between Anna and Marysville and it isn't even a village—it is unincorporated, officially a census-designated place. Population in the 2010 census: 366. Looking to avoid major metropolitan areas, Honda has successfully industrialized an enormous swath of rural west-central Ohio.

You might not recognize that, however, driving around the region. Change has certainly come over the last four decades. Marysville has grown substantially, expanding from a town of about six thousand when Honda officials started eyeing it, to a town of nearly twenty-five thousand today. Almost immediately after the Marysville plant first opened, the phrase "close to the Honda plant" became a selling point in the real estate ads in the Marysville paper.

On the other hand, Anna's mayor seemed pretty confident that Honda's engine plant wouldn't change the atmosphere of "basically a rural area." Egbert predicted: "I don't see us becoming 25,000 population. I don't see anything like that immediately." As he pointed out, "You can walk 500 feet from anyplace in town and be in a soybean field." He has been proved right to a large extent. Approximately twice as many people work at the engine plant each day as live in town. Most of those workers drive in from other small towns and from the rural hinterland, if a village of 1,500 can be said to have a hinterland. Locals gripe about the traffic in town when the shifts change and cars crowd the streets heading to and from I-75.

Roger Lentz might have been a little self-serving when he identified the good schools in Anna as one the reasons Honda came to town—after all, he had been a member of the school board in the 1980s. Still, as he reported, Honda contributed generously to the schools when it first came to town, though that arrangement ended in the early 2000s. As the seventy-seven-year-old sees it, Honda has been "a good corporate neighbor both in their investment in Anna and in helping bring supporting industries to the area."[29]

The on- and off-ramps that connect tiny Anna with I-75 are small tributaries in an enormous almost riverine watershed of American automobile manufacturing that covers much of the nation's midsection. I-75 and I-65 serve as the Tigris and Euphrates of the American car industry; while those two roads connect a whole host of cities, much of the manufacturing and many of the subsidiary suppliers are now located, like the Honda engine plant in Anna, in the small rural places along these spines. When I-75 was built through Georgia, it ran right past Ford's Hapeville assembly plant, south of Atlanta. When General Motors opened a plant to build Saturn cars, a highly touted managerial experiment for GM, it located the plant in Spring Hill, Tennessee, south of Nashville and right next to I-65. In 2020, Toyota announced it would build its new plant near Huntsville, Alabama, also

next to I-65. Take I-75 north from Anna and in about two and a half
hours you'll be in the Motor City, downtown Detroit. (An hour or
so beyond that and you're in Flint, where the sit-down strike against
GM in 1936–37 made the United Auto Workers a force to be reckoned
with.) Detroit, of course, isn't the Motor City anymore, not in any way
like it once was. The auto industry drained out of Michigan and out
of cities such as Flint and Toledo, and has relocated further south
along the two highways.

As Americans became an automobile people, starting in the 1920s
but even more so after the war, we have transformed physical space
for and with it in all kinds of ways. Among other things, the car enabled a decentralized population in a way that no other technology
ever had, facilitating a grand shift from the center out to the periphery. So there is something fitting that car manufacturing should follow the cars themselves. While the interstate highway system was
designed in part to connect urban centers, it is the space in between
those centers that has become industrialized in the second half of the
twentieth century. The landscapes themselves may not betray that
industrialization, but the social and economic ecology of these rural
places are products of American industry.

THE GRASS WILL ALWAYS BE GREENER

General Motors officials must have been shocked in March 2020 when
they opened a letter from Ohio Governor Mike DeWine. DeWine
wrote to GM that he wanted his money back—money that GM took
from the state of Ohio in the form of tax breaks the company had
received when it negotiated two economic development agreements
ten years earlier, worth $60 million, to be precise. In return for those
handouts, and among other things, GM had promised to keep the
Lordstown assembly plant open until at least 2027. Late in 2018, however, GM announced it was closing the Lordstown plant. So DeWine,
claiming the company leaders had broken their contractual promise,
announced he would claw back the money.

When the story broke in that COVID-19-addled summer, it was greeted with gasps in boardrooms around the country and with applause by those sick and tired of the pinstriped pinheads in those boardrooms. No one was quite sure whether anything like this had happened before. It violated the natural order of things. After all, corporations take from governments—local, state, and federal—but they don't give back. GM's lawyers busied themselves going over the fine print of the tax breaks they had negotiated while Twitterer-in-Chief Trump threatened, in a tweet, to end all of GM's subsidies.[30]

For its part, GM didn't try to counter with a legal argument. Instead, it asked Ohio officials to feel sorry for it. Profits were way down in the first quarter of 2020, and the market for the compact cars of the sort that Lordstown produced had softened—no doubt in part because GM has gone all in on pushing giant SUVs and pickup trucks. Given all these hardships, GM wrote: "We respectfully request your assistance to help us drive towards a full recovery by choosing not to require repayment of all, or a significant portion of, the tax credits."[31] Yes, having negotiated state "assistance" ten years earlier, having announced that it would close the Lordstown plant anyway, GM came back to Ohio asking for yet more assistance.

In the end, GM leadership needn't have worried. Two weeks after the initial story hit the national news, DeWine had sobered up from this momentary lapse and told the press that the state was "not actively pursuing" that $60 million after all. Instead, he announced, the state had been talking with GM about future expansion plans in Ohio. "What we're doing is having constructive conversations," he said, "about how we can turn [those] into things that are helpful to them and, importantly for us, to the state of Ohio. Our focus every day has to be on jobs."[32] He made those remarks after touring the Lordstown plant—not the shuttered part of it, but the part GM had sold to the Lordstown Motors Corporation, a new automaker hoping to enter the vehicle market with an all-electric truck.

Lordstown was and remains a rural place, still surrounded by plenty of cornfields and a lot of soybean fields as well. But it has also served as a symbol. The Lordstown assembly plant, even if its opening had been delayed, was at the vanguard of American industry's move out of urban areas and into the country, and certainly when it was announced it was the very biggest, highest-profile manufacturing operation to have made such a move. In the early 1970s, it became symbolic of the struggles unions faced hanging on to their workplace gains, and of the travails of the Rust Belt more generally. GM's closure of it was instantly caught in the maelstrom of Trump's bombast about reviving American manufacturing. Even the car models its lines produced—the Chevy Cruze being the last of those—tracked GM's and the nation's halting response to oil prices and its faltering, desultory commitments to fuel efficiency and greater environmental responsibility. That one part of the facility had been leased to an EV start-up might have made it a useful symbol of the larger energy transition the nation is undergoing, but as I write this, Lordstown Motors, which promised to manufacture small electric trucks in Lordstown, is floundering, its future far from bright.

Cars have played a large and thoroughly ironic role in the abandonment of rural places and in the increasing alienation many Americans have from those places. Before the creation of the highway system, roads took drivers into towns, and even the roadside space between towns facilitated the interaction between out-of-town drivers and locals. The big new roads, however, have made such interactions virtually impossible. Limited-access, high-speed freeways amount to corridors through rural space, and they reduce that space to an almost cinematic backdrop for those whizzing through them at 70 mph. Stops only come off the exit ramps; social interactions, maybe, only at gas stations, mini-marts, and chain hotels. Meanwhile, many of the towns bypassed by those big roads have shriveled, largely unseen and ignored by a national policy designed for drivers eager to get from point A to point B as fast as possible.

Those towns, in turn, have had their economic life pulled almost magnetically to the exit-ramp oases catering to drivers. In plenty of rural areas, these places provide the kinds of local jobs that used to be located on Main Street, while the Denny's or Applebee's just off the ramp put the local diner out of business. These ubiquitous clusters of retail and restaurants punctuate the drive for travelers, but they have also come to function as hubs for the people who live in the vicinity and with few other alternatives anywhere nearby—town centers, in a perverse way, for an automobile age.

In this sense, automobiles have not only transformed the physical spaces of rural America, they have fundamentally changed how Americans see and experience those spaces as well. The car enabled the decentralization of American industry into the countryside, and in some places that has brought some measure of prosperity. But the car may have taken away as much as it brought to rural places.[33] All of which is to capture a central conundrum of rural industrialization: while promoters of the idea believed it would "save" rural America while allowing industry to escape the various ills of the nation's cities, the places where manufacturers set up shop were no more removed from the big forces of American life than the metropolitan regions were.

As early as the late 1960s and early 1970s, even as Congress pushed for more industrialization of America's struggling rural places, analysts were quietly warning about the results. Sure, the land was cheap, and the workers—so desperate for any kind of job—probably wouldn't unionize, but isn't the first rule of economics that you get what you pay for? A report from the University of Texas published in 1972 found that cheap rural labor was often unskilled, untrained labor, restricting the kinds of manufacturing operations that could open in those places. The fact that these places often had inadequate public services, schools, health-care facilities, and the like made some firms reluctant to bring in their management teams or made it harder for small places to retain the plants that had opened.[34]

Worse, as small communities chased industrial development, they created their own catch-22. As the report concluded, rather than "building better schools and using public amenities to attract firms, many communities have extended direct financial inducements. It has been estimated that in the scramble to attract industry some 14,000 industrial development organizations have come into being to compete for 500 to 750 new plant locations per year. Many communities have even gone so far as to grant tax moratoria to new firms, thereby sacrificing many of the gains that industrial development was supposed to bring."[35] If a new manufacturing plant left rural communities exactly where they had started, what, in the end, was the point?

At the heart of this conundrum lies an ambivalence about the change factories might bring altogether, about what those repeated exhortations that industry would "save" rural America really meant. Senator Herman Talmadge inadvertently put his finger on the problem when he wrote for the US Chamber of Commerce in 1972. As he pushed business leaders to consider moving to the country, he assured them, "It is not the intention of this legislation to urbanize our rural areas. If that happens we will have failed. An important goal is to keep the charm and other qualities that make our rural areas so appealing."[36] While that sounded sensible in the abstract—after all, it wasn't just the cheap land and pliant labor that rural advocates were selling, it was that more ineffable but equally important "charm"—on the ground, the needle has proved tough to thread.

There are, essentially, two possible outcomes when a factory and the big company that builds it come to a small place: either that venture is successful or it fails. If it succeeds, then the place tends to grow, and that growth creates frictions large and small between newcomers and old-timers. The tax base may expand, but taxes altogether may go up; an influx of new residents can distort the housing market; and some people grouse that the "charm" of the place—the close-knit neighborliness, the slower pace, the established sense of civic order—has evaporated. And that, after all, is what Talmadge insisted could be avoided.

If a plant arrives and then departs, then the deindustrialization of a rural place can be even more brutal than it has proved to be in many urban locales. Much like the experience of areas that lost military installations, rural industrial sites are not likely to have a broader, more diversified economy to soften the blow of a plant closure. Nor is there often much left with which to rebuild the economic infrastructure or to replace the lost jobs and revenue.

None of this is speculative. By the 1980s, a USDA report noted, economic diversification in rural areas meant that the rural economy now mirrored the national one more exactly, "and [was] thus more directly affected by national economic cycles."[37] In fact, rural areas that industrialized in the middle decades of the twentieth century have been hit harder by the downturns than metro areas. Rural manufacturing contracted painfully during the downturn of the early 1980s and again during the recession at the turn of the twenty-first century, leading one analyst to conclude in 2004 that "rural areas have borne a disproportionate share of the recent manufacturing difficulties."[38] That was before the financial collapse of 2007, which hit already struggling rural manufacturing particularly hard. Rural counties lost one out of eight factory jobs alone as a result of the Great Recession. All told, between 2000 and 2017, rural counties suffered enormous losses of manufacturing jobs—some counties, like Monroe, Ohio; Harney, Oregon; and Jenkins, Georgia, lost virtually all those jobs. That, in turn, led to the closure of retail stores reliant on the income from those factories. And here's the kicker: most economic development policy remains predicated on the idea that over decades, agriculture will be supplanted by manufacturing, which, in turn, will be replaced by more highly skilled work in the service sector. But in many of those same counties, service-sector jobs have disappeared too. Those jobs depend on a requisite population density, and many of these counties just don't have enough people to support that kind of economy. In essence, many industrialized places in rural America have, in turn, deindustrialized; perhaps fittingly, commentators have started referring to the appearance of "rural ghettos."[39]

And then there are the costs to individual lives. According to one study, counties where an automotive plant closed between 1999 and 2016 had significantly higher rates of opioid overdose deaths than counties with auto plants that remained open. The study did not sort strictly by geography, but rural America has been ravaged by opioids since the turn of the twenty-first century.[40] This study strengthens the correlation between that crisis and the vagaries of rural manufacturing.

The deindustrialization of rural America is not a new problem. In 1951, even as the calls to decentralize American industry grew louder and the enthusiasm for it built, the sociologist W. F. Cottrell published a profile of an Arizona desert town he dubbed—unartfully, perhaps— "Caliente." Caliente was a railroad town, quite literally. Like any number of such dots on the map of the vast West, Caliente was established by a railroad company sometime in the last quarter of the nineteenth century (Cottrell wasn't specific about the dates or the geographic location) in order to service long-distance trains. More precisely, Caliente, sitting in a break in an eighty-mile desert canyon, served as a coaling station for steam locomotives. "Caliente," as Cottrell put it, "was a necessity."[41]

Initially, trains needed to refuel every 100 to 150 miles, and coaling towns were spaced accordingly. As steam locomotive technology improved, that distance increased to roughly two hundred miles, and thus "towns located at 100 miles became obsolescent . . . abandoned [and] crossed off the social record of the nation."[42] Caliente survived that round of technological erasure. World War II, however, accelerated the change from steam to diesel. Now trains could travel longer and faster between stops. Caliente was no longer a necessity.

Since the town's founding, however, its residents had established all the institutions of community life—churches and civic clubs and schools. It was "the average American community," Cottrell declared, "with normal social life, subscribing to normal America codes." Without the railroad, however, and with no other reason to be in that spot on the map, no one in Caliente could imagine a future. Caliente was faced with the prospect of "death by dieselization."[43]

In this sense, and from the beginning, industrialization of rural areas has often followed a boom-and-bust cycle. Remember that most of the "ghost towns" scattered across the West and which now attract tourists looking for that "Old West" experience began their lives as small-scale industrial sites, especially mining towns following a pattern that went like this: ore discovered; a flood of people, technology, and capital follows; lode plays out; people and money leave. The only difference between these abandoned mining towns and much of greater West Virginia is that the coal in that region has lasted a lot longer. Never mind the sentimental invocations of "hollers" and moonshine and kinfolk and the rest; much of the Appalachian coal country has been turned into a postindustrial moonscape of slag heaps, eroded hillsides, toxic retention ponds, and abandoned towns. These rural spaces have been shaped by exactly the same economic forces that have affected steel mills or automobile plants. And those rural areas may take much longer to recover than Pittsburgh has.

The population of Centralia, a tiny town in east-central Pennsylvania, peaked at almost 2,800 in 1890. Now it stands as symbolic of deindustrialization in rural America. The town sits on the northern edge of the Appalachian coal region. Men started digging coal out of the earth just before the Civil War, and they kept digging until the 1960s. Sometime in May 1962 a fire broke out in one of the coal seams, more or less right under the town. Townspeople tried to put it out on May 27, but two days later, flames were coming out of the ground again. People tried again to douse them. And again. And many times after that. But the fire could not be put out. It continues to burn to this day, and some estimates predict that there is enough fuel for it to burn for another 250 years. Centralia may be the most literally infernal location in the nation.

The town has attracted national attention on and off over the years. There were roughly 1,500 people living in Centralia when the fire broke out—already a thousand fewer than in 1940. Residents have been enticed, cajoled, and ultimately evicted, first by the federal government in the 1980s and then by the Commonwealth of Pennsylvania in the 1990s and 2000s. While most of the town's structures have been torn down, a few remain, attracting tourists to this ghost town. They come to watch the fire's smoke rise over the remote valley.

The Iowa State Fair. Brought to you by some of America's largest corporations. Photograph by Julianna Curtis.

PART III

RURAL INC.

> In spite of all the pleas for home-town loyalty and all the
> claims of economic solidarity within local communities,
> purchasing habits reveal a different story.
>
> LEWIS ATHERTON, 1954

The title of the book gave away the thesis. When Alfred Chandler published *The Visible Hand: The Managerial Revolution in American Business* in 1977, readers quickly realized its significance. A remarkable work of both original research and the synthesis of other scholars' work, *The Visible Hand* argued that "management," the reorganization of how businesses were run—not entrepreneurship or technological innovation or the invisible hand of some abstract market—had enabled the spectacular growth of American enterprises since the Civil War. Looking back from a distance of thirty years, Steven Usselman called it "magisterial," and it is hard to argue that we aren't still living with the managerial revolution Chandler identified in 1977.[1] Chandler's insight has become so fundamental to our understanding of how American big business operates that many people probably think about business enterprises in Chandlerian terms without knowing Alfred Chandler's name. One wonders how many of the thousands of students who pursue management degrees in American business schools every year have ever read *The Visible Hand*.[2]

Chandler saw his project as explaining in part how, between roughly 1840 and 1920, "the agrarian, rural economy of the United States became industrial and urban."[3] Read from a slightly different angle, however, *The Visible Hand* tells a story of how rural America developed precisely because of that managerial revolution. Take, for example, Chandler's analysis of the rise of mass distribution: "The transformation began as might be expected, in the nation's most important business—the marketing of farm crops," especially cotton and grain.[4] The revolution Chandler described began with the railroads and communications systems, but while those railroads might be headquartered in Chicago or Philadelphia or Minneapolis, the rail networks opened up rural space to make economic activity possible in the first place. In turn, retailers such as Sears and Montgomery Ward built their business by selling products through the mail to rural residents, a business model that relied on railroad and communications networks to work. Further still, meatpacking and tobacco provided two of Chandler's most important examples of the managerial revolution, and both fundamentally reorganized rural space. By the turn of the twentieth century, Americans likely bought their beef from one of six corporations that dominated the market. Armour and Swift each might have employed roughly a thousand office workers in their Chicago headquarters, but both companies consolidated a network of cattle ranches and grazing lands that spread across vast areas of the rural West. The cowboys who drove cattle from those ranches to centralized stockyards might have sung twangy songs around the campfire and slept under the stars, but they were, directly or indirectly, low-level workers for large corporations that dictated their pay and their schedules.

Likewise, the very names Peabody, Guggenheim, and Weyerhaeuser serve as reminders that the extractive industries that dominated certain parts of rural America have always been large corporate enterprises. Only businesses of enormous size could mobilize the capital, technology, and labor to dig coal out of the ground or cut down trees on an industrial scale. All of which is to say that rural people, whether miners, lumberjacks, or farmers, were just as enmeshed in the world of corporations as any urban factory worker or city office employee. "The United States was the world's first 'corporation nation,'" the historian Richard Wright has written, and that nation developed as much in rural places as it did in urban ones.[5] This section looks at several dimensions of that corporate takeover of rural space.

Chapter 6 looks at the ways corporate organization came to agricultural production, starting with agricultural cooperatives. Farmers have always banded together to form co-ops—sometimes to market farm products, sometimes to process them, sometimes to distribute them. Co-ops appealed because they enable producers to bypass the dreaded middleman and sell more directly to consumers. In so doing, presumably, farmers would receive more for their milk or wheat or hogs. The frustration that middlemen robbed farmers of profit lay at the root of much Populist anger in the 1880s and '90s. The passage of the Capper-Volstead Act in 1922 established the legal basis to create agricultural cooperatives and can be seen as the culmination of those late nineteenth-century complaints. But it also enabled some co-ops to incorporate and grow enormous, and that growth raised questions about whether farmers enjoyed special protections from antitrust laws.

Many Americans, from farming areas and elsewhere, have been deeply suspicious of the corporate ownership of farmland. Those fears crescendoed in the late 1960s and early '70s with congressional hearings and reports. In the end, Congress did not act, but plenty of states did. Across the 1970s, ten Grain Belt states passed laws prohibiting the corporate ownership of farmland, and somewhere in the agricultural hereafter, the Populists smiled. In fact, though, the vast majority of corporate farms have been "incorporated family farms," not farming operations owned by a faraway corporation whose shares get publicly traded. These family corporations were exempted from state laws as legislators drew an implicit distinction between good corporations and bad ones. The irony here is that while state legislators thundered against the corporate ownership of land, the grip of corporations on every other aspect of farming grew only tighter during the 1970s. By this point, everything about farming except the acreage itself had come to be controlled by large corporations, from the "input processing" at the front end—seeds, fertilizers, pesticides—to the back end, where farm products are transported, processed, distributed, and sold. It was not accidental or even incremental that this corporate takeover of farming should climax in the 1970s. Farm policy itself encouraged—indeed, cheered—all this, as did farmers. At least until farm prices collapsed yet again in the early 1980s.

Chapter 7 looks at how rural people shopped and how that shopping created some of the largest retail chain corporations in the nation. Twice over, in fact. In the first half of the twentieth century, Woolworth's and Penney's became ubiquitous, central to the lives of countless Americans over several generations. And while it might be easy to see these two corporations, with their headquarters in New York, as part of the urban incursion into small places, both empires were built in the opposite direction: Penney's and Woolworth's both started in small towns, expanded in small towns, and prospered by catering to small-town people and to those who lived in the rural areas surrounding those towns. Woolworth's and Penney's both struggled in the postwar period, but their decline mirrors almost exactly the rise of Walmart and Dollar General. Those two corporations have grown into retail behemoths exactly the way Woolworth's and Penney's did. Both have built vast empires—there are more than seventeen thousand Dollar General stores in the United States as I write this—primarily in rural America. Taking a look at these chain retail stores reminds us that rural America has never been averse to large-scale corporations. In these cases, rural America built them.

CHAPTER 6

WHO'S AFRAID
OF BIG?

Shortly before the Civil War, James Haggin and Lloyd Tevis left Kentucky for California hoping to make their fortune. They were lawyers by training, but not too long after they hung out their shingle in San Francisco, they invested in a mining company. Hearst, Haggin, and Tevis and Co. eventually became the largest privately held mining company in the country.

Having made it big in mining, the two—brothers-in-law by now—decided to go into the cattle-raising business. They bought acreage in Kern County, near Bakersfield, and soon realized, given the dry climate, that they'd be more successful using that land to mature their cattle. They bought ranchland in Arizona, New Mexico, and Oregon to establish cow-calf operations. In 1890 they incorporated their business under the name the Kern County Land Company. Already rich, the two grew even wealthier. Tevis went on to be president of Wells Fargo, and Haggin died among the ultrarich and their mansions in Newport, Rhode Island, in 1914.[1]

By 1960, the Kern County Land Company was something of a misnomer. The corporation still raised cattle, to be sure—forty thousand head of cattle each year got fattened for slaughter in its Bakersfield feed lot. But raising cattle constituted only one division of a wide-ranging corporation. The company farmed 11,000 acres itself and leased out an additional 115,000 to other farmers. Simultaneously, the Kern County Land Company had also become a property-development company and an investor in a California electronics firm. It operated 1,500 oil wells in Kern County and in several other states, and it had purchased the Walker Manufacturing Company, which made auto-exhaust systems in Racine, Wisconsin.[2] Kern County cattle, and the land they grazed upon, had become a diversified portfolio of corporate interests.

Success story or cautionary tale?

On the face of it, Messrs. Haggin and Tevis would seem to exemplify the spirit of their age: risk-taking entrepreneurial investors who manifested their destiny in the promised land of California, even if they never quite joined the pantheon of robber barons like Carnegie, Hill, or Stanford. Perfect examples of the go-west-young-man mythos.

They exemplified something else as well: the corporate rearrangement of rural space and rural production. In that sense, the story of Haggin and Tevis and their Kern County Land Company flew in the face of another American fable that we've discussed already. Whatever one calls it—the pastoral ideal or the agrarian myth or the Jeffersonian vision—rural America is supposed to be populated and worked by small-scale, independent producers, not impersonal corporate octopi.

Corporate management, corporate control, corporations altogether have generated uneasiness or hostility across much of rural America since the nineteenth century. Railroads in particular drew the wrath of the Populists of the 1880s and '90s, but their rhetoric was often directed more broadly at the emerging corporate order, most symbolically at New York banks. Their anger was not altogether misplaced. Across the nineteenth century, banks and insurance companies in eastern states provided loans to western farmers, and they often did so speculatively, driving up land prices as a consequence. Take one data point as a measure of the frenzy: twenty-nine million

of the thirty-eight million acres of public land sold between 1837 and
1839 were purchased by land speculators.[3] "The West and South are
bound and prostrate before the manufacturing East," thundered Mary
Elizabeth Lease in her speech "Wall Street Owns the Country," delivered over and over as she stumped for the Populist movement.[4]

However stirring that speech might have been, the situation was
more complicated. Rural America has been enmeshed with corporate
arrangements since at least the Civil War and probably before it as
well.[5] Far from representing an opposition or an alternative to what
Alan Trachtenberg memorably called the incorporation of America,
rural America has been at the forefront of that incorporation for a
very long time.

COOPERATION INCORPORATED

In the third week of November, duck callers from all over the world
gather in Stuttgart, Arkansas, to compete in the World Championship
Duck Calling Contest, as they have done every year since 1936. It was
a simple affair initially, but now it is part of a weeklong festival that
includes arts-and-crafts exhibits, a rally of off-road vehicles, and the
World Championship Duck Gumbo Cookoff.[6]

All that stakes Stuttgart's claim to be "the duck capital of the world."
The town also prides itself on being "the rice capital of the world"—
and that boast acknowledges the real business in town.

Riceland Foods Inc., whose international headquarters sits at
2120 South Park Avenue, just west of State Route 165, is a behemoth.
Formed initially in 1921—reorganized in 1926—Riceland is now the
world's largest miller and marketer of rice. The mill it operates in
Jonesboro, Arkansas, is reportedly the largest in the world. From
those offices in Stuttgart, Riceland products are moved all over the
country, and indeed all over the globe.

Walk two miles north to 218 East Harrison Street and you'll find
yourself at the headquarters of Producers Rice Mill Inc. Producers
started milling rice in Stuttgart in 1943 and expanded in the 1970s as

federal restrictions on rice acreage were lifted. As I write this, Producers mills more than sixty million bushels of rice annually. Between 1995 and 2020, Producers Rice Mill Inc. was also the second largest recipient of federal farm subsidies. First on that list stands Riceland Foods. Between them, they have brought nearly $900 million in subsidies to Stuttgart, nearly $100,000 for each resident of the town whose population isn't quite nine thousand.[7]

Riceland and Producers are both large, sprawling corporations. They are also farm cooperatives. For many of us, co-ops are small-scale operations. Grocery store co-ops emerged in the late 1960s and '70s as alternatives to chain supermarkets and were often the first places to market local and organic foods. But in the world of agricultural production, co-ops are big business, and they have been for a century. Indeed, farming cooperatives on a large scale began to emerge as a significant piece of the nation's agricultural sector after the First World War—precisely the moment when the federal government's attempts to reign in industrial trusts and monopolies faltered and waned.

There was not anything arbitrary, therefore, about the year Riceland formed or the year it reorganized itself. The first two decades of the twentieth century had been good to American farmers; those years have often been called "the golden age" of American agriculture. Climatic conditions in the Great Plains improved, immigrants pouring into industrial cities supplied millions of new mouths to feed, and the war itself was very good for business. Once the war concluded, however, the bottom dropped out of commodities prices, which fell to levels that hadn't been seen in twenty years. Rice, for example, sold at $4.50 per bushel during the war; by 1920, the price per bushel had dropped to 30 cents.[8]

Many farmers and farm state politicians offered the same diagnosis as they had in the 1880s and '90s: farmers were being ripped off by "middlemen" who robbed them of a fair price for the fruits of their labor. Senator Arthur Capper (R-KS) put this quite bluntly in an essay reprinted in newspapers around the country. The farmer, he wrote, "parts with his products long before the consumer sees them or needs them. A host of toll and profit takers meanwhile busy themselves with these products, transferring them from hand to hand and absorbing as much profit as they with their skill at that sort of thing are able to extract from the marketing business."[9] Co-ops seemed to be a promising way to eliminate those scheming middlemen. By banding together, farmers could work cooperatively to set prices, work out deals for distribution, and take care of their own marketing, and in so doing, put more money back into farmers' overalls. "Cooperative marketing or the collective selling of farm products is not merely an idea or a passing and popular fad," one Arkansas newspaper told its readers, "it is a business and economic necessity and must surely come, no matter if the number of middlemen be reduced or a change in methods must be made."[10] As troops came home and farm prices dropped, farmers started to mobilize to make agricultural co-ops a political issue.

Gathering in Chicago in 1919, farmers from thirty states formed the American Farm Bureau Federation, a lobbying group—though they didn't call themselves that—that would allow farmers to advocate for themselves. The statement they adopted read: "The purpose of Farm Bureau is to make the business of farming more profitable, and the community a better place to live. Farm Bureau should provide an organization in which members may secure the benefits of unified efforts in a way that could never be accomplished through individual effort." Farm Bureau members ratified that language in 1920, when the political lobbying went into high gear. In 1920, for example, the Texas Farm Bureau passed out a questionnaire to political candidates quizzing them about their position on agricultural co-ops.[11] Other state farm bureaus engaged in similar kinds of lobbying efforts. And to those who raised an eyebrow at the prospect of farmers organizing at a state or even national level, one farmer replied: "If a national organization is a good thing for merchants and bankers and manufacturers, it's a good thing for farmers, too."[12]

Farmers directed their efforts at a specific piece of legislation: a bill sponsored by Representative Andrew Volstead (R-MN) in the House and, fittingly enough, Capper in the Senate. Passing this bill became the most important rural issue of the day.

What held the formation of co-ops back to this point was that they ran the risk of violating the nation's antitrust laws by allowing farmers to collude on prices and production in ways that might prove to be monopolistic. Indeed, farmers had occasionally been prosecuted for just such behavior. The Capper-Volstead Act targeted that problem by granting agricultural co-ops exemption from antitrust laws. The language of the act stipulates that farmers "may act together" to market their products collectively.

The larger goal, however, of allowing farmers to "act together was to achieve the power of scale that enabled corporations to dominate other sectors of the economy, while also enjoying the benefits, legal and otherwise," that corporations did. Volstead explained this on the floor of the House when the bill had been put forward. "The objection made to these organizations [cooperatives] is that they violate the Sherman Antitrust Act," he acknowledged, "and that is upon the theory that each farmer is a separate business entity." As a result, Volstead went on, "when he combines with his neighbor for the purpose of securing better treatment in the disposal of his crops, he is charged with a conspiracy or combinations contrary to the Sherman Antitrust Act." But the way the law was currently structured, Volstead believed, put farmers as a distinct disadvantage: "Businessmen can combine by putting their money into corporations, but it is impractical for farmers to combine their farms into similar corporate forms. The object of this bill is to modify the laws under which business organizations are now formed, so that farmers may take advantage of the form of organization that is used by business concerns." On the other side of the Capitol, Capper, a more succinct orator, put things simply: the act's purpose, he told his fellow senators, "is to give to the farmer the same right to bargain collectively that is already enjoyed by corporations."[13] With farmers increasingly unhappy, President Warren Harding laid out an agenda of relief in January 1922 that included six items; among them was the promise to sign the Capper-Volstead

Act. Congress passed the bill, and Harding signed it the following month. Riceland (originally, the Arkansas Rice Growers Cooperative Association; the Riceland name came in 1970) formed as the enthusiasm for farm co-ops swelled in 1921.

P. G. Spilsbury, president of the Arizona Industrial Congress, stood before a convention of the state's wool growers in the summer of 1924 and told them that if "organized agriculture [was] to be permanently successful [it] must follow the principles determined by cooperative government and cooperative or corporation business," and that among those principles was "centralization of management under elective control of members."[14] The goal of forming agricultural co-ops, in other words, was not to beat larger corporations but to become more like them. And as a measure of just how snugly the agricultural co-op fit into the "business of America is business" ethos of the 1920s, Calvin Coolidge announced his support for a federal law to permit cooperative marketing in agriculture in a speech he gave in Chicago on December 7, 1925. "I propose actively and energetically to assist the farmers," Coolidge promised, "to promote their welfare through cooperative marketing," because in Coolidge's view, cooperative marketing would keep the government out of the farming business.[15] By the end of Coolidge's term, the US Department of Agriculture had created a Division of Cooperative Marketing.

Capper-Volstead did nod toward consumer concerns by saying the cooperatives could be forced to "cease and desist" should they be found to be acting in restraint of trade. For that reason, some in Congress wanted the Federal Trade Commission to take responsibility for overseeing agricultural co-ops. Farmers rebelled and insisted that the Department of Agriculture take charge of oversight, assuming that the USDA would be a more sympathetic audience. In the end, they got their way. But it took several years for everyone to figure out just how the new rules would work. In 1924, to take one example, the Armour Grain Company and the Rosenbaum Grain Corporation—two giants of the Chicago commodities world—came together to form a cooperative named the Grain Marketing Company. That seemed (to some observers, at any rate) like a shameless attempt to use the

Capper-Volstead law as a fig leaf for monopoly behavior. Newton Jenkins, counsel for the American Wheat Growers Association, railed in 1925 that the "operations of the Grain Marketing Company in the last year have in no way lessened the evils of speculative marketing" and that, as a co-op, Armour and Rosenbaum ran things exactly as they had done before they merged, "with the buyers' rather than the sellers' interest foremost."[16] The co-op dissolved in 1925 because it couldn't figure out whether the provisions of Capper-Volstead protected their operations or not.

In fact, not until 1939 did the Supreme Court define the antitrust boundaries of the Capper-Volstead Act with some more clarity. In a case brought against a coalition of companies engaged in milk production, distribution, and marketing for violating antitrust law, a lower court ruled that Capper-Volstead gave broad protection to agricultural companies and insisted that the real authority to regulate these companies and their operations lay with the secretary of agriculture. The Supreme Court disagreed. The *United States v. Borden* decision was issued in December 1939 and, in essence, ruled against the milk companies because only some of them were themselves co-ops. Others were not, and therefore those were subject to the Sherman Antitrust Act. The Capper-Volstead Act, the court concluded, did not immunize "any combination or conspiracy with other persons in restraint of trade that these producers [co-ops] may see fit to devise." In *Borden*, the milk producer's cooperatives had entered into arrangements with noncooperative distributors.[17] The court sent the case back for trial.

By the time the court ruled, agricultural co-ops had become a permanent fixture on the nation's economic landscape. During the campaign of 1928, the question of how best to aid farmers was being "contemplated by the platforms of the major political parties and discussed by their nominees." What was unarguable, however, was the extraordinary growth of farm co-ops. One tally counted one out of every four farmers enrolled in some sort of cooperative, and as the newsman Harden Colfax noted, "every form of legislation thus far proposed . . . contemplates transactions through groups, not individuals." What struck Colfax particularly was not the sheer number—more than twelve thousand, according to the USDA—but their size: more than one hundred of those twelve thousand did an annual business of over $1 million, and they had invested "more than $300,000,000 . . . in grain elevators, cotton gins and warehouses, live-stock yards, fruit-packing plants, creameries" and more. In less than ten years, these cooperatives had "leaped from an aggregate membership of 29,000 to close to 900,000" farms, or nearly half of the two million farms that had joined a co-op. That concentration, in turn, accelerated a reorientation in the way farmers interacted with markets. The very notion of "cooperation," Colfax observed, started to lose its local valence, and farmers started instead "thinking and acting in terms of State, region or Nation." The trend lines seemed clear enough to Colfax: "Many of the small, independent local organizations survive, but the tendency is strongly toward larger associations." "The era of the giant cooperative appears almost at hand."[18]

Co-ops also busied themselves in Washington. "In the past years," the agricultural economist E. W. Gaumnitz noted, "the leaders of the great agricultural selling cooperatives have taken a steadily increasing interest in national issues and legislation. They have conferred with high government officials, presidents down, and their advice has been sought and often accepted."[19] Gaumnitz made those remarks in 1936, by which point the concerns about the antitrust implications of co-ops had been replaced with a charge that co-ops drove up food prices in the midst of the Great Depression. In the face of these complaints, one newspaper editorialist felt compelled to leap to their defense. "Those who believe that the aim of cooperative marketing is to force prices sky high are mistaken," he wrote. Writing from the southern end of Maryland's eastern shore, he used dairy cooperatives as an example of how co-ops improved quality, facilitated better distribution, stabilized prices, and "conscientiously worked to give the public a better product at a fair price."[20]

In truth, life was difficult for farmers and consumers during the Great Depression—the page where this editorial ran, just to take a random example, also featured several notices for public auctions on bankrupt farms. But co-ops themselves, and especially the large ones that Colfax saw on the horizon, kept growing. Cooperatives couldn't join up with non–co-op companies to help control the marketplace— that much the Supreme Court made clear in 1939. But nothing in the ruling prohibited agricultural cooperatives from forming or acquiring other kinds of businesses, or even more important, from working with other co-ops to create more vertical integration. Arkansan rice growers came together in 1921 in order to market and sell their rice cooperatively. But the rice-milling operations had a vested interest in paying as little as possible for the product, and so the farmers in the co-op began leasing their own milling plants. And then, in 1939 (coincidentally, I suspect), the Rice Growers Cooperative Association bought its own mill in Jonesboro.[21]

After the Second World War, agricultural cooperatives continued to generate a certain amount of critical scrutiny—over how much taxes they paid and over whether they really did engage in monopoly practices after all. But they have successfully weathered those challenges and a number have grown into vertically integrated corporate behemoths. The Capper-Volstead Act is not the legislation for which Andrew Volstead is most famous, of course—that would be the law that enabled prohibition—but it has proved far more enduring. Since 1922, ag co-ops have been legal, and the Capper-Volstead Act has stood remarkably unchanged ever since. Cooperation has proved to be big business. Just ask the folks in Stuttgart, Arkansas.

CORPORATIONS DOWN ON THE FARM

Go to the local farmer's market on Saturday morning. You buy your sweet corn from the farmer who grew it. Same with your tomatoes, onions, and apples, as well, when they come in. You chat with the farmers and with the other shoppers. The trip each Saturday becomes something more than simply stocking up for the week; it creates a relationship with the food we eat that feels right in an almost moral way. We don't like to think that food is simply another consumer product, mass produced through industrial technologies, distributed and sold to us through corporate organization. The farmer's market takes us back to an earlier age. It stands as the antithesis of going to the supermarket.

In fact, as Jon Lauck has noted, "corporate attempts to take advantage of scale in American farming are as old as the Republic," though they largely failed, except in meat production, a handful of sugar and pineapple plantations in Hawaii, and some fruit, vegetable, and nut growers in California.[22] After the First World War, corporate ownership of farms became an issue of some public debate and even more so during the Great Depression. The idea that corporations would own farmland didn't sit right with many people or with many of their representatives. But it isn't clear that there was a genuine problem about which to get agitated. In Minnesota, for example, nearly 10 percent of all farmland was corporately owned by 1940. Whether or not that figure strikes you as large, it deceives a bit. Life insurance companies and the Minnesota Department of Rural Credit together owned over half that acreage, hinting strongly that farm foreclosures, rather than aggressive acquisition, led to this growth of corporate ownership. In fact, corporate ownership peaked in 1938, and by 1940 the trend line seemed to be heading down. As the agricultural economy improved, landowning corporations were eager to sell off their acreage. A report from the University of Minnesota Agricultural Experiment Station noted, "Corporate ownership of farmland in Minnesota is likely to continue to decrease if net farm income does not decline below the level of the last few years."[23]

After the war, corporate ownership of farms proliferated, but not in the way one might expect. In the 1950s, farm families discovered the advantages that incorporation provided, and many turned their farms into corporations. These so-called "closely held" corporations did not create an influx of new capital, nor were they designed to achieve efficiencies of scale, nor did they trade stock publicly. Rather, reorganizing the family farm as a corporation offered tax advantages and some liability protections, but perhaps most important, they made inheritance issues easier to resolve as one generation died and a new one took ownership. The more-conventional family partnerships dissolved upon the death of one of the partners; a corporation could potentially last forever.

In this sense, far from destroying small-scale farming, corporate organization was embraced after World War II to keep that way of life afloat. "Our society's concern over allocation and control of resources has led to a fear that the application of the corporate structure to agriculture would destroy the revered 'family farm,'" wrote the agricultural economist B. D. Crossman in 1953. But, he continued, "the farm corporation as a threat to the family farm, which is prized so highly in our society, is unfounded. The family farm may actually be perpetuated through the corporate device."[24]

By the late 1960s, however, corporations of the more stereotypical kind began acquiring farmland, and their arrival caused considerable debate and controversy. Cassandra came from California. In widely reprinted remarks, J. Blaine Quinn, master of the California State Grange, warned the nation in 1966 about his state's "corporate farm belt": "You drive for miles without seeing a home, church, school or business. . . . It is worse than feudal Europe and is a blot on the American civilization. In the name of all that's decent in American rural life let's not expand this pattern of corporate farming."[25]

A proposed large-scale and corporately owned hog operation in Traer, Iowa, in 1967 generated a fierce backlash. As local Don McLain put it: "What I really object to is the corporate nature of this setup. Most of the houses on this road are deserted or lived in by nonfarmers who commute to work in town. The very small farmer has been forced out and now the family farms are threatened."[26] The sense that Iowa farms were now under threat of corporate takeover prompted the Iowa Farmers Union to pass a resolution at its annual meeting that year urging the legislature to ban corporate ownership of farms.

The fear in 1967 that corporations would buy up America's farms stretched from the Farm Belt to Washington. Lyndon Johnson's secretary of agriculture, Orville Freeman, announced himself "deeply concerned over the increased movement by large diversified nonfarm corporations into agriculture."[27] At the end of the year, he ordered his department to undertake a study of corporate ownership.

The Senate, too, decided it needed to investigate. The Select Committee on Small Business's Subcommittee on Monopoly held two hearings, and senators left Washington to hold them, convening first in Omaha and then in Eau Claire, Wisconsin. Interestingly, when Senator Gaylord Nelson opened the proceedings, he made little mention of the economics of agriculture or the price of food. Nor did he comment on corporate bigness as a virtue or an evil. The committee, he told the room, wanted "to determine what the effect of corporation farming will be on small businesses in rural communities, what the consequences will be on the sociological and moral environment of rural America, what the implications will be on existing independent family farms and how we can expect our country's natural resources to be used by giant farm operators." Nelson then tipped his cards: "I suspect that if corporation farming becomes the wave of the future it not only spells the doom of small rural businesses and family farms but it raises other grave questions. . . . If corporation farming means fewer family farms and rural businesses then our already overcrowded cities will be the target for even more outmigration from the countryside. This further pileup of people in the cities will only compound the problems that have led to riots and civil disorder."[28] Small farms functioned as part of an economic matrix of small businesses, as Nelson saw it, and it wouldn't just be the farm kids who would move to the city—the feed-store operator, the local banker, and the teachers from the now-shuttered school would join them.

With the tone of the proceedings thus set, the subcommittee heard from a great many witnesses but heard largely the same set of warnings. Ben Radcliffe, president of the South Dakota Farmers Union, captured the essence of them in his testimony. South Dakota had lost more than six thousand farms between 1959 and 1964, a number that mirrored national trends. And for every six farms lost, South Dakota saw one other business close during that period. If one out of six businesses closed, then one out of seven South Dakotans left the state during the 1950s, a total of almost ninety-five thousand. More distressing still, 25 percent of those were young adults, "the real productive segment of any State's population." As Radcliffe put it: "The independent farmer in many rural communities throughout this great Nation could face oblivion unless the movement of nonfarm corporations into agriculture is halted." The question, as far as Radcliffe was concerned, was as simple as it was urgent: "Who shall control agriculture?"[29]

Tony Dechant played a prominent role in the subcommittee's hearings. And no surprise. Dechant served as the president of the National Farmers Union. In March 1968, Dechant's organization rallied its troops for battle against corporate farming. The Farmers Union issued a statement with this cry: "We urge every state [union] to conduct an educational campaign designed to bring pressure on state legislatures which will result in banning the super corporate farms."[30]

Legislatures in several farm states took up the charge. A year earlier, in fact, members of the Iowa Farmers Union had passed a resolution calling for a state-level ban on corporate ownership of farms, and as the 1960s turned into the 1970s, farmers and their allies in a number of farm states pushed their own state-level legislation to do just that. Writing in 1970, the lawyer Neil Harl noted: "In farming, the corporation has been even more controversial as a form of business organization. Few topics today evoke a more heated response in farm circles."[31] By 1974, lawmakers in Kansas, Minnesota, Wisconsin, Oklahoma, and North Dakota had all passed some version of anticorporate legislation.

In 1974, South Dakota joined them. The average size of a South Dakota farm had grown by a third since 1960, while the total number of farms in the state had shrunk by an almost equal amount. And as South Dakotans reckoned with these changes, they blamed outside corporations.

Such a bill had been put on the floor four times previously, and four times it had failed. Persistence paid off, along with a growing tide of anticorporate feeling in the state. As the bill was put to the South Dakota House in January, Governor Dick Kneip signaled that he would sign it if it passed. Ted Muenster, the governor's executive aide, echoed fellow South Dakotan Ben Radcliffe when he told the House Agriculture Committee that the fundamental question was "who shall own South Dakota."[32] The bill passed 39–27 in the House and then quickly in the Senate. Corporate ownership of land in South Dakota had been made illegal.

The debate over corporate farming in Nebraska came to a boil in 1982. As yet another "farm crisis" set in at the end of the 1970s, Nebraskans directed their anguish and frustration against corporate ownership of farmland as the source of their problems. Galvanized by a coalition of farm groups, more than sixty-one thousand citizens—swept up in "a prairie fire of populist discontent"—put their signatures to a ballot initiative to amend the state constitution.[33] They called it I-300.

The text of the amendment was unequivocal: "No corporation or syndicate shall acquire, or otherwise obtain an interest, whether legal, beneficial, or otherwise, in any title to real estate used for farming or ranching in this state, or engage in farming or ranching." But the text drew a clear distinction: "These restrictions shall not apply to: (A) A family farm or ranch corporation . . . (B) Non-profit corporations."[34] The target was obvious: not Family Farm Incorporated, but big outsiders, corporations coming into the state and buying up farmland, taking over farm production, and jacking the price of land up as a consequence.

I-300 split Nebraskans in predictable and not so predictable ways. Lining up to support the amendment stood farm groups such as the Nebraska Farmers Union, the National Farmers Organization, the Nebraska Grange, and WIFE—Women Involved in Farm Economics. On the other hand, the Nebraska Farm Bureau and the Nebraska Livestock Feeders Association vehemently opposed it. The measure also drew support from church groups, including the Nebraska Catholic Conference and the Nebraska Conference of the United Church of

Christ, while the Nebraska Realtors Association voted unanimously to express their opposition. Prudential—the Newark, New Jersey, insurance giant and owner of more than thirty-four thousand Nebraska acres—donated $125,000 to help defeat the initiative. It was the single largest campaign contribution in Nebraska history, and Prudential promised another $100,000 as the vote approached. In the end, opponents of I-300 spent nearly half a million dollars to defeat the measure; by contrast, the Committee to Preserve the Family Farm raised just under $35,000 for its advocacy work.[35] Money, at least in this case, couldn't buy the election: voters passed the initiative with 56 percent of the vote.

A SOLUTION IN SEARCH OF A PROBLEM?

As Senator Gaylord Nelson and his colleagues held their hearings in Omaha and Eau Claire during the summer of 1968, the study that Agriculture Secretary Orville Freeman had commissioned a year earlier came out. It was decidedly not a blockbuster.

The national survey concluded that while corporate farming was increasing, it had not made "serious inroads" into the traditional patterns and arrangements of farming in the United States. Corporate farming made up less than 1 percent of commercial farms; those farms accounted for less than 7 percent of all farmland, and those farms sold roughly 4 percent of farm products. In the data from the first twenty-two states in the survey, the USDA found a total of 150 large-scale corporate farms that each sold $500,000 worth of products. In fact, nearly three-quarters of corporate farms were owned by family-held corporations of exactly the type exempted by those state laws. When Nelson was asked to comment, he spun the results. "No one suggests that corporate farms have already taken over," he averred, "but this [report] confirms that the trend is increasing rapidly."[36]

The USDA released another survey of corporate farming; this one picked up from the first and ended in 1982, the year Nebraskans amended their state constitution. It reported an impressive increase in the number of incorporated farms—a whopping 178 percent from the 1968 figure. But it found roughly the same ownership patterns: 11 percent of those corporate farms were classed as "nonfamily"; some of those acres, as was the case during the 1930s, were held by banks or insurance companies dealing with some form of foreclosure. Meanwhile, the remaining 89 percent were family owned. Incorporation had always provided tax advantages for farm families. Lower corporate tax rates during the 1970s, however, combined with rising inflation that made personal income tax grow, encouraged family farms to become corporate farms. Large-scale, corporately owned growers did dominate in certain market niches—particularly, fruits, nuts, and sugarcane—and the visibility of those products to consumers "helped foster the impression that family farms are being threatened by large corporations." But the report was clear: "Despite the increase in farm corporations, most farms remain sole proprietorships and most incorporated farms are family ones."[37]

The fact that corporations were not aggressively buying up land in the nation's Farm Belt was not lost on some who were skeptical of anticorporate legislation. When the South Dakota House debated the anticorporate bill there in January 1974, Representative Don Jorgensen was among those skeptics. "I fail to see the concern," the Democrat from Ideal said. He continued: "This is unnecessary. There are fewer corporations with farm land in the state now than there were ten years ago. They just can't compete." His Republican colleague Walt Miller, from New Underwood, challenged fellow House members by asking: "I'd like one of the sponsors . . . to cite one example since last year of a corporation that has come in, bought the land and threatened the existence of a community." As the *Rapid City Journal* reported of the exchange, "No one responded."[38]

The phenomenon of the corporate farming conglomerate may have been exaggerated, but the evidence of rural decline was certainly real. The Iowa City newspaper man Jenkin Lloyd Jones sounded downright elegiac in 1965. "America's very small towns are in trouble. . . .

This is a sad fact of modern America—sad because of the sentimental legend, still strong among us, that the village represented peace and virtue and friendly help as opposed to the coldness and wickedness of the city," he wrote in an editorial. "Contract harvesting made possible the corporate farms where the empty houses warp in the sunshine and no man watches the wheat grow." Never mind that the rival *Des Moines Register* ran a story a few months later headlined: "Iowa Lags in Corporation Farm Development."[39]

The lawyer Neil Harl, analyzing the anticorporate groundswell in 1970, believed that "enthusiasm for limiting the use made of the corporate form in agriculture seem[ed] to be traceable to concerns about the changing rural environment and changing nature of the farm firm. The principal concerns appear[ed] to be related to 1) increasing size of farms, and 2) the decline of small towns in rural areas." That seems a sensible conclusion, as people across the middle of the country channeled their frustrations at rising farm costs, withering small towns, and the triumph of bigness altogether against corporations. But as Harl saw it, anticorporate legislation was unlikely to solve those problems. The year after the anticorporate bill became law in South Dakota, Curtis Jensen sounded even more doubtful about the efficacy of that state's legislation. Noting that it did "not appear that the existence of corporate farms in the state has had any marked effect on rural life," he characterized the bill as "prospective," an attempt to preserve what was, rather than fix something that had broken. Given that, however, Jensen wasn't optimistic that the law would even achieve its stated goal. The act, he concluded, might "prove to be an ineffective barrier to the entry of nonfarm investment. If in the coming years there exists the opportunity to reap huge profits in agriculture, there is little reason to believe the Family Farm Act will prove more than a minor hindrance to determined investors."[40]

Jensen may well have been proved right. In 1978, Dun and Bradstreet published one of their periodical business directories, this one inventorying "Million Dollar" firms. Of those, nearly eight hundred were engaged in agricultural production. They were all big, to be sure, and all had adopted the very latest technologies and efficiencies. But, according to one analyst, "many of these businesses embodied tangled operating arrangements," and the list "included corporate giants with subsidiaries engaged in food and fiber production." As the journalist Peter Meyer put it, by the end of the 1970s, despite the spasms of anticorporate politics in farm states, "almost everything [was] known about American land except who own[ed] it."[41]

LOOKING FOR CORPORATIONS
IN ALL THE WRONG PLACES

Drive across the agricultural midsection of the country—stay off the interstates—and you will see landscapes identical to the ones that surround the town where I live. Ohio, Indiana, Illinois, Iowa, Missouri, Minnesota—corn and beans, beans and corn, acre after acre for miles and miles. Monocultural, monochromatic, and depending on your aesthetic, monotonous. These are the rural spaces created by Earl Butz.

Newspapers often described Butz as "folksy," an aw-shucks, gee-whiz euphemism to describe a vulgar and deeply bigoted man. Born and raised on a dairy farm in Albion, Indiana, at the start of the William Howard Taft administration, Butz left farming for the groves of academe. After getting a PhD at Purdue University, Butz worked for a variety of farm organizations before being appointed assistant agriculture secretary by Dwight Eisenhower in 1954. When he left that post in 1957, he went back to Purdue as dean of the Agriculture College and stayed in West Lafayette until 1971. In that year, Richard Nixon plucked him to be his secretary of agriculture and Butz returned to Washington. American agriculture has never been the same since.

His nomination took Washington observers by surprise. Butz had already built a reputation as blustery and outspoken and vigorously opposed to the policies that had governed agriculture since the New Deal. Democrats—especially those jockeying for a possible presidential run—criticized him, but so did Republicans from farm states. He took his chair at his Senate confirmation hearings and said: "I feel like the man who walked into the post office, saw his picture on the wall and said he didn't know he was wanted."[42] He cleared the confirmation committee just barely, by a vote of 8–6.

Butz offended in part because he did not spout the time-worn bromides about the sanctity of the small, independent family farm. Small was not beautiful, whatever the economist E. F. Schumacher claimed in his 1973 book of that title. Small was inefficient, and Butz never shied from saying so. Butz had seen the future of agriculture, and it was big: big farms, big feedlots, huge per-acre yields. He'd said as much in the 1950s during his first tour in the USDA: "Agriculture is now big business. Too many people are trying to stay in agriculture that would do better someplace else." And then, sounding an awful lot like a famous scene from *Star Trek* years later, he intoned: "Adapt or die; resist and perish."[43] In subsequent years, he condensed that message to the more bumper sticker–size "Get big or get out," which became something of a personal slogan. The most Butz, charged as an enemy of the family farm, could muster in his defense during his confirmation hearings was to say: "The family farm must be preserved but it has to . . . produce more in the years ahead to survive."[44] That turned out to be a prophecy Butz's own policies would fulfill.

For Nixon, Butz's first task was to quell restive farmers ahead of the 1972 election. Fully aware that the 1960s had been another bad decade on the farm and throughout rural America broadly, Nixon worried that the anticorporate movement sweeping across farm states might translate into anti-Nixon votes in the election. Butz boosted farm prices by negotiating a blockbuster food deal with the Soviet Union, which was experiencing its own farm crisis.[45] Farmers cheered the announcement that thirty million tons of American grain would be shipped to the USSR. They voted for Nixon in November.

Almost immediately, in an agricultural version of Newton's third law, the Great Grain Sales of 1972 combined with rapidly rising inflation, price ceilings for farmers, and bad weather in certain farm areas to drive food prices up dramatically in 1973. Grain farmers may have been happy, but housewives now were not. They organized pickets outside supermarkets as beef prices, tracking the price of grain-based feed, skyrocketed. Meanwhile, in scenes reminiscent of the Great Depression, poultry farmers killed off their chicks because they could not afford to feed them those same grain-based feeds. "Like it or not," Lester Brown, an economist with the Overseas Development Council, said, "Americans are sharing food scarcity with Russia." Rumors circulated that a black market in beef had developed in Minnesota, and *U.S. News & World Report* warned: "Shortages may become so serious that rationing is a possibility later this year."[46] Nixon feared, rightly or not, that suburban consumers angry about the price of food would replace antiwar demonstrators in the streets, and he told Butz to placate them.

It was the moment Earl Butz had been waiting for. The mandate he had from Nixon to drive food prices down as low as possible allowed him to recast fundamentally the relationship between the federal government and the farming sector. In so doing, he dismantled the New Deal agricultural order.

That had been the goal of his boss and fellow Mormon Ezra Taft Benson during Butz's first tour at the USDA. Benson was convinced that everything about the New Deal amounted to communist infiltration (he believed the same thing about the civil rights movement— George Wallace had tried to persuade Benson to be his running mate in 1968). As USDA secretary, Benson held an unshakable, dogmatic faith that the "free market" would cure what ailed American farmers. He did away with—or tried to—a variety of government programs including price supports for commodities. He was once pelted with eggs by South Dakota farmers.

Benson's policies resulted in what the *New Republic* called "disastrous crop surpluses," and with surpluses came falling prices.[47] Surpluses have plagued American farmers from the very beginning of the nation. Initially, surpluses resulted first from ever more acres being turned over to farming; since the Second World War, surpluses

have been the consequence of ever-increasing yields per acre, thanks
to the saturation of American farm fields with fertilizers, pesticides,
herbicides, and other highly toxic if highly effective petrochemicals.
And surpluses have always generated a crushing paradox: they reduce
prices as more product comes to market. But at the same time, the
only way any individual farmer can earn money is to produce more.
To put this hypothetically, if the price of corn drops from a dollar per
bushel to fifty cents, cash-strapped farmers have to produce twice as
much corn to earn that dollar. Except that if every farmer feels forced
to do that, the supply of corn doubles and price drops still more. Iowa
corn grower George Naylor explained the dilemma by noting that the
law of supply and demand does not work on the farm. An ordinary
business firm, faced with economic difficulties, can lay people off or
shut down factories to support prices until "the market finds a new
balance between supply and demand." By contrast, "the demand for
food isn't elastic; people don't eat more just because food is cheap.
And laying off farmers doesn't help to reduce supply. You can fire me,
but you can't fire my land. . . . Even if I go out of business this land will
keep producing corn." In sum, as Naylor saw it, "the free market has
never worked in agriculture and it never will."[48]

Butz, from his post as assistant secretary in the mid-1950s, had seen
the problem of surpluses. As secretary of the USDA, he implemented
an ingenious solution that, in crude summary, went like this: keep
food prices permanently low by incentivizing farmers to produce as
much as possible, all the time. Pay farmers directly for that overpro-
duction and then export the surpluses overseas.

He had proved the effectiveness of that latter strategy with the
grain sale to Moscow, but the ramifications of it went beyond propping up grain prices. Butz was characteristically blunt about the foreign policy implications of massive food exports. He told the World
Food Conference, gathered in Rome in 1974 to address the issue of
global famine, that the United States wasn't interested primarily in
solving humanitarian disasters but rather saw food as "a tool in the kit
of American diplomacy."[49] That point of view was neither original nor

new; using food aid as part of the Cold War jousting with the Soviet Union dated back to the Eisenhower administration when Benson was in charge.[50] The promise of food could be used as leverage with nations in the developing world—given, should the political winds blow toward the United States; taken away, should they blow in other directions. Butz himself was quoted as saying: "Hungry men listen only to those who have a piece of bread." He wanted those hungry, and thus potentially communist, men to be eating bread made from exported American wheat. The farm fields and ranchland across the nation's rural midsection didn't just house the arsenal of the nation's ICBMs. Food itself could be deployed as a weapon in the global struggle against communism, and in this way, Butz enlisted American farmers as Cold Warriors.

The other constituent pieces of Butz's formula did represent a more dramatic break with the past. New Dealers also had recognized the problem of surpluses—and of good and bad years altogether—and devised several strategies to deal with it. Championed by USDA Secretary Henry Wallace, New Deal agricultural policy worked roughly like this: First, the government set a price floor on storable commodities based on the production costs of each product. Should the market price of corn (or wheat or sorghum) rise higher than that target, great. Farmers could sell and expect a profit in return. Should the price drop below the target, however, then farmers could keep their corn off the market by using it as collateral for a government loan to tide them over. If prices rose, then the farmer sold the corn, paid back the loan, and waited to see what the next season's harvest would bring. If he opted not to sell, he could keep the money by giving the corn (or wheat or sorghum) to the government. It would be stored against future demand in the quaintly named "Ever-Normal Granary."

Simultaneously, programs administered through the Soil Conservation Service and working hand in glove with the production limitation incentives of the Agricultural Adjustment Act subsidized farmers to take acreage out of production altogether.[51] That seemed an obvious way to reduce production, but it generated some initial controversy—paying farmers not to grow food even while some Americans went hungry was a tough public relations sell. The Soil Conservation Service, as its very name suggests, also had an environmental agenda. As prairie winds blew the topsoil from millions of acres in the Great Plains during the "dirty '30s," letting fields go fallow protected sensitive areas and gave overworked fields a rest.

Critics pounced on Wallace's proposals even before they had been fully enacted. The Stanford food economist Joseph Davis complained that the whole program was based on what he called "politico-nomics" rather than sound economics (as if there is ever really a distinction between the two). He predicted that "the ever-normal granary system . . . would not work well enough to endure long."[52] Davis got that one wrong. The system worked, more or less, across the middle decades of the twentieth century. In fact, the Agricultural Adjustment Act of 1938 (the one that replaced the AAA struck down by the Supreme Court) remained the country's basic framework for agricultural policy until the mid-1960s.[53] It was the system that Earl Butz inherited and the system he blew up.

The 1973 Farm Bill was the instrument of this dramatic reorientation of federal farm policy. It did away with the ever-normal granary and the loans that came with it. At the same time, Butz inverted the Soil Conservation Service's notion of land stewardship by exhorting farmers to plant fencerow to fencerow, another of his folksy mantras. Surpluses? Not to worry, Butz had two answers for that.

The first, as we've already discussed, involved exporting American farm products overseas, a faith that foreign markets—and starving people—would always absorb what Americans themselves did not consume. That was hardly a new idea. American agricultural exports propped up farm prices during both the war and its immediate aftermath. In 1965, even after agricultural production in war-devastated places had recovered, the US exported one-third of its wheat harvest. Butz only amplified the role of exports as part of a larger transformation of American ag policy.

His second goal was to replace the old New Deal loan arrangements with direct payments to farmers should commodity prices drop below the set floor. Farmers would be protected, consumers would get low prices at the grocery store, and food could be deployed as a weapon around the world. What farmer wouldn't want to plant fencerow to fencerow with grain prices running so high and with government payments to boot if prices dropped too low?[54]

The bill appealed to a range of important political constituents—not for nothing was it called the Agriculture and Consumer Protection Act. Consumers wanted cheap food, while farmers wanted to grow as much as they could whenever they could, and both objectives would help advance America's Cold War agenda. Everyone would come out a winner, so it seemed. The bill cleared the Senate by a vote of 78–9.

While the bill responded to a crisis in the nation's food economy, its roots lay much further back. Critics of the New Deal believed that the government had no role to play in agriculture—not so much for economic reasons, but for moral and mythic ones. Economist Davis bristled at the idea of a government telling farmers what they could and could not do on their land, warning farmers that they would be "selling their birthright for a mess of pottage."[55] Many farmers agreed and resented this intrusion of government into their farming practices. So too did laissez-faire ideologues like Butz himself, who preached over and over again that the reins on the "free market" should be released in the agricultural sector and that doing so would solve agriculture's problems. In this sense, the Agriculture and Consumer Protection Act finally let farmers loose, or so many of them believed. The act also stands as a crucial step away from a producer-based political economy toward one driven by consumer demand.

It isn't clear that Nixon, Butz, or any of their ideological compatriots saw the irony in their "market-oriented" agricultural policies, or whether they cared. Laissez-faire in 1973 meant not merely letting farmers do what they wanted on their land but subsidizing them to do it. No more "moral hazard" for farmers under the Butz regime, because the subsidy payments virtually removed them from the market mechanisms of supply and demand. Advocates of the 1973 legislation insisted that those direct payments would shrink and then disappear as the agricultural market came to an equilibrium. When Nixon signed the bill, he promised that government payment to farmers would be "reduced and in some cases eliminated during periods of strong demand and high prices such as we are now experiencing."[56] That never happened. And since 1973, those subsidies have amounted to billions of dollars—nearly $5 billion each year between 2004 and 2013, according to the Government Accountability Office.[57] A funny kind of "laissez-faire" indeed.

Butz's plan worked—at least, initially. Production jumped and harvest yields broke new records. Exports jumped too, thanks in part to a devalued dollar that made American products cheaper in overseas markets. Prices at the supermarket stabilized and farm income rose. The "market-oriented" policies championed by Richard Nixon appeared to have solved the apparently intractable agricultural puzzle. Farmers did okay for themselves during the 1970s, but the real winners were agribusiness corporations. The term *agribusiness* first seems to have popped up in a 1955 Harvard Business School publication as a way of describing the network of business entities necessary to put food on the dinner table.[58] That network had already coalesced by the 1950s—witness the B-school's use of the term—and it grew ever bigger through the 1960s. Butz's policy to promote maximum yields was a gift to agribusiness that continues to give and give.

The University of Iowa agricultural economist Earl Heady explained the interdependent agribusiness network neatly in 1976. At the front end of production was what he termed "the input processing industry." These companies provided the seed, the pesticides, the fertilizers, the machinery, and the fuel that were all necessary for "large-scale farming." At the back end was the processing company, "which takes over the products of farms, transports them to processing centers where they are cooked, canned, frozen, dehydrated, reconstituted, wrapped and labeled, and then distribute[s] them to wholesale and retail outlets." Oh, and in the middle were the farms themselves.[59]

And as tends to happen to things in the middle, farmers found themselves squeezed as corporations at either end of this production chain exerted more and more control. Heady pointed out for readers of *Scientific American* that "the cash cost of farming has risen so high that the break-even prices of farm produce . . . doubled over what they were in 1970." Much of that had to do with the rising price of oil—the basis for all the fertilizers and petrochemical pesticides now being used in greater and greater volume to compensate for depleted soils. OPEC's oil embargo affected American farmers at least as much as it did suburban commuters. Meanwhile, as Heady calculated, by 1975, "42 cents of each consumer dollar spent for food at retail prices went to the farmer and 58 cents went to the food processors."[60] Squeezed coming and going. In a nice touch, the Monsanto corporation took out a two-page ad and placed it in the middle of Heady's article. (Among many other things, Monsanto manufactured Agent Orange for use during the Vietnam; as that market wound down, it introduced its now nearly ubiquitous herbicide Roundup in 1974.)

The trends had been moving in these directions for decades. Mechanization arrived on the American farm in the decades after the Civil War. Internal combustion engines had replaced horses by the Second World War. Many of the industrial-scale food processors also dated back to the early twentieth century, and the farmers of the Populist movement rebelled against railroad corporations, which they felt gouged them on distribution costs. Americans of all sorts, but especially farmers, began their dependency on herbicides, pesticides, and petrochemical fertilizers—and therefore on the corporations that produced them—immediately after World War II.[61]

What was new was that the changes to federal policy over which Butz presided aligned federal goals with corporate ones, thus enabling agribusiness to cement its hold on American farm production and on farmers themselves. The demand for ever-increasing yields of corn and soybeans meant that many farmers replaced soil conservation practices by marinating their soil in more and more chemicals. Butz himself was unequivocal about that: "Without the modern input of chemicals, of pesticides, of antibiotics," he insisted, "we simply could not do the job"[62]—the job being to produce as much as possible to keep consumer prices as low as possible.

The bumper crops that those chemicals produced, in turn, meant lower and lower prices for corn and soybean processors. Those corporations turned all that corn and all those beans into any manner of processed caloric material—"food" doesn't really cover it. An early version of high-fructose corn syrup hit the American market in 1967, manufactured by the Iowa-based Clinton Corn Processing Company. It arrived in earnest in the mid-1970s as it replaced sugar in a host of food products, including soft drinks. Soybeans, in processed forms too numerous to count, wind up as the "milk" in your Starbucks latte, in animal feed, in industrial lubricants, and in the adhesives used to create particle board. That we are awash in processed foods, with all the implications they have had for our health, can be traced to the Butzian imperative to grow more.

Earl Butz caused these changes as much as any individual, but he is also a useful symbol. And at that level we can see Butz as a high modernist planner—and perhaps the last American high modernist at that. I'm borrowing this term from James Scott, who defined the high modernist approach to development as having three parts: the desire to impose order and rationality on the landscape; the use of state power to achieve that order; a civil society too weak to push back against these grand designs.[63] Scott's interest lay in the developing world; without stretching things too much, though, this analysis fits Butz and the agricultural regime he midwifed in the 1970s quite snugly.

Butz made no secret of his desire to rationalize American agriculture. He, and plenty of others, saw an inexorable logic to the ever-increasing scale of American farming, and his uncritical faith in science and technology to bring about that order is absolutely in keeping with that of other utopians of the mid-twentieth century. Butz used the hand-in-glove cooperation of government and private corporations as the instrument with which to rationalize American agriculture. And in the face of that collusion, farmers found themselves with little choice but to get out if they didn't want to get big. "A house is a machine for living," the modernist guru Le Corbusier famously wrote, and for Butz, farm soil was simply a matrix for growing carbohydrates (corn) and protein (soy). Local food and local flavor didn't interest him much.

Even at an aesthetic level, the rows of corn and beans laid out with unvarying precision and that stretch to the horizon have the clean, orderly geometry that rows of identical high-rises built by modernist architects and planners in urban environments. By the 1970s, however, modernist urban-planning ideas had been discredited and urban planners looked to shape spaces on smaller scales and with more attention to the local. Not so in rural spaces. Looked at with this eye, the rural expanses of the Corn and Bean Belt—from Ohio to Missouri to Minnesota—are not rustic, or quaint, or timeless, but modernist in every sense of the word.

Things went bad—for farmers, at least—in the 1980s. The fencerow-to-fencerow boom of the early 1970s prompted many of them to expand, enabled in large part by export demand and easy, low-cost credit. In other words, expansion meant taking on more debt: loans to purchase more land, newer equipment, even more fertilizer to wring high yields out of tired soils. Farm debt doubled between 1978 and 1984. But by the late 1970s, interest rates had soared, and so had oil prices again. A strong dollar discouraged other nations from buying American commodities, and in 1980 Jimmy Carter imposed a grain embargo on the Soviet Union as a reaction to its invasion of Afghanistan. Taking on debt enabled some farmers to get big, but it forced plenty of farmers out of farming altogether. And while that debt had a crushing effect on farm families, it also ricocheted back to the banks themselves, many with bad farm loans on their books. In 1985, sixty-two agricultural banks failed—more than half of the national total. The regime of high yields and low prices caught up with farmers, and the crisis of the 1980s arrived on American farms. By 1986, parity prices for farm commodities had plunged to 51 percent, matching the level they fell to during the worst of the Great Depression, and perhaps as many as three hundred thousand commercial farmers defaulted on their loans. Meanwhile, those who could leave, left. The USDA reported that nearly half of all rural counties—more than 1,100—lost population between 1983 and 1985. Things had not improved by the end of the decade either. Between 1989 and 1990, 1.5 million rural Americans left for metropolitan areas.[64]

It certainly felt like a crisis in farm country, but it might also have felt like déjà vu all over again. Roughly one hundred years earlier, Great Plains homesteaders had plowed up the prairie and become prosperous in so doing. They took out loans to expand their operations in the 1880s from bankers and mortgage brokers only too eager to issue them paper, and then found themselves saddled with debt when the farm economy took a sharp turn down. By 1890, Kansas stood as the nation's most mortgaged state, and some central Kansas counties recorded as many as three mortgages for every four farms.[65] This mortgaging sucked American farming into the vortex of finance capitalism in the late nineteenth century, not the late twentieth.[66] In other words, American farming has always been part and parcel of national, and international, financial systems, and American farmers have always been tethered to financiers (and financiers to farmers, for that matter).

The debt problems of the 1880s generated a political response. Farmers organized: farm co-ops, lobbying efforts, and ultimately a political party that articulated an economic vision to make their lives better—no coincidence that the Populist uprising of the 1890s was rooted precisely in places like central Kansas. The debt crunch of the 1980s, however, did not generate anything like that. By one estimate, only 2 percent of rural Midwesterners took part in some sort of protest and fewer than 1 percent joined a political action group. Farmers at the center of their financial crisis also reported feeling ostracized and shunned by the neighbors. And while some activists—notably, Jesse Jackson—tried to mobilize people in farm country, those efforts hardly gained traction even among those most burdened by debt. Residents of farm communities in western Minnesota hit hard by the 1980s debt crisis, for example, saw the protesters as "outsiders" and "radicals" and would not be "caught dead" at one of the rallies Jackson organized.[67] Racism surely played a role in the negative reaction of those Minnesotans to Jackson's efforts, but their own failure to respond politically to the farm crisis bespeaks a withered political vision quite unlike that of their forebears a century earlier.

If the farm crisis of the 1980s did not produce much by way of an effective or even coherent political reaction, it did produce a number of extraordinary writers. Sarah Smarsh, born in rural Kansas in 1980, and Tara Westover, born in 1986 in remote Idaho, both published memoirs in 2018 that detail the agonies of rural life.[68] Smarsh in particular describes the grinding effects of rural poverty and the toll that precarious life takes on women—the isolation, the absentee husbands/fathers, the endless, casual misogyny taken for granted. Both women, it is worth noting, felt compelled to flee those rural environments. Escape offered them their only shot at a future.

"Farm crisis," however, hardly describes what happened to agribusiness in the 1980s.

It stands as a bitter irony that even as farm interests mobilized in the late 1960s and early 1970s against corporate ownership of farmland, they seemed remarkably unconcerned about, or perhaps did not recognize, the extent to which corporations took greater control of everything else about farm production. Had there been a movement in the 1970s that merged the environmental concerns about pesticides and fertilizers with ways to support small-scale production, reinforced by a more aggressive regulatory posture toward the oligarchies controlling agricultural processing, we might have a very different food system today. As it stands, organic growing accounts for less than 5 percent of the total, and the tomatoes at your local farmer's market, delicious though they are, don't register on the graphs of the nation's food production.

We should see something else as well as we gaze out over those endless acres of corn and soybeans. If the New Deal disproportionately targeted rural America, then rural America was where the New Deal order was first dismantled and replaced with the economics of the New Right. Before Ronald Reagan shredded the social safety net, attacked labor unions, and rewarded the rich at the expense of everyone else, Earl Butz did away with the New Deal on the farm and introduced neoliberalism to rural America. And if you watch those fields over the course of a growing season, you can see that, far from being a "free market," the market is structured to benefit a small number of enormous corporations. Corporations control the seed that goes into the ground, the chemicals that saturate the soil, the equipment used to plant, spray, and harvest, the trucks that haul the product away, and the processing operations that turn the raw material into something profitable. As Iowa farmer Naylor put it: "Agriculture's always going to be organized by the government; the question is, organized for whose benefit? Now it's for Cargill and Coca-Cola. It's certainly not for the farmer."[69]

Earl Butz wasn't around anymore when the wheels fell off the farm wagon. He told one racist joke too many, and they finally caught up with him in the court of public opinion. He was forced to resign in 1976. Those jokes did not result in a federal indictment, but Butz's tax returns did—in May 1981, he pled guilty to tax evasion and was sentenced to five years in prison. He served thirty days. As farm foreclosures made national headlines and as Willie Nelson organized the Farm Aid fundraiser, Butz returned to West Lafayette and assumed a role as an éminence grise in agricultural circles.

On January 31, 2008, the *Wall Street Journal* ran a story about the record prices of American commodities. In 2007, farmers had put in ninety-three million acres of corn—a 20 percent increase from the year before—and many were looking at ways to plant even more in 2008. Tim Recker figured he could add another three acres to his farm in Arlington, Iowa, by demolishing two old barns and a workshop building.[70] Boom times again, fencerow to fencerow. I don't know whether Earl Butz saw that story; he died two days later, the oldest ex–cabinet member in American history. But if he did read it, he surely smiled.

CHAPTER 7

CHAINS 'R' US

In the midst of the Great Depression, Representative Wright Patman had figured out the problem.

Patman had arrived in Washington from his sprawling rural district in northeast Texas in 1929, and the Great Depression hit before he had served a year in office. Plenty of people in Washington and elsewhere struggled to figure out what caused the economic collapse and, more to the point, what might be done to end it. By the middle of the 1930s, Patman decided he knew the answer to both questions: chain stores. Their rapid growth since the First World War had created the economic problem; crushing them through legislation would fix it.

In 1938, Patman proposed a bill that would do just that (though it didn't get a hearing until 1940). Realizing that it would be unconstitutional to ban chain stores from operating in more than one state, he figured that he could tax them out of existence. Several states had already passed taxes on chain stores operating within their boundaries. Patman saw an opportunity to do the same thing nationally.

In his formula, chains would have to pay a $50 tax on every store in the chain over fifteen; stores in excess of five hundred would pay

$1,000 per store. Then that figure would be multiplied by the number of states in which the chain operated. The numbers got big pretty quickly. Woolworth's, for example, operated 1,864 stores in 1940. The "excess store" tax for Woolworth's would have amounted to $1.65 million. But Woolworth's stores could be found in all forty-eight states and Washington, DC. So multiply 1.65 by 49 and the new tax would have come to nearly $81 million—almost three times Woolworth's net profit that year. Patman did offer the chains an escape route of a sort: the tax would be deferred for two years, during which time chains could liquidate themselves.[1] If the 1935 Revenue Act was called the "Soak the Rich" tax, Patman wanted to soak the chains to the point of putting them out of business altogether. Some commentators called it the "death sentence bill."[2]

Wright Patman was born in Hughes Springs, Texas, a place that didn't have a thousand people when he grew up there at the turn of the twentieth century, or when he came back to start his law career after college. Born in 1893, just as the Populist movement hit its crescendo, Patman seems to have imbibed the kind of anti-urban rhetoric his parents might well have heard in that part of Texas during those campaigns. As Congress prepared to hold hearings on his proposal, he railed: "There are about 20 large interstate concerns which operate out of New York City [and] they are trying to run roughshod over independent business and locally owned business in this country."[3]

He believed national chain stores were ruining the country, especially the small places like his hometown. His crusade against chain retailers would save those small towns, farmers, and the unemployed more broadly. Patman claimed that chain stores bore direct responsibility for putting seven million to eight million Americans out of work, though how he came to that figure wasn't entirely clear. Nor was it clear where he came up with the figure $3 billion, the amount he believed farmers lost each year because of chain stores. And then there was the nation's youth. As millions of young people left farms, Patman intoned, chain stores robbed them of other economic opportunities. "If you have the chain system operating from one end of the country to the other," he told Congress, "the local print shop is gone, the local lawyer is gone. They do not need him. In addition to that the insurance agents are gone. He cannot go into the grocery business or the drug business."[4] Patman insisted that if the chains could be broken, prosperity would return to America in a year or two.[5]

You can't blame Patman for trying. The remarkable growth of national chain stores had happened during his own youth, changing the world in which he had grown up. In 1920, the twenty largest chains operated roughly ten thousand stores around the country. By 1925, that number had more than doubled, to twenty-five thousand. As the Great Depression began, twelve thousand more had opened. Some had their origins in the late nineteenth century, like Kroger grocery stores. There were already forty stores when the company incorporated in 1902; by 1930, there were more than five thousand. As it happens, the first J. C. Penney store also opened in 1902. The company incorporated about ten years later and in 1930 operated 1,452 stores nationally.[6] Patman was doubtless right that chains had put some number of small, independent groceries, clothing shops, and variety stores out of business on Main Streets across the country, and as he battled against them, their growth seemed unstoppable.

Likewise, Patman had reason to believe that his bill would become law. In fact, he initially offered his "death sentence" as an amendment to a bill Congress passed in 1936. The Robinson-Patman Act outlawed discriminatory pricing in an effort to boost small buyers as they competed with large ones. Some large buyers had been getting lower prices from wholesale distributors and manufacturers that were not offered to smaller concerns. Robinson-Patman made that illegal. At the start of 1940, Patman seemed quite confident that he could get this bill passed too.

In the end, however, Patman's tax didn't even make it out of the House Ways and Means Committee. Flexing the muscle that made Patman so upset in the first place, the chain stores' interests mobilized. The New York–based Institute of Distribution published an impressive book about the value of chain stores and presented it to Congress just before the hearings opened. Cleverly titled *Keep Market Street Open*, the book marshaled a closeout sale's worth of data, some of it in graphic form, to make the case that "chain stores are a good thing." The institute left no angle unexamined: chain stores bring capital into town; chain stores keep business and purchasing power in the towns; chain stores enlarge opportunities for competitors; chain stores provide equality of opportunity for consumers. And on it went for over one hundred pages. In a graphic that might have responded directly to Patman's dig at New York, the institute asked "who controls chain stores" and showed that "more than 85% of company directors live[d] outside New York City."[7]

Once the committee took its seats, first up to testify in opposition to Patman's bill was Earl Sams, president of the J. C. Penney Company. In summarizing the complaints that his fellow chain owners had about the proposed tax, Sams testified that putting chains, his included, out of business would only drive up the cost of living for average Americans. That, in turn, "would deal a staggering blow" to the rest of the economy; further, the tax plan would only benefit "a small minority group of self-interested middlemen and another small minority group of ill-advised marginal retailers."[8]

Theodore Christianson, former governor of Minnesota and now working for the National Association of Retail Druggists, attacked chain stores in his congressional testimony as monopolistic. "While I have no objections to chain stores as such," he told the congressmen, "I do object to monopoly." Chain stores as they existed in 1940 might not yet have constituted an actual monopoly, but their expansion and the rate at which they merged constituted a "potential monopoly"; the Patman tax would nip that in the bud. "We need to lock the barn door before the horse has been stolen," Christianson urged.[9]

But the political winds shifted across the 1930s. By the end of the decade, New Deal economic and regulatory policies had tacked away from attacks on big business and toward stimulating consumer demand.[10] The testimony over Patman's "death sentence" bill serves as one marker in the transition from a producers' vision of economic well-being to an increasingly consumerist one. Busting trusts—certainly, potential trusts—took a back seat to promoting consumer spending. And as plenty of witnesses testified in 1940, consumers spent their money at chain stores. When Patman first offered his bill in 1938, it had seventy cosponsors; by the spring of 1940, only five congressmen seemed prepared to support it. Even Henry Wallace, Roosevelt's secretary of agriculture, wrote a letter opposing the bill.

That the head of one of the nation's leading chains should lead the charge against Patman's "death sentence" comes as no surprise. But the coalition that came out in opposition to the bill was considerably broader than only the chain stores themselves—certainly broader than those who testified in favor of the bill. More significant still, despite the fact that Patman saw chains as an attack on American farmers, farm organizations were part of the coalition opposing the bill, including three of the biggest: the American Farm Bureau, the National Council of Farm Cooperatives, and the National Grange. In summary, farm organizations believed that the chains lowered distribution costs for farmers, something they had been struggling with since the Civil War. Large-scale chains also enabled farmers to deal more effectively with surplus. And chains offered good prices for farm products, as a letter from Minnesota dairy farmers who marketed twenty million pounds of butter through chains attested. Finally, of course, farmers and rural people more generally were consumers as well as agricultural producers. They had to buy things too. Chains offered more variety at better prices, so the testimony went, and that counted for more than the sentimental attachments to the locally owned Main Street shops. Chain stores were where rural people had their most regular contact with the new world of large-scale corporations and the managerial capitalism that those corporations produced. They seemed to like the experience.

Patman simply got it wrong to cast his fight against chains as an urban vs. rural, Wall Street vs. Main Street struggle. Chain stores had not arrived on Main Street in an act of hostile takeover resisted by the locals. Indeed, beyond serving rural customers, a number of the most consequential chain stores had their corporate roots firmly in rural soil, including two of the very biggest in the twentieth century, each of which came to symbolize small-town Main Street in the twentieth century: Woolworth's and J. C. Penney.

―――――――――――

At the beginning of 1901, an eighty-year-old father came to New York City to tour the new house his son had recently purchased. Not just any house, but an extravagance on Fifth Avenue's "Millionaire's Row." The son wanted to show it off to his dad as a demonstration of just how successful he had become. "This must have cost a mint of money Frank," the father said to his son, "you always did like to lay it on thick."[11]

"Frank" was none other than Frank Winfield Woolworth, who had started in the five-and-dime business in 1879 and twenty years later presided over a sprawling and profitable archipelago of Woolworth's stores. Neither father nor son commented on the irony that nothing in the new mansion could be found in any of those stores—not the red-and-gilt wall paneling, not the Louis XVI sofas. Woolworth had hired the architect Cass Gilbert to design the faux French château at Eightieth and Fifth and liked the result so much that he hired Gilbert again to design a new company headquarters. When this gothic skyscraper, this cathedral of commerce, opened in Lower Manhattan in 1913, it was the tallest building in the world, and remained so until 1930—"a lasting monument," as one news story put it, "to one man's faith in the value of nickels and dimes."[12] The vast bulk of those nickels and dimes had come from small towns and the hinterlands they served.

When Wright Patman complained about those "20 large interstate concerns which operate out of New York City" that he hoped his tax plan would force out of business, Woolworth's certainly fit the bill. But before he moved to Manhattan's Millionaire's Row, and before he put his name on the world's tallest building, Woolworth had started out as a farm boy who built his success catering to rural residents just like himself.

Woolworth had grown up on a farm in Jefferson County, well upstate in New York—his father still lived there when he came to tour the new house—and eleven miles or so from Watertown, the county seat. Frank remembered farm life as miserable and cold, and he wanted no part of it. Faced with the prospect of being shipped off to work for wages on his uncle's farm, he persuaded the owner of a store in Watertown to take him on as an apprentice. He never again picked up a pitchfork, except to sell one.

By 1879, Woolworth had accumulated enough experience and enough ambition to start out on his own. Initially, he looked for places like Watertown—county seats or small cities that served as commercial hub to an agricultural region. He tried a shop in Utica, but that failed after some months, and so he moved south, to Lancaster, Pennsylvania. He took a lease on a storefront on North Queen Street, and the store he established became his first success. Lancaster sat at the center of Pennsylvania's Amish community, and Woolworth's proved "highly popular with the Pennsylvania Dutch housewives."[13]

Failure in Harrisburg and York, success in Reading and Scranton—Woolworth's grew fitfully as Frank scouted locations and tinkered with the formula for five-and-dime merchandising. In 1884, he made a move to Erie, opening with six times as much stock as he had when the doors on North Queen Street opened. The store remained virtually empty during that first day, but by evening "farmers' wagons had been rolling into town for shopping expeditions." Store saved.

That story reads much like one from the annals of J. C. Penney. When Penney's conducted customer research in 1928 to determine why some of its stores prospered while others struggled, the investigators determined that the dairy farmers surrounding Little Falls, New York, and "people from outlying towns have saved the day for their store."[14] This rural spending accounted for an estimated 60 percent of the store's sales. Farmers made the J. C. Penney store in Little Falls viable.

James Cash Penney grew up in as equally a remote corner of rural America as Frank Woolworth had: on a farm outside of Hamilton in Caldwell County, northwestern Missouri. There were about a thousand people living in Hamilton when James was born in 1875. (There are about two thousand living there today.) Needing more money, the family sent young James to clerk at a dry goods store in town. He never went back to farming. Penney would look back on his childhood with the rose-colored nostalgia about small-town life that had become formulaic, but by the time Penney was twenty-one, he left Hamilton behind and headed west, first to Colorado, next to Utah, and then to Wyoming.

By 1899, Penney was working for a syndicate of mercantile stores that called themselves the "Golden Rule Merchants." The syndicate operated stores in boomtowns across the vast West, in places such as Lemmon, South Dakota, and Great Falls, Montana. The stores promised low prices for new shoes and fashionable clothing, among other things. After Penney persuaded the Golden Rule partnership to let him take charge of his own store, he opened it in Kemmerer, Wyoming.

When Frank Woolworth arrived in Lancaster it was a small but bustling market town and county seat. Compared with Kemmerer, however, it was a metropolis. Kemmerer was little more than a camp on the edge of a recently opened coalfield. Penney had actually bought some property in the area on his own in 1900, anticipating a coal boom. Partnership papers were drawn up in January 1902, and Kemmerer's new Golden Rule store opened in April. J. C. Penney launched his clothing empire from that coal camp of nine hundred people.

The Golden Rule stores didn't just bring East Coast fashion to the rough-and-tumble places of the Euro-American frontier. They brought urban money as well, in the form of credit from banks in New York, Boston, Chicago, and St. Louis. By 1898, the syndicate was purchasing nearly a million dollars' worth of merchandise financed through those banks and having it sent west. Syndicate members traveled to New York twice yearly on buying expeditions and used the Broadway Central Hotel, close by a number of garment manufacturers, as their base of operations. The logic seemed marvelous to the *Daily Herald* of Provo. "Instead of buying for one or two stores as the ordinary merchant does," the newspaper told its readers, "the 'Golden Rule' invades the eastern markets prepared to do business upon an immense scale." The syndicate descended on Boston and Chicago on similar buying trips each year as well.[15]

Like Woolworth, therefore, Penney built his chain of stores through the networks and experience he acquired working for an earlier chain; like Woolworth's, the Penney's chain grew initially in small places serving rural populations. In fact, as the Golden Rule partners scouted locations for Penney's first solo venture, they wanted him to open in Ogden, Utah, an established town of twenty thousand. Penney thought Ogden was too big: a bigger town meant a bigger store, which meant taking on a bigger debt. Just as important, Penney preferred small places, according to his biographer. He knew them, and they felt familiar. After all, Kemmerer had about as many people as his hometown of Hamilton did.

Penney started expanding in the same region of the West, becoming majority owner of Golden Rule stores in Bingham Canyon, Utah, and Preston, Idaho, in 1908. In June 1911, J. C. Penney incorporated his retail enterprise as the "J. C. Penney Company," and he did so in Utah.[16] By that point he controlled twenty-eight stores under the Golden Rule name, most operating in small towns across western states. With offices in Salt Lake City, Penney had become the pride of Utah. Ten years after he took charge of his own store in Kemmerer, Penney's was now doing upward of $1.5 million in business annually. The press fawned over him. "It seems little short of marvelous," a widely reprinted article opined, "that one man could accomplish what Mr. Penney has accomplished in so short a period."[17] By 1916, Penney ran 128 stores—a remarkable expansion in a scant five years— and "practically all [were] doing business in the small-town field."[18]

Those Salt Lake City offices did not last long. The directors of the new corporation met in New York City in November 1913 and at Penney's urging relocated to the Big Apple permanently. Salt Lake City houses were sold, Manhattan apartments were rented, and the company started operating out of offices on Fourth Avenue early in 1914, almost the same moment that Frank Woolworth moved his corporation to the big city too. By the time Penney's marked its twenty-fifth anniversary in 1927, its offices occupied an eighteen-story building in Midtown.

It took fifteen years before Woolworth decided to try his luck in major cities. Between 1895 and 1897, in the midst of the economic slump that began in 1892, he established himself in Brooklyn, Manhattan, Boston, and Philadelphia. Still, Woolworth remained committed to smaller towns. Up-and-coming places, as he saw them, where the stores would cater more often than not to a mix of town residents and more-rural people who came into town to shop. For example, by the mid-1930s, Woolworth's operated two thousand stores around the country, but only five in Boston.[19] J. C. Penney followed much the same pattern. By that silver anniversary, Penney's did have stores in Portland, Salt Lake, and Denver, but Penney himself still believed that small towns—fewer than twenty-five thousand people and often fewer than eight thousand—best fit his model of retailing. There were doubtless financial reasons for this, like the cost of retail space, but Penney explained that the intimacy of small towns and the personal relationships his staff could cultivate in those places was good for business. "The success of the Penney stores," he told *Chain Store Age* in 1925, "has been due in a large measure to the personal contact with the communities which the managers have been able to develop."[20] And, he explained, he always scouted not just the town itself but its surrounding region when choosing a new location. One Ashtabula, Ohio, shopper confirmed the wisdom of Penney's strategy: surveyed in 1927, she reported that her mother "comes in two miles to Penney for the clerks."[21]

In fact, it took professional market researchers a few decades to catch up with the location model that Woolworth and Penney had come to intuitively.[22] In 1926, the J. Walter Thompson Company published a major study of American retailing using census and other kinds of statistical data. The purpose of the exercise was to redraw the American map where "the chief emphasis [was] placed on people as markets rather than as political groups" so that retailers could better understand where the customers were. "The main purpose of this new re-grouping of population figures," Thompson explained, "is to get away from the meticulous and misleading intricacies of trying to handle smaller towns by themselves without relation to their rural, dependent population."[23] Rural shoppers, already a mainstay of the success of Penney's and Woolworth's, were officially on the national retail map.

During a whirlwind two weeks in 1904, Woolworth completed the most rapid expansion of his empire to date. Recognizing that it no longer made sense to look for new locations on his own, he took a train from New York headed west. When he came back, he had purchased twenty-one existing five-and-dime stores, many already operating on the chain model and many of them in exactly the sort of places Woolworth had first had success. County seats, market towns, small cities with a rural hinterland close within orbit: Joliet, Illinois; Fargo, North Dakota; La Crosse, Wisconsin; St. Joseph, Missouri.[24] The unprepossessing five-and-dime had gotten into the mergers and acquisitions business in a big way.

And no one in those towns (at least, to judge by newspaper accounts) seems to have expressed much concern that Woolworth's had arrived. Besides, Woolworth bought fourteen of those twenty-one stores from the Buffalo-based firm of Pfohl & Smith. Their store in St. Joseph had only been open for three years before Woolworth bought it. After he took possession, he kept his new store in the same location but "so materially increased the scope of business" that the store now occupied four thousand square feet.[25] St. Joseph shoppers were already accustomed to spending their money in chain stores owned by "Eastern firms." Woolworth's promised to provide a better version of that experience. Penney's, too, expanded through acquisitions, as well as by opening entirely new stores. In 1927, fittingly enough, Penney bought out the twenty stores that remained as the Golden Rule Syndicate for the sum of $2 million. With that purchase, J. C. Penney now owned nearly nine hundred stores around the country.[26]

Likewise, when those shoppers walked into Woolworth's, whether in St. Joseph or Sioux City, Iowa, or Pueblo, Colorado, they purchased items manufactured in large industrial cities or even from Europe. Just as Penney had done, Woolworth had set up wholesale purchasing agreements with a variety of manufacturers both in the United States and in Europe before he ever opened stores in New York or Philadelphia. The Christmas tree ornaments someone in Sioux City bought, for example, doubtless came from a single factory employing more than two hundred people in north Philadelphia.[27] The Woolworth's and Penney's chains may have caused some uneasiness as they dominated the retail ecology of rural areas, but many consumers seemed pleased with the service and the bargains. "Just the store for working people who get the most for their money there," said one J. C. Penney's shopper, while another noted that the hired men at his father's mill operation shopped at Penney's.[28] Chain stores, whatever their virtues for consumers, connected small places with national and international products. Farm families and others who did their shopping in town participated fully and enthusiastically in the incorporation of America in the late nineteenth and early twentieth centuries and in the move toward a consumer economy.

FROM SMALL TOWN TO SUBURB

Even as the attacks against corporate chain stores ebbed after the war, their defenders insisted on pointing out that the worst predictions made during the 1930s had simply not come true. The pace of chain store proliferation, spectacular in the first three decades of the twentieth century, reversed itself in the next two. Or, at least, seemed to. The twenty largest retailers ran 37,524 stores in 1930. By 1949 that figure had dropped to 20,047, 41 percent fewer. That much was true.

Driving that drop was store consolidations, not simply store closures. Fewer stores, but bigger ones.

The grocery business led the way, and its transformation can be summarized in the word *supermarket*. The elements that combined to create the supermarket had evolved during the 1920s and '30s. Technologies of transportation, refrigeration, and food preservation made it possible for a single store to sell meat and vegetables in addition to dry goods. Experiments in self-service and huge volume, and the accompanying lower prices, all came together in the late 1930s to create the first supermarkets.

Supermarkets required enormous square footage. Their footprints were routinely four to five times as large as those of the smaller grocery stores they replaced. That demand for square footage, in turn, led to a rearrangement of space in the locales where grocery stores were supplanted by supermarkets. In short, supermarkets didn't—couldn't— open downtown. They opened on the edges of town or even further out, as those places became suburbanized in the postwar period. Out there, they did not have to squeeze into an existing street grid or worry that customers couldn't find parking.

Other retailers did much the same thing after the war. Lancaster, Ohio, fit Woolworth's criteria as an up-and-coming place when he opened a store there on West Main Street in 1907. The seat of Fairfield County and the Hocking Glass Company, which had been founded just two years earlier, the town served as the focal point of a rural, agricultural hinterland. Lancaster hosted its first agricultural county fair in 1851, and the event takes place each October to this day. Woolworth's lasted for fifty-three years on West Main and then in 1960 decamped for the new Plaza Shopping Center.[29]

Small places such as Lancaster, Ohio, also suburbanized after the war. That process accelerated when Route 33, which originally went through the center of town, was rerouted around it. So while the new suburban shopping mecca in Lancaster was only about a mile and half away from the town center, the road created a more convenient center of gravity. This reoriented the way people inside of

Lancaster and in its hinterland did their shopping. Once they all met downtown; now they went to the mall, where there was more parking.

Just after the war, Penney's sales still rested on the small-town foundation upon which J. C. Penney had built it and those sales remained robust. Of the 1,600 stores in the Penney's archipelago, fully a third of them served customers in small towns of 2,500 to 7,500 people.[30] By the 1960s and '70s, however, "up and coming" had become "down and out" in many of the places Woolworth's and Penney's operated. The fastest growing retail chain of the 1970s was Kmart, which bypassed downtown altogether and staked out its claim in the new shopping centers mushrooming on the suburban periphery.[31] Penney's tried to adapt by turning its stores into "anchors" of new suburban malls, and it did so first in King of Prussia, Pennsylvania.

King of Prussia was never a place in any proper sense of the term. In fact, it was simply the name of an eighteenth-century tavern located near the Schuylkill River twenty miles northwest of Independence Hall in Philadelphia, right next to Valley Forge. By 1963, that tavern site sat at the juncture of the Pennsylvania Turnpike and the Schuylkill Expressway. Which is probably why the Kravco Company chose that dot on the map to build an enormous shopping mall. And the King of Prussia mall was where Penney's experimented with its first mall-anchor store. When it opened for business in August, it was the largest of the nearly 1,700 Penney's stores and a prototype for Penney's future.

Scale wasn't the only thing that distinguished the new mall-anchor model from the older Main Street version of Penney's. J. C. Penney had made a point of becoming part of the towns in which he opened stores—he placed a high value on having his sales force know their customers and their communities. At King of Prussia, however, there was no town or even any community. Instead, as company president William Batten estimated, one hundred thousand people lived within a five-mile radius of the mall, and these new suburbanites were all potential customers.[32]

Fortune noticed Penney's move from small towns to the suburban hinterlands in 1967. At that point, Penney's still operated 1,200 stores in small and midsize towns. Those stores averaged twenty thousand to fifty thousand square feet. The new anchor stores ran to 175,000 square feet, and this was where Penney's saw its growth. The chain planned to open forty-two of the big new stores by the end of 1967 alone. *Fortune* approved. The "logic of markets and merchandise" made the move to "metropolitan-area shopping centers" eminently sensible for Penney's.[33]

When Penney's stores all over the country marked the seventy-fifth anniversary of the company in April 1977, its store in Dover, Ohio, operated on West Third Street in the center of town as it had when it opened in 1925. Woolworth had built his emporium empire moving from east to west; Penney did so in the opposite direction. The Penney's in Dover was among the earliest that the corporation opened east of the Mississippi River. Dover had been a canal town in the east-central part of the state before the Civil War, but those canals were abandoned by the early twentieth century. Roughly nine thousand souls resided in Dover when Penney's came to town—just the kind of place J. C. Penney liked.

All was not well in downtown Dover at the start of 1977, however. In January, Stan Kutz, head of Dover's Business and Professional Association, said that the economic situation in downtown "right now is stagnant." And he predicted "a marked deterioration" in the coming years if something wasn't done to improve the shopping district. In 1970, Kutz told the group, downtown Dover generated 5.6 percent of retail sales in the entire county. By 1977 that had dropped in half. There was more than a little irony in this assessment. In addition to his role as chairman of Dover's chamber of commerce, Kutz managed the J. C. Penney store in Dover, and just a few weeks earlier Penney's had announced it was leaving downtown Dover and moving its store to the new Miracle Lane Plaza. The West Third Street building sold at auction in late September and the new Penney's opened on October 1. Bidding started at $100,000. No one bit on that price, though, and the auctioneer settled for $66,000, an indication of the southward direction of downtown real estate values. "It's a little sad," offered Fred Leaders, who came to watch the show. He had been Penney's very first manager in Dover.[34]

Miracle Lane Plaza wasn't that far away—less than two miles, in fact—from 125 West Third. But it was on the other side of the Tuscarawas River from central Dover, and it was built on the new suburban model. The plaza's twenty-eight acres afforded ample parking and road access and space for stores to sprawl. It had opened in 1959, and when it did, it helped drain the retail life out of Dover's central business district. By 1977, Miracle Lane was already in need of its own reinvention, and Penney's came in to provide an anchor store. In this move from Main Street to the mall—and like much of rural America, as we'll see—Penney's suburbanized without really having urbanized first.

In the 1980s, Woolworth's started closing their iconic downtown stores. Closing the stores became both cause and effect in many places. Squeezed by the Kmarts and other stores in new shopping centers, Woolworth's declining sales acted as a barometer for the general retail health of a central business district (CBD). But as those stores closed, life in the CBD doubtless got worse. The actual and symbolic effect of those closings sent a shudder through many towns.

I don't use the word *iconic* as empty filler or glib banality. When four Black students from North Carolina A&T State University sat down at the lunch counter in the Woolworth's in Greensboro and asked to be served, they chose that spot precisely because Woolworth's was centrally located in town, both physically and imaginatively. This behemoth New York–based corporation—probably the world's largest retailer in 1960—had become an intimate part of the lives of ordinary people in small and midsize towns spread across rural America.

Those people mourned the loss of their downtown touchstone when they closed. Woolworth's acquired his store in Decatur, Illinois, on his 1904 buying spree. It sat on North Water Street, just off the square, in the center of town. This location was already a five-and-dime, owned and operated by John Carey. Carey himself had arrived in town in the 1890s and "built up a fine trade" on North Water Street. "His retirement from the local commercial world," the local paper reported, "will be regretted by his acquaintances and patrons."[35] News of the sale ran next to a story fretting about the "vitality" of the seed corn being used by farmers in the area. That article serves as a reminder that Decatur was exactly the kind of place where Woolworth had built his success: the seat of Macon County, in the center of Illinois, and surrounded by farmland.

Woolworth's served customers on North Water Street for more than eighty-five years; in September 1990, the company announced the end of that run. Amelia Jones was "shocked" when she heard the news, and Angie Bond, a receptionist in downtown Decatur, got nostalgic, despite being only twenty years old. "My mother used to take us to the lunch counter when we were little. It's sad," she told a reporter.[36] The store would close on January 19, 1991. Frank Woolworth had grown his eponymous empire by selling to a clientele of frugal farmers and price-conscious townsfolk (preponderantly women, as far as we can tell). He hit upon that model in the 1880s. By the 1980s, it no longer worked.

The announcement may have stunned the town, but it shouldn't have. Things in downtown Decatur weren't good by any measure at the end of the twentieth century. The town's population peaked in 1980 and had declined nearly 11 percent during the '80s. A number of downtown stores had shuttered before the announcement from Woolworth's, and the Woolworth's store itself had been struggling for several years; the one in Lincoln, Illinois, about thirty-five miles away, had been closed already. "Everything's leaving downtown Decatur," Bond lamented. Donna Barnes, another downtown worker, wasn't all that surprised at the news "with the situation downtown."[37]

Woolworth's might have been the first experience people in Decatur had with a nationally scaled corporation, but it certainly wasn't the last. When Woolworth's came to town in 1904, Decatur could not yet claim to be "the soybean capital of the world." In fairness, no place could. The advent of large-scale soy production didn't begin until the 1920s and '30s, but when it did, Decatur was at the center of it. In 1939, Archer Daniels Midland, already one of the biggest agricultural corporations in the country, opened a soybean processing facility in Decatur "because of the availability of raw material," according to Steven Archer in the company's 1939 annual report. Thirty years later, ADM moved its corporate headquarters to Decatur, and its bean-processing plant in the city was the largest in the world.[38] Several manufacturing corporations opened in Decatur as well, making auto parts and other metal castings among other things. By the second half of the twentieth century, very little about life in Decatur—from grocery shopping, to buying life's little necessities, to working at a soybean plant—had not been corporatized.

RURAL RETAIL, THE NEXT GENERATION

Sam Walton (1918–1992) and Cal Turner Sr. (1915–2000) were almost exact contemporaries, born in Oklahoma and Tennessee, respectively. They both grew up in modest circumstances, and both died fabulously rich. And while you've undoubtedly heard of Sam Walton, you probably haven't heard of Cal Turner. Walton and Turner were both, in the Orwellian babble that passes for literacy in marketing classes, "value retailers." Walton, of course, founded Walmart, the low-cost retail behemoth. Turner founded Dollar General. As I write this, there are almost 4,800 Walmarts doing business in the United States. There are nearly eighteen thousand Dollar Generals.

In some ways, the rise of these two discount retailers parallels the stories of J. C. Penney and Woolworth's. Both grew in rural soil and in the small and midsize towns that served as hubs for the surrounding rural areas. As Penney's and Woolworth's struggled to redefine their niches in the nation's retail ecosystem in the postwar period, they tried to establish themselves in the burgeoning suburbs, even in the suburbs of a place as small as Dover, Ohio. In a sense, Walmart and Dollar General have filled the rural space Penney's and Woolworth's once occupied, and they have done so with spectacular success.

Walmart has been the subject of several important studies and a great deal of journalism.[39] I won't retread that ground. Dollar General, however, has not received the same level of attention. This seems remarkable, given its size and the extent to which it defines how people across rural America now shop. More than that, those eighteen thousand Dollar General locations map rural poverty to an exacting degree. If Woolworth sought out the up-and-coming in rural America, Dollar General searches for the down-and-out.

Dollar General started as J. L. Turner & Son, a wholesaler. It got into retail in 1954 with a few dozen small department stores. The following year, Cal Sr. had the idea of turning those stores into dollar stores: everything priced at a dollar or lower. The first of those conversions happened in Springfield, Kentucky. The company changed its name to Dollar General, and its growth since then has been astonishing. It went public in 1968, at which point it was operating about two hundred stores. All headquartered in the Turners' hometown of Scottsville, Kentucky, population about three thousand.

Before the phrase *value retailer* was coined, analysts weren't quite sure what to make of Dollar General (and similar retailers such as Family Dollar). This tickled Cal Jr., who joined the company in 1965 after college and a tour in the navy. As the company grew in the 1970s, Turner recalled, "New York didn't understand us. They viewed the company outside the normal parameters of retailing." Financial analysts evaluate a company by, say, comparing its price-earnings ratio against those of other companies in the same sector, but, as Turner chortled, "we weren't really part of a sector." And it seems true, so far as I can tell, that as Dollar General marched steadily toward a place on the Fortune 500—in 2021, in fact, it cracked the Fortune 100—it did so largely under the media radar. Writing in *Forbes*, Kenneth Fisher chided this Wall Street provincialism. "Wall Street has a perverse tendency to bypass firms that serve primarily out-of-the-way little towns," he wrote. Too bad, he noted, because "there are stocks of good companies tucked away in places—maybe up to 30,000 in population—you or I rarely hear of, but the firms are doing good business, growing and, best of all, selling for cheap." Even today, the Dollar General profile can be a bit confounding to those who aren't familiar with it. "Dollar General was like a child whose parents were 7-Eleven and Wal-Mart," explained David Perdue in 2019. Perdue was Dollar General's CEO between 2003 and 2007 before he became a hard-right US senator from Georgia.[40]

Like Woolworth and Penney before them, the Turners found that plenty of money could be made in those small towns. And like Woolworth's and Penney's, Dollar General expanded first by opening its own stores—in this case, primarily across the rural South—and then by acquiring other discount retailers. In its early days, in fact, Dollar General had been "inevitably opposed to acquisitions," Cal Jr. explained, "especially when they would involve taking over someone else's problems."[41] But by the late 1970s, the company reversed course and started buying up assets and expanding aggressively out of the South. Dollar General opened its first store in Iowa in 1988. The *Des Moines Register* sounded a tad alarmed when it reported that "the South is invading Iowa," but the locals seemed pleased enough. Dave Johnson, an Albia, Iowa, development official, believed that Dollar General had found that "small towns aren't necessarily dead." For its part, Dollar General found that Iowa fit the company's demographic model. Stores kept popping up, and thirty years after that first one, Dollar General operated more than 250 stores in the Hawkeye State.[42] A few years after it "invaded" Iowa, Dollar General ventured further west, into Nebraska, the twenty-fourth state in which it operated. True to form, it opened a number of new stores across the state within several months of the first one.[43]

If you ask anyone inside the company, they'll explain the formula of Dollar General's success in making money in rural America: buy cheap (often discontinued items, closeouts, slightly damaged items, out-of-season goods), sell cheap, and reduce operating costs relentlessly. Turner himself defined the niche Dollar General occupied

this way: "Operating in markets other retailers didn't want, occupying buildings they bypassed, buying merchandise they ignored, and
serving customers they overlooked." By the mid-1990s, according
to one survey, Dollar General's prices were 5–10 percent lower than
Walmart's.[44]

Reducing operating costs started with those rural locations. The
real estate was cheap, and Dollar General often occupied extant buildings vacated by other stores. The company invested almost nothing in
renovation—in the early decades, they even built their own shelving
to save on the cost of buying it—and signed short-term leases, nothing longer than three years. Then those stores were staffed typically
with no more than two employees: a manager and a clerk, with an
occasional second clerk during busy times of the year. In the 1980s,
Cal Jr., now running the company he inherited from his father, cut operating costs further by more or less giving up on advertising and by
closing the "loss elimination" department, making those two employees responsible for controlling the "shrinkage" in each store. In 1992,
operating costs as a percentage of sales dropped from 23.6 to 22.4,
and Turner believed he could drive that figure below 20 percent.[45]

I've been unable, despite my best efforts, to access whatever corporate archives Dollar General might maintain. Instead, I have relied
to some degree on Cal Jr.'s remarkably and probably inadvertently
revealing memoir. On page 201, for example, he appears to admit
that Dollar General committed securities fraud when it filed the paperwork for its first public stock offering in 1968. At issue is what
Cal Sr. did or did not tell his son about the company's ownership
structure and whether the failure to disclose a "silent partner" was
illegal. Indeed, the entire book stands as a 243-page monument to the
enduring torments of the Oedipus complex. Cal Jr. titled the book *My
Father's Business*, playing on the idea that he had taken the business
over from his father while alluding to his deeply held religious faith.
All sons struggle with their fathers, but I'm not sure Cal Jr. realized
that the title he chose metamorphosed his father into God and himself
into Jesus Christ.[46] In an episode that could keep a team of Freudian

analysts busy for a long time, Cal Jr. tells a story of being sent to Chicago to meet with bankers and then being instructed by his father to purchase a present that he, father, could give to his wife—Cal Jr.'s mother—for her birthday. "Buy her some nice lingerie or something," Dad told his son.[47]

Cal Jr. subtitled his book *The Small-Town Values That Built Dollar General into a Billion-Dollar Company*. What those small-town values are, however, he never quite says. Apparently, the phrase has become such a cultural shorthand that merely to invoke it conveys what it means. Cal Jr. seems deeply proud of his, and his company's, roots in tiny Scottsville, and he reports that the family was all broken up when he moved the corporate headquarters to suburban Nashville in 1986. Beyond that, things are more than a bit hazy. Small-town values apparently don't include being honest with federal regulators. Dollar General did "spectacularly well" in the late 1990s, in Turner's telling. Shortly after that, the SEC swooped down on Dollar General for issuing false earnings statements during exactly those years. Small-town values don't seem to include being honest with children either. In yet another of those unintentionally revealing stories, Cal Jr. describes a visit to a fourth-grade class in an underresourced Nashville school. He buddied up with one of the students, who asked him at the end of the day whether he was rich. Cal Jr., whose worth at that point probably ran into eight digits, said no. "I knew when I said it that I was being dishonest. To this day, I think I blew it."[48]

Values to one side, Dollar General has made a tremendous amount of money in small towns, but it has cared very little about the towns themselves. In this regard, Dollar General's approach is quite different from Woolworth's. Frank Woolworth had encouraged his store employees to be active members of the communities in which they worked. He envisioned his stores as centers of their towns and placed them in central locations. They were substantial, and they meant something important to those towns. When they closed, people mourned the loss. Dollar General stores are the opposite in almost every way. "No frills" is the euphemism often used to describe these sad and shabby boxes filled with merchandise. They attempt no connection to the places they serve, and no one mourns when a Dollar General closes.

And close they do, at an astonishing rate. Closing stores quickly is as integral to the success of Dollar General as opening them. Cal Sr. was unsentimental about this when he spoke to the *Wall Street Journal* in 1971. "Too many merchants are filled with false pride and hate to close a store," he told the reporter, sounding more like a Kentucky preacher than a hard-nosed businessman. "I'd rather fold my tent and live to fight another day." At that point, Dollar General was closing about a dozen stores each year—by my estimate, 3–5 percent of the total number. In the first six months of 1975, Dollar General opened twenty new stores and closed fifteen. In 1995, Dollar General closed forty stores while opening nearly four hundred. At that point, more than 2,400 Dollar Generals dotted the landscape in twenty-three states.[49]

Those short-term leases made it easier to close up and leave. If a store wasn't showing a profit after year 2, it would "just pick up their tent and move," according to Kathie Gambill of Nashville-based Equitable Securities. "Shucks," Cal Jr. explained—he insisted on using words like "shucks" despite his Vanderbilt BA—"that's just a simple redeployment of assets." Even if locals wanted to mourn the closing of a Dollar General, there wasn't time to do so. As Cal Jr. explained to another journalist, "We're kind of gypsies. We can close a store and be gone in 24 hours."[50]

That nimbleness has clearly been good for Dollar General's bottom line and for its shareholders, who have seen almost consistently strong performance. What it has done to the rural communities where Dollar General folded its tent is less clear. Walmart has been criticized for forcing out smaller, local retailers in the places it has opened. In certain regions, some have charged, Walmart will open more stores than it knows the area can support. Once all the local competition has been driven out of business, Walmart in turn will close its own stores and replace them with one of its "superstores," at which point, consumers have no other option. At the start of 2016, for example, Walmart announced that it would close more than a hundred of its "Wal-Mart Express" stores—the smallest variant of the Walmart model—forcing people in those areas to travel further to find a larger Walmart. Others have disputed that analysis. "There is very little compelling evidence that Wal-Mart crushed small businesses," according to Ball State University's Michael Hicks. "On the contrary, Wal-Mart killed Sears and Kmart."[51] The same chicken-and-egg ambiguity surrounds Dollar General's impact on the places it operates. The presence of a Dollar General or Walmart store may well make it impossible for any smaller, local retailer to survive, but there is plenty of evidence that Main Street shops had already closed by the time either arrived in town.

Dollar General may not be a beloved local institution, but in plenty of rural places, it is a necessary one. The stores carry some grocery items—cereal, Pop-Tarts, microwave popcorn, canned soup, and the like. Dollar General has been quick to insist that it does not see itself as a grocery store. "We do have an offering of food products," company spokesperson Crystal Ghassemi explained, "but it's a small amount aimed at helping customers fill in, not fill up." Nevertheless, in some number of these small places—how many is exceedingly hard to say—Dollar General may well be the only place to buy food at all. That's true in Manson, Iowa, where Dollar General opened in 2017 even as the mayor lobbied unsuccessfully to bring a grocery store to town. The grocery store in nearby Rockwell City closed in 2019, while the Dollar General remains. All told, nearly a hundred rural groceries closed in Iowa in the 2010s. It is an underappreciated irony of American life that some of the nation's most arid food deserts sit smack in the middle of farm country. Meanwhile, Dollar General kept opening new stores.[52]

Underneath the lease arrangements, underneath the closeouts and irregular merchandise and low operating costs, Dollar General's success has, from the very beginning, been built on a foundation of poverty. Small-town rural poverty. Carl Sr. may have had a legendary nose for bargains, but the company as a whole sniffs out poverty

whenever it expands into new markets. Cal Jr. couldn't quite allow
himself to acknowledge that the people who shop at Dollar General
are predominately poor, preferring instead to refer to his customers as
"struggling." Others have not been so coy. *Fortune* was perfectly can-
did that Dollar General's strategy was "to locate stores in low-income
neighborhoods in rural towns," and noted that, coyness aside, Cal Jr.
had "spent his life courting the low-income customer." *Stores* magazine described Dollar General as "locked in the low-income niche."
By 1998, the *Wall Street Journal* concluded that Dollar General's "customers are generally poorer than Wal-Mart's."[53]

Putting accounting fraud to one side, a big reason that the 1990s
were so good for Dollar General is that the working poor found themselves stuck and strapped. "Our customer has always had a hard time
getting by," Cal Jr. noted, but now, with more people concentrated
in low-paying service jobs, it was "even harder to get by in the late
1990s."[54] *Fortune* put it this way in 1998: "For every middle-class
mom Kmart attracts with its Martha Stewart bedding, it alienates a
minimum-wage worker struggling to make ends meet on $5.15 an
hour." But poverty is lucrative, and, as the *Journal* went on, "for five
years [Dollar General's] stockholders have been more richly rewarded
than those of any other retailers, with a 44.7% average annual return."
Dollar General's stock performance during the 1990s ranked as ninth
best in the nation and first among retailers.[55]

Given Dollar General's reliance on poor people, it comes as no surprise that the chain would eventually turn its attention to depressed
urban neighborhoods, and in the mid-1990s, it took its first tentative steps into those places. Initially, the first few opened in public
housing projects—in Nashville and Columbia, South Carolina—and
involved a social service agenda, including a program to help local
residents get GEDs and job-skills training.[56] In the 2000s, it dropped
those philanthropic pretenses and entered urban markets with its
characteristic vengeance. There are now roughly a dozen Dollar Generals in the impoverished West Side neighborhood of Dayton, Ohio,
a city of 140,000 people. Those stores, in turn—in cities such as Dayton,

Cincinnati, St. Louis, and Baltimore—have become magnets for crime, and at truly horrific levels. In 2017, there were thirty-two reported armed robberies at eighteen Dollar General stores in Dayton alone. All told, according to statistics tallied by the Gun Violence Archive, fifty people were killed in Dollar General stores between 2017 and 2020.[57]

Crime is a complicated phenomenon to be sure, but police, policy makers, and city leaders agree that Dollar General's modus operandi, the very things that have made it such a runaway Wall Street success, has contributed to making the stores such dangerous places for customers and especially for employees. If crime is often opportunistic, Dollar General stores offer ample opportunity: the unrelenting demand to reduce operating expenses means that the stores are routinely understaffed, with little or no security—in the form of either personnel or technology—and usually in physical disarray. Taken together, Dollar General stores are the perfect physical environment for smash-and-grab crime. Back at corporate, Dollar General has offered little but indifference to the mayors of cities where it operates. In 2019 filings, Dollar General warned that its "financial condition [would be] affected adversely" if it had to pay for more store security. All of which led Nan Whaley, the exasperated mayor of Dayton, to say, "They don't even care that [their employees] are being held up at gunpoint." Those employees are overwhelmingly women, and they are paid badly even as they are overworked in chronically understaffed environments. Dollar General's 2019 filings complained about the rise in hourly wages across the nation and promised even more "productivity initiatives" to squeeze even more work out of fewer employees.[58]

As he took over the company from his daddy, Cal Jr. went to a management seminar and fell in love with mission statements. After some verbose casting about, he settled on "God-honoring change" as his own. For the company: "Serving Others." In his memoir, he explains the connection he saw between that mission statement and his overworked, underpaid female workers: "I think retailing done as Serving Others has a feminine quality, a mothering dynamic. A store becomes a 'home' to customers, a place where they are always welcome. When they go in, they are greeted in a way that says, 'You are special.'"[59] It's hard to know quite what to say after reading that fatuous description of the feminized rural poverty to which Dollar General has contributed, but the Labor Department had a response of a kind. In December 2021, it issued a press release titled "History of Violations: Dollar General Continues to Put Workers at Risk."[60]

This seamless connection between Christian sanctimony and the exploitation of female labor is another thing Dollar General shares with Walmart. Each has couched its business model and practices in explicitly Christian terms, and each has tapped into notions of Christian service and sacrifice, particularly those of the white women each employs. The historian Bethany Moreton, who has examined this nexus of Walmart and Christianity, relates a wonderfully telling anecdote from a female clerk at a Missouri Walmart. Not quite awake, she began her morning prayer: "Dear Father. We thank you for shopping Wal-Mart."[61]

Dollar General's arrival in low-income urban markets signals that poverty is something shared across the much-discussed urban-rural divide. Dollar General has certainly figured out how make a profit in each area by operating in exactly the same way. In this sense, the journalist Alec MacGillis is right when he wrote, "The glowing signs of the discount chains have become indicators of neglect, markers of a geography of the places that the country has written off."[62] Yet at another level, those thousands of stores, whether in inner-city Baltimore or in Gettysburg, South Dakota, stand as the predictable, almost inevitable consequences of the economic policies the nation has pursued since the late 1970s. Todd Vasos, CEO of Dollar General, said as much to the *Wall Street Journal* in 2017. The future looks great for Dollar General because "the economy is continuing to create more of our core customer."[63]

John Luther Turner started what became Dollar General in 1939 with a $10,000 stake. He used that money to buy up the stock of small stores in small towns in Kentucky and Tennessee bankrupted by the Depression. Cal Sr. accompanied his father to these auctions and recalled, "It was a most sobering thing to see a man 60 years old standing in front of his store the day of the auction. That really tears you up."[64] Though the experience of watching their small-town neighbors suffer may have been sobering, the Turners continued to buy and buy, usually for pennies on the dollar, profiting handsomely from the economic misfortune of their rural brethren.

For well over a century, rural poverty has been viewed as a crisis demanding a solution, an aberration from the natural order of things. For the Turners, it has proved a golden opportunity. A small-town family that created an enormous corporation built on taking advantage of the economic hardships of other small-town residents. Whereas Woolworth's profited from the up-and-coming, Dollar General relies on impoverished people, and it needs them to stay impoverished. "Our low-income customer base is part of a growing market," Dollar General's chief administrative officer said, tone deaf to the commentary he was making about rural America and about American society altogether.[65] Small-town values, I suppose.

One last crop as rural space morphs into suburbia.

PART IV

THE SUBURBANIZATION OF RURAL AMERICA

What I think is happening is that rural and urban are meeting under a variety of conditions and in a variety of ways.

ROGER ANGELL, 1953

When we get to the postwar period in my American history survey course, I discuss the racialized development of the postwar suburb through the use of redlining and restrictive covenants. To illustrate this, I show a slide of a deed with the racially restrictive language usefully highlighted: "#14: RACIAL RESTRICTIONS. No property in said addition shall at any time be sold, conveyed, rented or leased in whole or in part to any person or persons not of the White or Caucasian race."

One year, however, one of my students noticed restriction 15, the one that comes next in the deed. It prohibits animals. More specifically, it stipulates that "hogs, cattle, horses, sheep, goats or similar livestock" are not permitted in this particular development, though residents can have up to twenty-five chickens. My student—who, like most students in the class, grew up in the suburbs—chuckled at the idea that pigs might run around her community had they not been excluded.

Restriction 15 stuck with me after that class. We have a pretty good idea that racially restrictive covenants were common across suburbia and remained so even after the Supreme Court declared them unconstitutional. Language forbidding nonwhite people from moving in still sits in the deeds of suburban homeowners, whether they realize it or not, to this day.[1] How common prohibitions on cattle and sheep were, or are, I don't know. Such edicts have not attracted much attention from the courts, and probably less from historians. We tend to still talk about postwar suburban growth largely in relation to urban dynamics: jobs and population moving from the center out, political splits between urban Democrats and suburban Republicans, racial hostilities between the chocolate cities and the vanilla suburbs, as the funk musician George Clinton put it memorably in 1975.[2] But restriction 15 points to something significant: postwar suburbia grew almost entirely on farmland, and restrictions like these ensured that the land would not be used for farming again. Physically, socially, and economically, suburban development transformed rural places at least as profoundly as it changed American cities. The chapters in this section begin a sketch of those transformations.

Chapter 8 attempts a kind of geographic and demographic accounting. It is obvious enough that suburban development overwhelmingly happened on agricultural land, and from a developer's point of view, that was very convenient. The land was already cleared, and often the drainage problems had been solved. Better yet, a developer could deal directly with a farmer eager to sell. But the land upon which new houses sprouted was certainly not empty. The arrival of suburbs disrupted rural communities in all sorts of ways. At the same time, those new houses didn't fill up only with people fleeing the urban center— the numbers simply don't bear that out. While hundreds of thousands left big American cities in the decades after the war, rural counties across the country but particularly in the South, Midwest, and Great Plains hemorrhaged population as well. Take Atlanta, for example. The city itself lost about seventy thousand people during the 1970s, while the Atlanta metropolitan area grew by roughly half a million. As the student of Atlanta's history Kevin Kruse notes, "Clearly, the suburbs were not populated solely, or even mostly, by people fleeing the city."[3] Some of those souls doubtless moved to the region from cities (or suburbs) in other states, but some number of them left rural places and became suburbanites. (And some of them might have been tempted to bring their pigs with them.)

Overlooking the rural influx into postwar suburbia has, in turn, meant we haven't fully understood the political dynamics of the suburbs during those same decades, and this is what I consider in chapter 9. It is certainly the case that rural suburbanites shared racial animosities and anti-urban biases with those white city dwellers who moved to the suburbs to avoid having Black neighbors. But rural residents also held what we might broadly call "conservative" beliefs about a number of other issues. Rural residents—whether they found themselves surrounded as new developments grew up around them or whether they themselves relocated from rural places to new suburbs—seem to have been more resistant to raising taxes (school expansion was usually the flashpoint issue on that front), to zoning and other sorts of land-use regulation, and even to the expansion of basic services such as roads and sewers made necessary by rapid residential growth. Added together, these rural political positions amount to a hostility to government altogether, and my sense is that we can find at least some of the roots of the right-wing antigovernment backlash of the late twentieth century in the mixing of rural and urban that took place in the postwar suburb. That story is crucial for us to reckon with more fully.

CHAPTER 8

CREATING
POST-RURAL SPACE

It turns out to be harder than one might think to tally how many acres of American agricultural land have been developed since the end of World War II. Part of the problem is definitional: what counts as agricultural, what counts as developed, and what falls between the cracks of those categories? Another part of the problem arises when the intensely local control over land-use decisions and accounting crashes up against the sheer scale of the country. But let me try a quick sketch of the changes in rural land use at the end of the twentieth century anyway.

The United States Department of Agriculture has divided the nation's acreage into five agricultural uses, plus a sixth category simply called "developed." Those five agricultural uses are cropland, pastureland, prime farmland, rangeland, and forestland. When the National Agricultural Lands Study announced its findings in 1981, it had determined that between 1967 and 1975 farmland had been converted to nonfarm uses at a rate of three million acres a year. In the next ten years, the Census of Agriculture tallied that land in agricultural use declined by forty-one million acres. But the census does not investigate what became of that land, and so while some of it may have been developed for residential or industrial uses, some may have been put into the Conservation Reserve Program or been reclaimed by forest.

To get a better sense of just what happened, we turn to the National Resources Inventory (NRI; also run by the Department of Agriculture). By their count, the amount of developed land in the country increased by fourteen million acres during the period of 1982 to 1992. An area roughly ten times the size of Chicago, in other words, built on and paved over every year. Even this, impressive as it is, probably is an underestimation. As Richard Olson and Thomas Lyson have observed, "The NRI clearly undercounts developed land" because it does not include within its "residential" stock-taking "most land located within large lot subdivisions."[1] So the McMansion itself gets included, but its three-acre lot does not.

The phrase *urban sprawl* has always annoyed me a bit. It is a shorthand for the proliferation of suburban residential and commercial development after World War II that happened on a mind-boggling scale. To my ear, *sprawl* is almost onomatopoetic in its ugliness, but the *urban* part of the phrase implies that the ugliness is somehow the city's fault.

In fact, urban boundaries around most major cities haven't moved much—certainly not in the Northeast and the Midwest. It is true that Sun Belt cities such as Houston, Los Angeles, and even Columbus, Ohio, have grown through aggressive annexation, allowing them to redraw their borders ever outward. The lines that hem New York and Boston, however, as well as Chicago, Milwaukee, Cleveland, and Detroit haven't changed in decades; in the case of Philadelphia, not since 1854. Cities, in the main, haven't sprawled—but suburbs certainly have.[2]

One way to define *sprawl* is to think about it in terms of land-use density and efficiency, and here those fourteen million acres take on even more significance. In 1982, the amount of "built land" in the country—including housing, roads, factories, parking lots—averaged

0.34 acres per person. During the ten years surveyed by the NRI, the population of the nation increased by roughly twenty-three million people. At the land-use rate measured in 1982, the amount of additional built land in 1992 would have come to only 7.8 million acres. We can deduce, therefore, that those 6.8 million "extra" acres came from an even less efficient use of land than in 1982. Not just more houses, but bigger ones; not just more roads, but wider ones; not just more shopping malls, but more expansive ones, surrounded by even larger parking lots.

We can be confident that this dramatic increase in per-person land use came in the form of suburban sprawl by looking more closely at the hinterlands of large urbanized areas. The population of the five counties surrounding Philadelphia grew by 3.5 percent between 1970 and 1990; the amount of developed land in that region increased by 34 percent. Chicagoland added 4 percent to its population during those two decades, while its developed land increased by 46 percent. By the turn of the millennium, according to the American Farmland Trust, most of the twenty "most threatened" agricultural regions were around major cities or along urban corridors.[3]

Staring out at all that sprawl from some vantage in the central city, you see land-use patterns considerably less dense than where you are standing. Looking at it from the other direction—from the point of view of those farm fields, and the small settlements interspersed between them—suburban development has often meant an increase in residential density, a wider range of services, an expansion of all kinds of amenities. In this sense, suburban development has meant the wholesale transformation of agricultural land into spaces not exactly urban but certainly no longer rural.[4]

There are surely several different kinds of development patterns that shaped postwar suburbia. Outside of Chicago, for example, towns that served as stops along the Northwest railroad line grew rapidly and the space between them filled up, so that a train trip on that line today rolls through wall-to-wall suburbs from the edge of the city all the way out to Harvard, Illinois, less than ten miles from the Wisconsin border. In other places, such as Hendricks County, Indiana, just west of Indianapolis, suburban development began as auto-centric, so development proceeded as new roads were built and older ones were widened. In Sun Belt suburbia, city boundaries expanded around separate suburban municipalities in crazy-quilt fashion. Regardless of the local terrain, postwar suburban development almost always started with agricultural land, graded, plowed, and staked, to yield one final crop: of houses, strip malls, shopping centers, and parking. That land was hardly "empty" to start with, though it is surely ironic that many developers viewed it as such, given that the farms they erased were established on land that nineteenth-century settlers viewed as virgin too, once Native people had been removed from it. In any event, as the suburbs advanced, rural communities and the patterns of rural economic and social life retreated.

Rather than thinking of postwar suburban growth only as urban expansion, like undoing a belt after an overlarge Thanksgiving dinner, we should see it as part of the larger transformation of rural America that had begun before the Second World War but accelerated after it. Just as manufacturing firms did, suburban developers sought out rural sites because the real estate was cheap, because the attached regulatory strings were far fewer than back in the city, and because federal policies made it financially attractive to build on the metropolitan edges. Without being too hyperbolic about it, suburbia is where the rural has morphed and vanished, the pasture and cropland replaced with lawns. Rather than thinking of the little boxes and the cul-de-sacs and the split-level ranches as "sub-urban," we might better think of them as "post-rural."

SUBURBANIZATION AS A TWO-WAY STREET

For his part, Harvey Branigar admitted he had no idea why business was booming.

Taking reporters on a tour of newly developing suburban areas in the hinterlands northwest of Chicago in 1955, where demand for new housing created "unprecedented home building and buying," he confessed: "We just don't know where all the families are coming from."[5] No one did, apparently, but Branigar's confession is remarkable nonetheless. As head of the Branigar Organization, he was building houses as fast as he could, and even he didn't know who was buying them.

It was easy enough to connect the growth of the suburbs with the population loss of the nation's older industrial cities. As people left Chicago in the decades after World War II, they bought Harvey Branigar's new houses. In fact, however, the numbers simply don't add up. Consider these figures: cities that shrank between 1950 and 1970 lost almost two million residents, while suburban areas ballooned by thirty-five million. Nationally, between 1960 and 1966, the white population of the nation's big cities declined by nine hundred thousand. The suburban population, however, grew by an astonishing ten million in those same years.[6] No amount of baby-boom fecundity can explain the difference between the flight from the cities and suburban growth around them.

Simultaneously, as study after study reported, the rural population continued to shrink. The 1960 Census reported that of the 1,520 counties in the eighteen states that roughly constitute the middle of the country, from Mississippi and Louisiana to North Dakota, Montana, and Minnesota, 61 percent lost population during the previous decade; a whopping 92 percent of counties in Arkansas. During that same period, population in the metro regions of those same states grew robustly. So while thirty-seven of eighty-seven counties in Minnesota shrank, the Twin Cities area grew by 29 percent. Two-thirds of counties in Kansas were smaller in 1960 than they had been in 1950, but the Wichita region grew by over 50 percent. The rural exodus did not abate during the 1960s. According to the *Monthly Labor Review*, "Between 1960 and 1966 the average loss of farm population was 804,000, or 5.9 percent, a rate that shows an increase in off-farm migration during the 1960s." Multiply 804,000 by six years and you get a rough total of nearly five million people who left the farm. By that point, only 6 percent of the nation's population still lived on a farm.[7] If those uprooted rural residents didn't go to central cities—which were losing population, after all—then we can safely assume that many of them wound up in one or another suburban ring. We might also conclude (at least, from a strictly demographic point of view) that the in-migration from the countryside has been as least as significant in the development of suburbia as out-migration from the city.

Clues that suburbanization was a process with both urban and rural dimensions were there for anyone who bothered to look in the middle decades of the twentieth century. In a study of population movement within Ohio toward the end of the Great Depression, Warren Thompson counted that just over seventy-six thousand people had moved from nonmetropolitan areas to what he called "metropolitan subregions." Of those, a tick over 40 percent relocated not to the cities themselves but to their "rings." Urban population, in fact, shrank between 1935 and 1940, according to Thompson's tally: "The central cities lost population in their interchange of migrants with nonmetropolitan subregions, while the rings, particularly the other urban communities and rural-nonfarm communities, gained, to offset in part, the losses of the central cities."[8] Due north, Amos Hawley studied exactly the same question during exactly the same period in Michigan and found a remarkably similar pattern. "For some years," he wrote, "rural to urban migration in the nation as a whole has shown a growing tendency to stop short of the largest cities, gathering instead in the incorporated and unincorporated areas within easy access to large cities." Further, Hawley found a marked drift from the northern part of the state toward its southern urban areas. These appeared to be workers (and their families) displaced as timber and mining in northern Michigan played out. Once the mines and mills closed, those rural industrial workers had to move to "areas dominated by fabricating and service industries."[9]

What happened in Ohio and Michigan seems to have happened across large swaths of the country. In his wider survey, the demographer Donald Bogue noted that the onset of the war caused "an almost unprecedented desertion of population from certain very rural areas." Those people went many places, to be sure; they certainly made their way to the emerging suburban areas not just around major cities but especially around smaller ones. Cities as small as five thousand had experienced "extensive suburbanization," according to Bogue, and he found that suburbanization "was a major development in the vicinity of cities of 10,000 or more inhabitants at all distances from the metropolis." More significantly for our purposes, Bogue was certain that "cities of 10,000 or more inhabitants which have already been shown to have grown faster than the total population *were also accumulating rural populations about themselves at a very rapid pace*" (emphasis original).[10]

Rural populations had been declining in certain areas since the early twentieth century, and the First World War only accelerated the trend—Joe Young and Sam Lewis asked the question: "How Ya Gonna Keep 'Em Down on the Farm (after They've Seen Paree)?" in 1919—as the mechanization of agriculture consolidated farm operations and made farmworkers increasingly redundant. Those who left rural places during the early years of the twentieth century went in large numbers to the big city to make their fortunes, and literature from that era tells that story. Carrie Meeber gets on a train in her small Wisconsin farm town headed for Chicago at the beginning of *Sister Carrie* (1900), and George Willard does the same thing at the end of *Winesburg, Ohio* (1919). The train conductor in Winesburg, Tom Little, knew exactly what was going on as he punched George's ticket: "Tom had seen a thousand George Willards go out of their towns to the city. It was a commonplace enough incident to him."

Those who looked at population mobility during the 1930s, however, noticed something new. Rural people were still on the move, but rather than getting off the train in Chicago or Cleveland, they were getting off a few stops before the end of the line. Or they were driving their Model Ts, taking advantage of newly paved roads, to relocate on the urban periphery. Even before the Second World War, migrants from farm fields and coal country and from played-out timber stands were reshaping the space around American cities.

The Second World War, however else it shifted people from one place to another, did not change the essential trajectory of rural people moving toward, if not quite into, urban centers. Recognizing, perhaps, that the older urban-rural conception of the population and space no longer sufficed, the federal government issued standard definitions for "metropolitan areas" in 1949.[11] Thus, the Census Bureau could now parse population numbers with some more geographical specificity. So when the bureau reported in 1955 that the total population of the country had increased nearly 8 percent since 1950, it also reported that metropolitan areas had grown almost twice as much (13.7 percent). City growth was much smaller, at only 3.8 percent, so the bulk of that growth happened in the surrounding "rings": 19.1 percent in the "metropolitan ring urban" and a whopping 46.5 percent in the "ring rural." Conversely, rural population—defined as those who resided outside standard metropolitan areas—grew only by 0.5 percent.[12]

Taken together, these numbers reveal a pattern. The great age of urban population growth across the nation's industrial heartland had come virtually to an end (though Sun Belt cities grew dramatically), while rural areas grew barely at all in the aggregate (and shrank in many places). As the historian Christopher Clark has pointed out, after the immigration restrictions imposed by Congress in the 1920s, "rural areas became the nation's chief 'reserve' sources of wage labor," and that labor pool landed in post-rural spaces. This motion from rural to suburban doubtless contributed to a racial sorting as well. Rural Black southerners still migrated into cities in the 1950s and '60s, but white rural folk wound up in the suburban rings.[13]

Scholars looking at these population shifts immediately after the war recognized that those metropolitan rings grew with influxes both from the central city and from the surrounding hinterlands. Myles Rodehaver studied what was then commonly called the "urban-rural fringe," in this case around Madison, Wisconsin. In 1947, he found that "fringe settlement" was decidedly "two-directional." Fully 30 percent of the residents he surveyed had moved inward from less densely populated areas in the Wisconsin countryside. In 1951, the sociologist Nathan Whetten could announce confidently that "the suburban movement is undoubtedly a two-way process." He went on: "Not only is the population from the city moving out to the nearby rural areas but the adjacent farm areas confronted by the expansion of the cities are themselves caught up in the suburban movement." Noting that the percentage of nonfarm rural residents had risen from 39 to 57 between 1920 and 1950, Whetten sketched a process of rural suburbanization: "This may begin when a daughter from the farm family finds employment in a city office building, or a son gets a job in a department store. Part of the farm is later sold off as building lots; the agricultural enterprise becomes a part-time farm and the farm family gradually takes on a semi-urban orientation."[14] Notice that rural suburbanization takes place on two levels: farmland becomes suburban housing, farm people become suburbanites.

Outside Lansing, Michigan, E. H. Moore and Raleigh Barlowe found much the same a few years later. "Southern Michigan has experienced considerable suburbanization in recent decades," the two wrote, and they echoed Rodehaver almost exactly: "This movement has stemmed from two directions—from the outward movement of city dwellers to rural areas, and from the increasing tendency for rural people to work in the city but to continue their residence in rural communities." Almost wistfully, they described traveling on rural roads "that once ran through open farming country" but now bore the hallmarks of postwar American prosperity, lined "with suburban homes, occasional business establishments, undeveloped lots, and signs announcing that farm frontage is for sale."[15]

Another study of suburbanizing Michigan, this one published in 1962, hints at the importance of the Second World War in driving this traffic. Alaiedon Township, a farming area southeast of Lansing, had already seen the arrival of new residents during the 1950s, some who commuted to urban jobs, others who combined those jobs with some level of part-time or hobby farming. These new arrivals "apparently moved from other areas to Lansing to take off-farm jobs during World War II, then bought acreage in Alaiedon Township to farm while they continued working at their off-farm jobs."[16] While wartime workers who didn't serve in the armed forces might have taken factory jobs in Detroit or Chicago or Philadelphia, once the war was over, some number of them moved back outside the city limits, suburbanizing it in the process.

In fact, the two-way street that fed the growth of the postwar suburbs had several lanes, and I want to propose a four-part typology of suburban people, especially those who moved to suburbs in the 1950s and '60s. First are those who left the central city in search of more space to start a family or to "escape" the Black family that moved in down the block, or both. Many of these retained connections to the city, at least initially, commuting in each day for a job or returning to a parish church on Sundays. The second group are those who moved into a central city, maybe for a job or for college, and then left soon after for a suburb. They might be tallied as part of the white-flight phenomenon, but they were hardly urbanites to start with. They had perched in the city for a few years, then rather than moving back to the rural place from which they came, they bought a new house in a nearby new suburb. A third category of postwar suburbanites had never lived in the central city at all but moved from one suburb to another. Josephine Chapman was one such. Born in Sicily, she came to the United States in 1947 at the age of ten, part of that postwar wave of immigrant-refugees who crossed the Atlantic after the war. She grew up in Wyandotte, Michigan, a suburb south of Detroit where her Sicilian family settled initially, and graduated from high school there. At the age of twenty, she married Edward Chapman and moved to Belleville, a smaller south Detroit suburb. She lived there for the rest of her life and was not quite sixty when she died in 1997.[17]

Finally—and to an extent not fully appreciated by sociologists or historians—some large percentage of those who moved into suburbia were themselves rural. Some of these lived on a family farm and watched suburbia grow up around them as they sold off their own acreage to housing developers. Others came to the subdivision as displaced rural residents who could no longer make a living out in the country. Through some combination of ambition and necessity, they left their family farm or small rural town and moved to a new suburb.

The residents of Richfield and Brooklyn Park, both suburbs of Minneapolis, embody this typology, and both provide a nice laboratory in which to study the rural dimensions of postwar suburban growth. Richfield sits immediately to the south of Minneapolis. Established in the 1850s, it remained a small town surrounded by farms until the 1940s. Then the population exploded. From 3,800 residents in 1940, Richfield grew a whopping 190 percent in that decade. By 1947 more than a hundred houses were being built each month. Things didn't stop in the 1950s as the population grew by another 365 percent. Brooklyn Park, located on the Mississippi River upstream from Minneapolis, grew similarly—130 percent during the 1940s; 230 percent during the 1950s. Minneapolis itself was not a major destination for southern Blacks during the Great Migration—fewer than ten thousand migrants arrived there.[18] As a result, neighborhood-based interracial frictions were not as common or as consequential in Minneapolis as they were in Detroit and Chicago and Philadelphia. White flight doubtless occurred, but race did not play as significant a role in reshaping the residential landscape around Minnesota's biggest city as it did in other urban areas.

As Richfield and Brooklyn Park transformed with astonishing speed from small farm communities into bedroom suburbs, some "old-timers," whose families had been in Richfield for a few generations, remained. Donald Elsen, born in 1926, a third-generation Richfielder, was one of those. So was Lawrence Molsather. His parents were Norwegian immigrant farmers; Lawrence grew up in a house in Richfield built by his father that did not have indoor plumbing. Thomas Saylor was also born in Richfield in the 1930s, and he spent his entire life there. All three watched suburbia grow up around the farm fields of their childhoods. In Brooklyn Park, William Schreiber also grew up on a farm, and he watched the bumper crop of new houses with a certain resignation: "We and the others who have been here a long time knew what was going on. But we're a small percentage now," Schreiber told a reporter, and he predicted that "pesticide spraying, dust and noise from tractors will be irritating to city dwellers. . . . If there are complaints all the time, it's not worth it."[19] Donald Tessman's family had been farming in Brooklyn Park since the 1870s, just a few years after the Dakota War had made it possible for Euro-Americans to settle there in the first place. He decided to cash in on the housing boom by selling off seventy of his acres, room enough for 350 new houses.

Florence Sherman, who moved to Richfield in 1952, might have counted among Minneapolis's urban exodus statistics. Born in 1926 in Plainview, a farm town of about 1,300 people then, Sherman got a teaching license from the University of Minnesota in 1945. She stayed in the city for just a few years before becoming a suburbanite. After growing up on a farm near Ada, in the Red River Valley hard by the North Dakota border, Art Kvamme also came to the big city to attend the University of Minnesota. He moved out to Brooklyn Park in 1956 and served as its mayor in the early 1960s. Similarly, Sherman Booen, born 1913 on a farm outside Glenville, Minnesota, one hundred miles due south of Minneapolis, went off to war and then moved to Richfield in 1945 right after his discharge. Though the Twin Cities provided his job opportunities, he retained his rural attitudes. He told an interviewer, "I didn't see any reason to go to Minneapolis, and Richfield was a new area and I liked it here. I liked to be as far as I could get from a big city. . . . I wanted to be outside the city and that was Richfield at that time. That's for sure." Likewise, Loren Law and his wife, Arlene, grew up in Bordulac, North Dakota. The war brought them to Minneapolis, where Loren worked at the airport. They moved to Richfield in 1941. As Loren explained, "I guess coming from North Dakota and living in a small town I think it appealed to both Arlene and I."[20] Suburban Minneapolis exemplified the urban-rural fringe, shaped by rural people who had either migrated from elsewhere or who stayed put even as farms turned into housing.

This rough-and-ready typology describes where postwar suburbanites came from. There is, of course, another way of thinking about the people who moved into new developments. The mass-produced, monocultural nature of most suburban building—houses for sale within a narrow price range—has meant that residents of any particular development are likely to be members of the same class. If you can't afford a house in Foxe Hunte Acres, you must look at a more down-market place. If, on the other hand, your annual income allows for a bigger mortgage, you're likely to be steered by your realtor to Foxe Hunte Run Hills just a few miles away.

This is worth keeping in mind as we consider where rural migrants landed once they left. The junior executives and their wives who left the city for a suburban house moved to one kind of place. That sort of suburb, observable at least from the 1920s, became to a certain degree fixed in the American imagination as the typical suburb. Historian Robert Fishman captured this nicely with the phrase *Bourgeois Utopias*.[21] To some extent, I suspect, "leafy" and "affluent" still define the suburbs for many people.

The displaced miners and farmhands and the residents of shriveling small towns without any economic opportunities—the white ones, anyway—moved to quite different suburbs. *Farm Journal* editor C. P. Streeter conducted a survey of farm families around the country in 1967 on their experiences with suburbanization and noted that "in some areas, there is an influx of the relatively unskilled and the poor into abandoned farm homes and trailer camps and 'cracker box houses' as one Missouri woman described them."[22] These were not Organization Men or June Cleavers, they were workers in the Fairless plant, rural migrants leaving even less tenable rural situations than the ones they found in those cracker-box houses.

An estimated 1.5 million Appalachians left the 250 mountain counties of nine southern states during the 1950s alone—roughly 20 percent of the total—and moved north and west. These were impoverished white people, and journalists in the early 1960s fixated on the creation of a handful of "hillbilly ghettos" in a few northern cities—Cincinnati, Chicago, Detroit, and Cleveland—where Appalachian men sat around in bars "drinking draught beer and listening to sad hillbilly songs that sum up their yearnings for the hills they left behind." If that sounds patronizing, other journalists described these places in language that verged on panic. Noting that thirty-thousand "hillbillies" now lived in Chicago, *Newsweek* reported: "The Southerner appears slovenly, primitive, and decidedly dangerous to their new Northern neighbors." Gerald Johnson of the *New Republic* sounded an even louder alarm. "If children grow up in an environment productive of ignorance and superstition, malnutrition, and infection," he wrote, describing his view of these white rural migrants, then when they did arrive in industrial cities, "they will bring their ignorance, superstition, weakness, and infections with them."[23]

But as the historian James Gregory has pointed out, "scholars should have been combing the suburbs instead of dense urban neighborhoods" if they wanted to learn about what happened to migrants from Appalachia. After all, in 1960, only 37 percent of white Appalachians in the midwestern states where they relocated lived in one of the region's cities—roughly the same percentage who had moved to the suburbs from the hollers.[24] The so-called working-class suburbs filled up with rural people at least as much as with urbanites.

The growth of these working-class suburbs was often linked to the decentralization of industry. Levittown, Pennsylvania, had been conceived initially as just such a working-class suburb designed to attract workers at U.S. Steel's huge new plant. On the other side of the country and also in the early 1950s, Ford Motor Company closed its assembly plant in Richmond, California, a small industrial city that had quadrupled in size during the war, and replaced it with a brand-new facility fifty miles away, in what was then rural Milpitas. New tract housing popped up to accommodate Ford workers, and quickly the place took on the outward appearance of a typical postwar suburb. But those houses were not filled by what people thought of as typical suburbanites. A survey of Ford workers in 1957, shortly after the new plant had opened, revealed that 54 percent of them had been born on farms and nearly 60 percent had been raised either on farms or in towns of fewer than 2,500 people. They had come from all over the country to Milpitas, but the survey sample showed "a very heavy representation of persons from Arkansas and Oklahoma."

This was decidedly not a white-collar suburb, and these "Okies" and "Arkies" had not "to any marked extent, taken on the patterns of behavior and belief" associated with those kinds of suburbs. Roughly 350 miles south, in the working-class Los Angeles suburb of South Gate, much the same thing happened. Many of those who moved to South Gate came originally from the Great Plains, according to the historian Becky Nicolaides, while across the Los Angeles region, working-class suburbs drew displaced rural people from agricultural work in the Central Valley to jobs in wartime (and postwar) plants.[25]

The same pattern of country-to-suburb migration seems to have taken place in the South as well. When George Wallace ran for president in 1968, he drew much of his support in southern metropolitan regions "from first-generation farm and small-town migrants who remained attached to traditional, fundamentalist cultural values and beliefs," according to the political scientists David Knoke and Constance Henry.[26] Wallace was going to do well with white Alabamans regardless of where they lived, but it is intriguing to think about how these migrants shaped the political culture of the state's suburbanizing areas in other ways as well.

Given all this, I want to suggest two ways in which rural people influenced the politics of post-rural space. First, as new suburban growth surrounded and swallowed up rural land, those areas retained at least for a time rural attitudes toward taxation, land use, and other forms of regulations. Those issues emerged as central to the suburban success of the Republican Party. There may well be other issues—I'm thinking particularly of religion—where we need a deeper understanding of the rural roots of the suburbs in order to more fully understand the conservatism of the second half of the twentieth century.

Simultaneously, we know that rural people have been in motion for over a century. They may have once joined newly arrived immigrants in industrial cities, but probably since the 1930s at least they have been moving into working-class suburban developments from Levittown, Pennsylvania, to Milpitas, California. It should come as no surprise that they brought their worldviews with them from

Arkansas or Kentucky or central Pennsylvania or northern Minnesota. It seems perfectly plausible that postwar suburban enclaves in any number of metropolitan regions were formed by rural migrants and that their political cast reflected those rural origins. In 2015, the Southern Baptists held their annual meeting in Columbus, Ohio, and why not? There are now more than 700 Southern Baptist churches in the Buckeye State, 120 of them in the suburbs surrounding the capital city itself, reflecting the enormous influx of white southerners into central Ohio since the 1960s. Grove City, a working-class suburb just to the south, is derisively referred to by some in Columbus as "Grovetucky."

While post-rural space was occupied both by city dwellers and rural people, by white collar and blue collar, those groups differed in other ways as well. Rodehaver's study of the area around Madison found that those who moved out from the city did so because the housing market in the capital had become painfully tight (the postwar expansion of the University of Wisconsin was underway already) and new housing in the formerly rural hinterlands offered more space for less money. For the rural transplants, however, "employment and educational opportunities available in the nearby city" stood as the primary reasons they relocated. Interestingly, that relocation took place later in the life cycle; heads of household were older than they were in the formerly urban families. Once they arrived, Rodehaver found, they earned less money: "Average income for rural families was substantially lower than that for the urban families." And they appeared not to have brought that fabled rural sense of community with them: "The families which moved from rural places belonged to fewer organizations and they attended meetings of such organizations with less frequency. In addition, they evinced less interest in the affairs of local government."[27] Twenty years later, the *Monthly Labor Review* came to much the same conclusion: "On the average, migrants reared in rural areas have less income, lower skilled jobs, and less involvement in the community than those raised in cities."[28]

The portrait Rodehaver painted of these post-rural people—older, less successful, less educated, and less civic-minded—is not flattering, to be sure. But it does rhyme with the transformations taking place in rural America at that moment. We know that farm jobs had been disappearing for some years already, and with them the ancillary agricultural jobs in market towns and smaller cities. The increasingly industrial, consolidated agricultural economy created large numbers of displaced workers just as declining employment in extractive industries did. Those workers, having calculated that they had few prospects where they were, made the decision to leave (and did so not at the start of their family cycle but some years later). They arrived in suburbia with less education and fewer skills, and without adequate training to take any but the low-end jobs in a metropolitan job market. Nor does it seem that these transplants viewed the suburbs as "home"—at least, initially. Migration from depressed rural areas, in other words, and from heavily industrialized rural areas already experiencing rural deindustrialization helped fill up the new suburbs. When they arrived, these workers "tend[ed] to leave their families behind and go home on weekends." Only after establishing some job security did they send for their families to move to suburbia with them.[29]

Andy Keyso was born in 1941 in a small Pennsylvania coal town in Schuylkill County (his mother had been born in the adjacent town of Minersville). When Andy finished up a four-year tour with the air force in 1963, his father was already an unemployed coal miner. Andy figured he would join his dad on unemployment and started to fill out the paperwork when an aunt who lived in Levittown, Pennsylvania, invited him to come visit. He did, got a job at the new U.S. Steel plant, and worked for U.S. Steel for thirty years. Along the way, he bought a house in Levittown and died there in 2013.[30] Joseph Yesenosky was another suburbanite from a depressed rural area. Born in 1918 to a coal-mining father in a remote corner of southwestern Pennsylvania, Yesenosky spent a year in the army during World War II, and then settled with his wife and children in Levittown.[31] When he died there in 1996 his family asked for donations to be sent to the Ave Maria School in Ellsworth, Pennsylvania—back in the place where he had grown up.

We don't know much about how the exodus from rural America changed the places they left, but these characterizations suggest that

struggling rural communities were made much worse by the depar-
ture of the talented and ambitious. Edward Alsworth Ross described
rural towns of Indiana, Michigan, Illinois, and Missouri as "communities which remind one of fished-out ponds populated chiefly by
bullheads and suckers," and that was in 1923. As unflattering as Rodehaver's description of rural suburbanites was, there is some evidence
that those rural residents who did relocate were more ambitious
and striving than those they left behind. Writing about "the shrinking south" from which he came, Hodding Carter noted that between
1950 and 1956, the white population of Mississippi had dropped by
fifty-one thousand. "More alarming than their numbers," he wrote
in a 1958 dispatch, "is the caliber of the white emigrants. . . . [They]
are on the whole, better educated than the average of those who stay
at home." Across the Mississippi River in Arkansas, *Business Week*
found much the same thing. During those same years, white people
started leaving the state at the same rate as Black people, and while it
was clear that "the biggest loss since 1950 has been in the rural farm
population," the magazine focused on the college graduates and pro-
fessionals who left and the brain drain from the state they created. As
he traveled through the South, Hodding Carter felt haunted: "The
ghosts of departed people are walking the dusty road of the rural
Deep South."[32]

THE RECEDING RURAL

The influential sociologist Leo Schnore summed up the emerging
picture of metropolitan growth in 1958. "As far as migration and mobility are concerned," he wrote, "decentralization has two sources—
outward *relocation* from the center and growth via *accretion* at the
periphery. As yet, however, the relative contribution of these two distinct types of movement has not been firmly established."[33] Schnore
worked with a common assumption: that suburban growth took place
on what amounted to an empty canvas. This simply wasn't true.

If arrivals from the countryside helped fuel the growth of metropolitan "rings," then that growth simultaneously displaced, or swallowed up, the rural people who lived there in the first place. Since the suburban developers preferred farm fields, most of those displaced were small-scale producers who had participated in a locally focused food economy that was itself in eclipse around the country.

Consider the Moehlings. They started farming in the village of Arlington Heights, Illinois, in about 1910 on a hundred acres that Mr. Moehling's father had purchased twenty years before that. By 1956, Arlington Heights boomed as a suburb of Chicago, and the Moehlings found what remained of their farm surrounded by all the manifestations of suburban development: a new hospital, a new Episcopal church, a new radar installation for O'Hare Airport, and lots of new houses. Though the 1918 barn still stood, there wasn't really any land left to farm. The Moehlings' son, Melvin, farmed 160 rented acres nearby, but that land, too, had been sold to a developer. Farming across Chicagoland was disappearing rapidly.[34]

Hendricks County, Indiana, due west of Indianapolis and once almost entirely agricultural, suburbanized furiously in the postwar decades. By 1960, 40 percent of the houses across the entire county had been built within the previous ten years. Livestock farmers, as a consequence of that residential growth, had reduced the size of their herds, and crop growers were farming on smaller, more scattered acreage as pastures and farmland were sold out from underneath them. The number of farmers declined by 30 percent during the 1950s, while the county's nonfarm population grew by 115 percent. Between 1954 and 1965, fifteen thousand flat, black-earth farm acres had been turned into residential lots.[35] Throw a dart at a map of postwar suburban America and the place you hit will have experienced a version of this farm-to-suburb transformation. Call it "the receding rural."

A University of Pennsylvania study of lower Bucks County, Pennsylvania, just north of Philadelphia, noticed this phenomenon.[36] Just after the Second World War, U.S. Steel announced the building of a new plant—the Fairless Works—and the company began buying up "spinach fields" and other small-scale truck farms for its behemoth new facility on the Delaware River. This was farm country, and old farm country at that. The Ivins farmstead was among those that U.S. Steel purchased, along with the gravesite of Joshua Ivins, died 1814, age "123, three months and nine days," according to his headstone. U.S. Steel broke ground on the plant in late winter 1951, though farmers had already put a spinach crop in. Eventually hundreds of farmers sold up to create the 3,800-acre parcel that U.S. Steel required—many no doubt feeling that they were doing a patriotic service. U.S. Steel promoted the new plant as vital to the nation's Cold War needs. As a company press release put it: "On farm lands that formerly produced many bushels of spinach and asparagus a big plant is rising which will produce many tons of steel—steel for the nation's defense."[37] No better example of how the industrial part of the military-industrial complex transformed rural space.

By 1953, the changing social dynamics could be tracked through the local newspapers. "On a typical day in April 1953 . . . ," the Penn researchers wrote, "the area's newspapers, old and new, were likely to be carrying feature stories about the new developments and their impact on the area. . . . Farm news and syndicated boilerplate had been replaced by stories of new plants coming into the area, disputes between one or another developer and the municipalities, discussions of how to pay for the new schools." In summary, the Penn study noted: "The new developments, large and small, displaced much farmland. . . . As a result of the new developments, the value of farmland has often increased to about four times the pre-World War II level."[38] Since the nineteenth century, American farmers have viewed land both as the source of the commodities they sold and as a financial asset in and of itself. The postwar suburban boom hastened the transubstantiation that turned land into cash as farmers saw their opportunity to sell up and took it.

The farmer who struggles to hold on to the family farmstead in the face of development pressures has become a staple of our rural romance, but farmers themselves could also be calculating. North of Lansing, Michigan, farmers who found themselves in the path of suburban growth indicated a willingness to sell if they could get the "right price." Thirteen hundred miles to the southwest, in Bell County, Texas, Oscar Lewis found little by way of sentimental attachment to the land on the part of what he called "old-line Americans." Czech and German farmers, Lewis discovered, seemed to see themselves as stewards of the land, whereas among those ethnically indistinct—presumably meaning those who had moved into Texas from other parts of the South—"there has been a tendency to sell, especially when offered good prices." In fact, Lewis reported, "in speaking with a few old-line Americans who were forced to move off their land to make room for Camp Hood, the only complaint heard was that they didn't get enough for their land," not that they had been forced to sell in the first place. Truck farmers who worked the region northwest of Chicago found themselves getting a pretty penny indeed. Between 1950 and 1955, prices tripled, from $500 an acre to $1,500, as developers fed an insatiable hunger for new housing. One Maryland farmer summed it up in the mid-1970s: "Ninety percent of land use is making a buck."[39]

Large-scale suburbanization might be a new phenomenon in the postwar era, but farmers who saw their land as a financial asset, and who pulled up stakes and moved on once they got the right price, certainly were not. Not in the vast agricultural interior of the country, at any rate. According to Richard Hofstadter, what developed in the United States in the nineteenth century "was an agricultural society whose real attachment was not to the land but to land values."[40] In fact, this impulse to see land as one more commodity goes back to the start of the nation itself. Land sales in the trans-Appalachian West helped pay off the money the United States had borrowed to fight the Revolutionary War. The historian Philip Deloria neatly noted that the United States positioned itself from the very outset "as a land-speculator with continental ambitions."[41] As Native people were cleared militarily from the space, it wasn't settlers who followed so much as real estate investors. The urge to flip property for a tidy profit seems to be woven into the national DNA.[42] When Michigan State University researchers ventured into the farm fields of Alaiedon

Township in 1962, about ten miles away from campus, they found that attitude alive and well. Alaiedon was already changing with the arrival of new suburban residents, but a much bigger tide of suburbanization seemed ready to wash over the township with the opening of a new highway. In the face of this, longtime full-time farmers expressed little interest in zoning changes that might preserve their agricultural land. Instead, "they wished only to continue farming until they could sell at a top price."[43]

More calculating still, some farmers who were getting ready to sell up well might have let their land deteriorate in a practice referred to as "mining" the soil. In Michigan, suburbanization prompted "poorer farming practices" among those who hadn't yet sold off their land. As development pressures caused land values to rise, for example, farmers often gave up soil conservation practices such as crop rotation and resorted to cash-cropping instead. "Judging from observations made by rural residents regarding the condition of the soil on their places," the researchers E. H. Moore and Raleigh Barlowe discovered, "it would appear that 'mining of the soil' actually prevails on those farms where the owner plans to plat or subdivide his land within a few years."[44]

Where those farmers who cashed out went was not something researchers seemed to care about much in the 1950s. "In the limited fringe areas," two of them predicted grimly in 1953, "the chances of survival for rural people and the rural way of life are slim." To the authors of the Fairless plant study, the farmers seem to have more or less melted away. "Some of the displaced farmers have moved further north," they wrote, raising the question of what happened to the others. At any rate, they appear not to have taken jobs with U.S. Steel or the ancillary industries that the Fairless Works attracted. "Workers for the new industries," the study found, came primarily from two places: nearby Philadelphia and "depressed areas (such as the Pennsylvania anthracite region)."[45]

By the turn of the twenty-first century there were exactly two farms left in Falls Township, Pennsylvania, which encompassed Levittown and was next door to the now-shuttered U.S. Steel plant. A total of about 150 acres. The Sadowski farm had been in the family since 1920; third-generation owner Lenore Sadowski wanted to sell the 37.5 acres to the township to preserve it as open space, a last remnant of the farm fields that just fifty years earlier had defined the area. When the *New York Times* covered the groundbreaking of the Fairless plant in 1951, it had predicted "rural life to vanish," which proved correct—this rural area became entirely suburban. Lenore Sadowski explained to the press why she was to trying to preserve this piece of undeveloped land by saying, "That's what we want. There are enough houses around here."[46]

Before the farms of Brooklyn Park, Minnesota, had been turned into houses, they produced potatoes. As the farms were sold off, locals started a "Tater Daze" festival in the mid-1960s, complete with a tractor pull, to remind the newcomers of what once had been. It only lasted a few years, discontinued in the early '70s. At about that moment—1974—radio listeners were introduced to another small farm town in Minnesota. Garrison Keillor started reporting the news from Lake Wobegon, his hometown, every Saturday on his variety show *A Prairie Home Companion*. Keillor created an entire world in Lake Wobegon, a fictional town of fewer than a thousand nestled among the Minnesota wheat fields, in his telling, in the way that Sherwood Anderson invented Winesburg, Ohio, and William Faulkner imagined Yoknapatawpha County, Mississippi. Year after year, decade after decade, he made Lake Wobegon come alive for his listeners, at least for twenty minutes each week. He made gentle fun of the place and told his tales of rural life with his tongue firmly in cheek. But Keillor himself had grown up in Brooklyn Park, moving there as a small boy in 1947, just as the suburban boom was taking off. His parents, John and Grace, moved to Brooklyn Park from an even more rural county to the north, and they finished building their new Colonial Revival/Cape Cod at 200 Brookdale Avenue North in 1952.[47] Lake Wobegon, the little town that time forgot and that the decades couldn't improve, sprang from the imagination of a kid who grew up in one of the fastest growing suburbs in the state.

CHAPTER 9

THE POLITICS OF POST-RURAL COMPLAINT

THE RURAL AND THE RACIALIZED SUBURBS

Eva Kurswidas was born the child of Lithuanian immigrants in 1912. Her parents had made their way from Lithuania to the coal country of Schuylkill County in central Pennsylvania, where her father worked as a miner. Eva was born, fittingly enough, in a town called Lower Shaft. She managed an eighth-grade education and then married Adam Dombroskie, four years her senior and himself the child of Polish immigrant parents who tried their hand at farming. Adam worked on the family farm into his young adulthood, but at some point during the Great Depression, he, too, found work in the mines, employed by the Tancredi Coal Company. He joined the United Mine Workers, though he managed only fourteen weeks of work in 1939.[1] In 1940, Eva and Adam lived in a rented house in West Mahanoy Township in Schuylkill County. They stayed there for thirteen years, at which point the family packed up and moved 120 miles to the southeast, buying a house at 19 Dewberry Lane, in the Dogwood Hollow section of Levittown, Pennsylvania.

And on August 14, 1957, Eva was arrested and charged with disorderly conduct.

Eva Dombroskie (though apparently not her husband) emerged as one of the leaders of the racist backlash in Levittown that confronted William and Daisy Myers when they became the first Black people to buy a house there. She appears to have committed no act of violence that day, but as an angry mob of several hundred gathered into the evening, she screamed "profane language" in an attempt to "incite other residents."[2] She pleaded guilty and paid her fine.

Mary Brabazon was among the others arrested and ultimately enjoined by the local court from harassing the Myers family. Brabazon (née McMenamin) also came to Levittown from a tiny dot of a place in Schuylkill County. Born in 1927, she left the area when she married and moved with her husband to Philadelphia in 1948.[3] Just a few years later, they decamped for Levittown.

It isn't clear whether Dombroskie or Brabazon knew Howard Bentcliff before the ugly events of 1957 in Levittown, but they certainly got acquainted as a consequence of them. Bentcliff, too, found himself hauled before a judge for his role in the harassment and intimidation of the Myerses. Bentcliff grew up in Philadelphia and was still living in his parents' house there in 1940 though he was twenty-eight years old.

Among other things, Bentcliff stood accused of spraying "KKK" on the home of Lewis Wechsler, a sympathetic neighbor of the Myerses and himself a Jew. Wechsler also found a Molotov cocktail on his driveway. Perhaps Bentcliff's real moment of fame came when he collapsed of a heart attack while acting as his own defense attorney during his trial. The judge had to declare a mistrial after Bentcliff was picked up off the courtroom floor and taken away by medics. He later pled guilty to burning two crosses—on the lawns of other white Levittowners who befriended the Myerses—and to the spray-painting. He was fined and given probation, though the judge seemed less than pleased with his own lenient ruling, telling Bentcliff, "I'm giving you a break because of your health. You should go to jail."[4]

Hundreds of Levittowners snarled and cursed at the Myers family, but in the end, only eight were arrested for their actions. Of those, at least two came to the famous suburb via some rural place and more specifically from the played-out coalfields of Pennsylvania. That they were women should surprise no one, considering just how many women joined the KKK in the 1920s, and just how enthusiastically they participated.[5]

During the trial, Mary Brabazon insisted that she was opposed to any sort of violence on religious grounds and wished no ill upon the Myerses. "I would rather move myself than have any violence happen to the Myers family," she testified and added that she and her family were "in the process of moving now." The house might have been on the market when she took the stand, but she didn't move immediately. The Brabazons jumped the river and moved into Levittown, New Jersey, in August 1959.[6]

Racial exclusion sits at the center of many cul-de-sacs in suburbia, the result of white racial fear but even more because of the racially discriminatory nature of mortgage lending. That was true at the beginning of the postwar suburban expansion, and it remains true to a dispiriting degree today. Those sociologists who concluded that "the house" or "the neighborhood" or a chance to raise the kids with a yard drove suburban growth failed to recognize the extent to which the very definition of a good home in a good neighborhood was racially inflected in the first place. The attraction of racial homogeneity created the "pull" to the suburbs as much as anything else. This much the white-flight thesis gets absolutely correct. But as the episode in Levittown in 1957 suggests, rural residents brought their own racial fears and hatreds with them from places where they might not ever have encountered a person of color. Josephine Chapman, the Sicilian immigrant child we met in chapter 8, had a moment of national fame in 1972 as George Wallace's campaign manager for the Michigan Democratic primary. The frothing-at-the-mouth segregationist had Chapman to thank for his stunning victory there.

As we've seen, several different groups made up the population of new suburbs. They found common ground in a shared commitment to racial exclusion and a more general anti-urban hostility. Race, however, was not the only contentious issue that roiled the postwar post-rural spaces. Land use and zoning, schools, environmental regulations, taxation of any sort—all these created political frictions that pitted different kinds of suburbanites against one another. If we were to dig deeper into the rural nature of suburban development, we might discover how rural hostility toward taxes and regulation and government altogether have shaped the political dynamics in the suburbs. Reorienting our perspective so that we look from the fringe toward the center rather than the other way 'round, we might discover that postwar suburban politics were an extension of rural political values into post-rural space—not just a product of the racial animosities that city residents packed up with them in their moving vans. That admixture of urban and rural attitudes in the new suburbs helped curdle the midcentury liberal political consensus.

ALL POST-RURAL POLITICS ARE LOCAL

Farmers in Alaiedon Township, Michigan, in 1962 reported that rising taxes, not an influx of nonwhite people, worried them most as the area seemed on the cusp of suburban development. That fear was not at all hypothetical. One farmer reported that between 1940 and 1960, the tax bill on his farm acreage had risen over 400 percent.[7] Interviewees may very well have been shy to report their racial animosities, though in 1962 Michigan was certainly no stranger to racial conflict. It was rising property taxes, however, that cut most immediately into the economic viability of these farms, stirring their fear and anger.

In his study of the Flint, Michigan, area in the mid-1950s, Thomas Brademas found a fundamental disjunction. In what he called the "fringe" region around Flint, people found themselves living under increasingly urban conditions—higher residential density and increased car commuting, for example—but they did so "under a government set-up designed to satisfy rural needs." Rural areas had not built the kinds of infrastructure and amenities that urbanites now took for granted (though many areas did now enjoy electricity, thanks to the New Deal's Rural Electrification Administration). "Most of the homes in the fringe are without public water supply and there is no sewerage system," Brademas noted, and he went on: "There are few paved roads and there is almost no regulation of building construction and none of land use." Nor was this condition specific to Flint. Any rural area, Brademas was convinced, that became suburbanized experienced the same disconnect: "In short, what has and is happening to the Flint, Michigan areas is repeated to a greater or lesser degree in almost all of our metropolitan areas today."[8]

Fights over such issues certainly happened as Richfield, Minnesota, experienced its dizzying growth. In 1951, the town council erupted into conflict over whether to build or expand sewer and water systems to service the rapid increase in houses. LeRoy Harlow recalled: "The newcomers who wanted all the amenities of city living clashed with the old-timers who wanted things left the way they were." As Richfield's first city manager, Harlow had a ringside seat when council meetings devolved "into endurance contests as the two sides slugged it out in debates over controversial issues such as water and sewage. The gatherings often lasted until after midnight. More forum than meeting, these affairs drew crowds so large that fire trucks had to be driven outside to allow the council to meet in the fire hall." But he, like Brademas, was certain that these fights were a "miniature of what happened . . . wherever developers built on what was formerly farmland at the outskirts of large cities."[9]

The suburbanization of rural space created legal frictions in three broad areas: annexation and incorporation, zoning, and nuisance laws. Annexation enabled suburbanizing areas to tie into all the municipal services of some larger entity; incorporation allowed those areas to retain a measure of political independence but necessitated creating new governmental structures. Both came with higher taxes, or so older inhabitants feared. Zoning laws imposed regulations on how land could be used, and farmers—indeed, many rural residents—objected on principle to any kind of land-use restrictions. In a similar way, nuisance laws could limit what rural people did on their land.

Local government structures in newly suburbanizing areas might not have had the capacity to replace outhouses and septic tanks with municipal sewer systems, but more to the point, rural people—either those who were already living there or those who migrated in from elsewhere—often did not want to pay the increased taxes required. In Hendricks County, west of Indianapolis, farmers complained about rising property taxes in the wake of new residential development, though while they didn't actually pay more in taxes than farmers in adjacent counties, they did benefit from inflated land values.[10]

In the burgeoning areas surrounding Flint, newly arrived residents in the 1950s found the same inadequate governmental structures. In fact, those structures had not been significantly altered in one hundred years, though "extraordinary population growth and urbanization have taken possession of the fringe area."[11] Those structures groaned under the strain of delivering services the new residents expected as the area transformed from a sparsely inhabited agricultural one into a more densely populated residential one.[12] Yet despite the mismatch between governmental capacity and resident demand, residents still felt good about their township form of government. The sociologists Basil Zimmer and Amos Hawley were left scratching their heads at the results of interviews they conducted with more than four hundred people. Informants consistently rejected alternatives to the antiquated and now too-small township arrangements such as annexation and incorporation. They concluded, sounding a tad condescending, "that fringe residents, at least in the Flint metropolitan area, are not well enough informed to make mature judgements about the governmental forms and procedures needed to deal with local problems."[13] Seeking an explanation for this apparent contradiction, Zimmer and Hawley discovered that their interviewees still clung to another aspect of the rural myth: small government is necessarily better government. "Most of the responses clustered around negative aspects of bigness," they found. In addition, "frequent references were made to 'red tape,' inefficiency, and lack of contact with people."[14] In other words, residents believed in the romance of face-to-face democracy and wanted the personal connection with government officials that small governing units allowed, even as they acknowledged that those officials could not actually solve the problems at hand.

New school facilities also caused conflicts outside of Lansing over taxes and more broadly over what we might call culture. "So long as the areas were inhabited almost exclusively by full-time farmers," Moore and Barlowe found, "the country school houses were usually considered large enough to accommodate all the students." But, they observed, "once the rural residents started their migration into the area, many of the school facilities became inadequate. School consolidation has provided an answer to this situation, but some 'old-time' residents have not been convinced that this is the best solution."[15] The clash over schools in this corner of Michigan echoes what Herbert Gans found in Levittown, New Jersey, at about the same moment. Initially, Levitt representatives has assured the existing school board "that its essentially rural educational values would be perpetuated in the new Levittown," but once the new arrivals started putting their children into those older schools, rural-suburban conflict flashed and the district superintendent found himself in the middle of it. As Gans saw it, much as with public facilities more broadly, new Levittowners expected more for their children than the rural parents who were there already and were already sending their kids to the schools. But the superintendent simply could not or would not adapt his previously rural experience to the wishes of the new arrivals. As Gans reported it: "Because the superintendent had spent his life in rural education, he was intensely concerned with average students, retarded children, and slow learners."[16] Thus he could not satisfy the generally more-affluent, more-aspirational parents. Just south of Minneapolis, voters in Richfield rejected a ballot measure to build a new—and needed—high school during the war. In fact, the town didn't have one at all, and an ad that ran in the *Richfield News* asked imploringly, "Can anyone imagine a village of nearly 10,000 residents without a high school?" Apparently, plenty of people could, since nearly ten years and more than seven thousand new residents later, Richfield "ranked among the largest communities in America *without* a high school."[17]

Nor were rural residents, especially those still farming, keen to create zoning codes to regulate land use as that use changed dramatically and rapidly. They feared that their farming—especially animal operations—might be zoned into oblivion. Cities had pioneered zoning laws during the Progressive era, but as late as 1951, only thirty-eight states had passed enabling laws to even permit rural zoning. Even that number, however, overstates the case: by 1951, only 178 rural counties in the entire nation had actually enacted zoning regulations.[18] Back in Michigan, for example, farmers who found themselves surrounded more and more by suburban development "felt that zoning would take too many rights away from the individual, and that they themselves were capable of coping with any problems the suburban movement might create."[19]

Resistance to any kind of land-use regulation sometimes came back to bite rural residents. Without it, farmers could sell off land that might then be developed in almost any way, exerting yet more pressure on those farmers who remained to sell up. Even more, many rural residents quickly discovered that the money behind big development ran roughshod over whatever control they thought they might have. "If Lower Bucks County had been master of its own fate," University of Pennsylvania researchers noted about the area surrounding U.S. Steel's Fairless plant, "its citizens might have debated seriously whether or not to admit any more new subdivisions or new industries which could upset the present balance. As it was, however, United States Steel had already begun to acquire the spinach fields and other truck farming lands on which the Fairless Works are operating today."[20] Farmers might have felt that zoning would take away their rights, but many discovered that developers and their new neighbors could take away their livelihoods.

Conflicts between the new residents and the rural residents who resented all the changes their arrival brought happened regularly—a "revolution," one writer called it in 1970, "albeit subtler and less violent" than that taking place in American cities, but a revolution nonetheless where "expanding urban centers [met] the resistance of rural America . . . the lines of battle [had] been drawn."[21]

Those battles often involved nuisance laws as rural space was transformed into post-rural space. Many nuisance laws had been on the books for years, designed to create more livable environments in densely populated areas. As suburbia rolled over farmland, those laws were sometimes invoked by new residents against the farmers already operating in the area. Take, for example, the Jordan family, pig farmers in rural Preble County, Ohio, thirty miles west of Dayton and abutting Indiana. In 1965, they found themselves with new neighbors as a "beautiful little subdivision" had been built nearby. But the Rockhill family, having built a house in that development for $35,000 (roughly $300,000 in 2021), found their suburban idyll spoiled by the smells vented by industrial fans from the Jordans' pig barn. They sued the Jordans in Preble County Common Pleas Court under Jefferson Township's zoning resolution article 8, section 5, which defined "nuisance" behavior. They won, and the Jordans were enjoined from operating their pig farm.[22]

How many such cases have made their way through court, I cannot say. But while the specifics undoubtedly differed as different judges interpreted different local laws in different ways, the same irony lies underneath all these conflicts: suburban development, from its very beginnings in the mid-nineteenth century, sold itself as an amalgam of country living and urban convenience. But the image of country life that new suburbanites brought with them often collided with agricultural realities. As one Nebraska farmer put it, "Town people will pay extra for a lot facing a farmer's pasture so they can see those pretty cows. But when a dairyman spreads manure or a hog farmer builds a manure lagoon, they want to sue him."[23] In other words, many new suburban residents expected to move into a Currier & Ives print; they found themselves next door to the noises and smells of an industrial operation.

No one understood that better than farmer Ray Dettmering.

On April 26, 1990, police in Matteson, Illinois, arrested Ray Dettmering, booked, photographed, and finger-printed him. He was charged with disorderly conduct, and while no one could be completely certain, Dettmering may well have made Illinois legal history as the first person to be charged for plowing too loudly.

Matteson had been a small agricultural village thirty miles due south of downtown Chicago. At the outbreak of World War II, fewer than a thousand people lived there. By the time Ray Dettmering was arrested, Matteson had grown to nearly 11,500 people. In this, Matteson was absolutely typical of countless towns swallowed up by postwar suburban expansion, not just around Chicago but all over the country.

The spring months of 1990 had been very wet in Illinois, and as a consequence Dettmering had to wait until the ground dried before he could plow. He was thus several weeks behind his planting schedule. To make up for lost time, Dettmering needed to plow at night. That's what upset his suburban neighbors, and that's why several of them called the cops. "It was so loud," Doris Norton, one of those neighbors complained, "we couldn't even hear the TV." Taking his stand, Dettmering vowed to plow on, even if that meant racking up more fines. "It's worth it to me," he said, adding: "The people around here will just have to get used to it." The farms had been there before the subdivisions, after all. "It's not like these farms snuck up on them."[24]

Plenty of people remarked on this at the time. Illinois Farm Bureau lawyer Dan Leifel summarized this succinctly after Ray Dettmering's arrest: "A lot of people are searching for a glorious escape into the open country," he opined. "They see farming as an ideal, pastoral life. They're not always aware of the hard work or the other things that go with it."[25] In this sense, the Currier & Ives reference really is apt. As suburbanites moved into their new houses, they wanted to see the country (their gauzy imagining of it, at any rate) through a picture window; they didn't want to hear it or smell it.

The transformation of rural spaces into post-rural ones forced people to confront political organization and consolidation—questions such as whether to incorporate unincorporated areas, whether townships would be designated villages or even cities by the state, the creation of local governmental structures to deal with increased demand for services, and more. Given that suburbanization happened in much the same way all over the country—new arrivals from the urban core and from the surrounding countryside converging on once-rural places—we can assume that conflicts over these issues happened everywhere, though it would be exceedingly difficult to catalog them all. Suffice it to say that intrasuburban conflict was probably as fierce as the hostility new suburbanites had toward the central cities from which some had fled and for which others had disdain in the first place. The fights over sewers, schools, and services were nothing less than the urban-rural conflict fought on post-rural terrain.

NOSTALGIA, LOSS, AND GRIEVANCE
IN POST-RURAL AMERICA

Suburban development is built on a basic irony. If those suburbanites who left the city were drawn by the promise of more space, less traffic, fewer people, lower crime rates, and all the rest, then many seemed resentful as their suburb filled with more and more development. Indeed, there is almost something of planned obsolescence in the promise of suburbia.

Different kinds of suburbs have emerged at different moments across the late nineteenth and twentieth centuries, driven by new technologies of communication and transportation. Dolores Hayden has provided a perfectly serviceable seven-part typology of the suburbs: Starting with "borderlands" in the early Republic; proceeding to the picturesque suburbs of the mid-nineteenth century; followed by the street-car suburbs; the "mail-order" suburbs of the turn of the twentieth century; "sit-com suburbs"; then the "edge nodes," starting in 1960; and, finally, the "rural fringes," a phenomenon she dates to 1980.[26] By that point, of course, the ripples-in-the-pond model no longer applied in most places as suburb-to-suburb commuting and suburb-upon-suburb development became more and more significant.

However much one might quibble with this periodization, the larger point is that each phase of suburban growth was spurred to some extent by a dissatisfaction with the previous one. The open space, the quiet life, the easy traffic—those all evaporated as more people moved in looking for exactly those same things. Suburbia as a dream not just unfulfilled but unfulfillable, an ever-receding horizon of disappointed expectations chased deeper and deeper into rural America.

But irony moving in exactly the opposite direction bedeviled those rural residents who found themselves surrounded as new suburbs grew up in the old familiar places. For these people—especially local boosters and small-town burgermeisters—post-rural suburbs represented a kind of triumph: population growth, economic development, and all the rest, as opposed to stagnation, depopulation, and decline visible so painfully in other rural towns. Yet even so, many of those "old-timers" were unhappy with the results. The last spud came out of the ground in Brooklyn Park, Minnesota, in 1992 when Calvin Gray, the only remaining commercial potato grower, threw in the towel. "It's progress, I guess," he laconically told a reporter.[27]

By the turn of the twenty-first century, as the sociologist Sonya Salamon observed of the small towns she studied in rural Illinois, the strategy of "smoke-stack chasing" in order to promote industrial development in the countryside had largely been replaced with one that "market[ed] a town as a package that delivers 'small-town life' to urban, middle-class families." Salamon made the mistake that so many others have in believing that the residents being drawn to these small towns came from the central city, while, in fact, many (maybe most) likely had relocated from another suburb. Nevertheless, the result for small towns has been the same: "Suburbanized, homogenous rural neighborhoods are oriented outward toward the metro area anchoring the region, rather than inward."[28] Of course, Arthur Morgan, as we saw, had made a similar point in 1953.

More kids in the local schools, more shoppers in local stores, an expanded tax base—this was exactly the goal of local chambers of commerce and Washington policy makers alike. Yet many said these small towns had lost the social cohesion and community spirit that had defined them, though I suspect this was more imagined than real.

The population who had moved to these now-suburbanized places, Salamon concluded, "exhibits less trust than an agrarian-community population does, avoids neighborly contact and conflict, and focuses on possessions rather than social acts to validate the family reputation." What remained, however big and economically robust, felt hollowed out: "The place name is the same, but the nontown suburbanized culture is not what old timers equate with their formerly authentic hometown."[29]

The boundaries that define DuPage County, Illinois, shape an almost perfect square, except for a tail that juts out from the county's southeast corner—a good example of the rectilinear geometry imposed on the spaces across the middle of the country. In the southwest corner of the county sits Naperville, also laid out in the grid pattern so common in nineteenth-century towns. In this and many other ways, Naperville was typical of towns scattered across the agricultural Midwest, and it remained so through the Second World War. In 1951, Naperville's city council vowed to get rid of the outhouses that still remained on Water Street.[30]

By the late 1950s, however, the town cheerleaders trumpeted that it was "First in DuPage and First in Progress." And who could blame them? New houses, new schools, new businesses, and new people. Naperville was still a prairie village at the end of the Second World War. Then the town's population almost doubled between 1950 and 1960. Naperville was booming.

Underneath the cheers, however, flowed a current of uneasiness. Mayor William Zaininger had been born in a Naperville of about 3,500 at the start of the First World War; in 1960, he presided over a town of thirteen thousand. Even as he trumpeted all the "progress" happening in the town thanks to a coordinated master-planning process, he acknowledged that the forces shaping Naperville's destiny were "beyond the control of our city government." Naperville, "like so many other small communities in this area, [had] been forced to change from a small town to a suburban city which [was] part of a large metropolitan complex." The challenge, as Zaininger saw it, was to accommodate all this growth while still retaining "the character of the community."[31] Zaininger did not elaborate on just how those two things could be simultaneously accomplished.

Though he did not say so specifically, that "character" to which he referred was surely a rural ideal—or, "the refinements of gracious rural living," in the words of the *Naperville Clarion*. Preserving those refinements, even as Naperville transformed into a modern suburb, was "what the citizens of Naperville [were] planning for the future of their city." Naperville confronted the dizzying expansion of the Chicago metropolitan region, but the *Clarion* explained a tad smugly that the town was "profiting by the mistakes of its neighbors," who had simply not planned "for the tomorrow that is today." And as if to reassure the town, the *Clarion* insisted that even adding more than three thousand new houses in an eight-year span had been accomplished "while carefully preserving its charm and attractiveness."[32] Napervillians themselves—some of them, at any rate—looked around them and did not like what they saw: the unregulated growth, the ugliness of untrammeled sprawl, the loss of . . . gracious rural living.

Whatever one meant by "gracious rural living"—and in all honesty, what did that phrase really mean?—agriculture would not be a part of it. The new housing in Naperville, however well planned and tasteful it might be, went up on farmland. In this, Naperville was no different than any of its neighbors. Flip to the classifieds in the *Chicago Tribune* on October 24, 1954, to pick a date randomly, and Naperville's J. P. Phelan was ready to sell you "farms in Naperville—vacant property, ideal for subdivision."

Unlike Park Forest, where William Whyte's Organization Man went home each day, or the Levittowns or many of the other suburbs built immediately after the war, Naperville continued to grow. A key accelerant for the second generation of Naperville's growth came in 1964, when AT&T built a research facility on the northern edge of town, next to a recently completed highway. In the nineteenth century, a railroad stop could make or break the fortunes of a small town. The interstate system played a similar role after the Second World

War. Towns adjacent to that sprawl-facilitating network of high-speed roads had a much better shot at economic growth than those places bypassed by the highways. Amoco followed AT&T with a research building of its own in 1969. By 1982, I-88 as it runs west from Chicago through DuPage, Kane, and DeKalb Counties had been dubbed the Illinois Technology and Research Corridor.

In the thirty years between 1960 and 1990, Naperville exploded from a town of thirteen thousand people to a city of more than eighty-five thousand. During the 1980s alone, the population doubled and the market value of the real estate tripled, from $1 billion to $3 billion. Naperville thus stands as a quintessential example of the "exurban" boom of that decade. When *Newsweek* wanted to run a story about the new exurbs in 1988, it sent reporters to Naperville. Exurbs— "where 'the commute' can be as far as 90 miles"—might be new, but the issues facing Naperville were not. They were exactly the sort of tensions that we have seen almost everywhere as rural morphed into post-rural. "Once sleepy roads are congested with traffic," *Newsweek* found, "and while there is more tax money there is also a greater demand for government services." But by that point it had become apparent that "the qualities that attract baby-boomers—peace, quiet, and simplicity—tend to erode as communities grow."[33]

The locals were not happy with all the growth, even if their leaders professed to be. "Natives find it difficult to see 'progress' in the change," the magazine reported. "I think the new homes are pretty," said seventy-six-year-old Marjorie Osborne, who lived in Naperville's historic district, which she helped establish in 1986 as a response to the rapid influx, "but 100 years from now will anyone see anything special in them?" After talking to the "natives" in Naperville, *Newsweek* concluded that all the new arrivals were "changing the essential character" of Naperville and towns like it.[34]

But then again, Marjorie Osborne wasn't exactly a "native." She and her family had moved to Naperville from California in 1951, part of that first wave of postwar suburban growth. She might well have been one of those who confidently believed that Naperville could grow and yet retain its small-town charms. In essence, she wanted to preserve the Naperville of her youth, oblivious to the irony that plenty of "natives" had doubtless grumbled when her family arrived. That confident insistence of the 1950s—that Naperville could strike the right balance—had been undone by the 1980s. The prairie village had become the fourth largest city in the state, and no one was talking much about "gracious rural living" anymore.

Forty miles due north, in Barrington, Illinois, Herb Walbaum doubtless sympathized with Marjorie Osborne. Walbaum had lived his whole life in Barrington, a small town of 1,400 when his family moved there in 1911. At that point, Barrington sat at the far reaches of the train line running northwest out of Chicago and was surrounded by farmland. After the war, it grew substantially, and the agricultural space between those railroad stops filled in as well. A familiar story, to be sure. Interviewed by the *Chicago Tribune* in 1991 at the age of eighty-two, Walbaum complained that he once "knew everybody by name." Now that was no longer true, as this "sparsely populated farm community . . . filled with orchards and dairy farms" had been replaced with housing developments. "It's been a constant struggle against the developers," Walbaum lamented.[35]

Except that Walbaum *was* one of those developers—or, at least, he had been. In 1934, shortly after high school, he started his own cement contracting business and claimed to have poured the foundations for fifty homes in Barrington before the war intervened. When it was over, Walbaum got into the development game, helping to build on a 1,200-acre tract. In 1950, he founded Barrington Realty and ran it well into his seventies. If you bought a house in the environs of Barrington, Illinois, in the decades after the war, there's a good chance you met Herb Walbaum. And he never stopped "marveling" at all the new growth in which he played his part. "He would constantly drive around watching new developments as they were happening," his daughter Mary reported.[36]

Technically speaking, Walbaum no longer lived in Barrington when the *Tribune* came to talk with him. He had moved to Barrington Hills immediately to the west. Barrington Hills had been incorporated in 1957 with a zoning innovation requiring that building lots be a whopping five acres each—a place for people who thought Barrington itself was already too crowded, and a foreshadowing of the large-lot exurban development that would run rampant in the 1980s. For Walbaum, five acres gave him space to keep a horse.

The horse, and the cowboy boots he wore every day until his death, weren't exactly affectations of country living so much as palimpsests. Walbaum entered this world in 1910 on a farm his German-speaking immigrant parents had bought just a few years earlier. They themselves had been farming in the area since their arrival in the region in the late nineteenth century. Before he could walk, his father was killed by a lightning strike while trying to fix a tractor, and his widowed mother could not run the farm on her own. She moved the family to town, where they stayed. In a single lifetime, Herb Walbaum lived the trajectory from farm to suburb that characterizes the story of much of post-rural America. He embodied an emotional arc as well: from the struggles of farm life to the prosperity of midcentury suburbia, to the nostalgic dissatisfaction with those suburbs as they kept insatiably gobbling up rural space.

PLACES VS. SPACES

This rural civilization, whose making has engaged mankind since the dawn of history, is passing away.

FREDERIC HOWE, 1906

A thought experiment: Stand by a country road and imagine counting the cars. Initially, one goes by every hour. The following month, three go by every hour. And so on for several months until the traffic is bumper-to-bumper. Is this place still rural, and if not, when did it cease to be?

Conceptualizing rural places can become a version of what philosophers call the sorites paradox. You have a pile of sand—say, a million grains. You remove one grain; what remains is still a pile of sand. Remove another, and it is a pile still. Proceed this way and ultimately you have one grain of sand left. It is clearly no longer a proper pile. Yet are you still calling it a pile? The problem, of course, is deciding when the pile has ceased to be a pile, since any definition—half of the original? a hundred thousand grains? a dozen?—is arbitrary and subjective.

While I hope this book has prompted you to rethink what rural means and what its history has been, I want to finish with a nod to the sorites paradox: What happens if we think about rural spaces by starting with the assumption that there isn't a "rural" in the United

States, not in any meaningful sense, at all? What's more, what if there really never has been?

This is certainly the conclusion I've drifted toward as I've worked on this project, but it's not an original thought. "It is contended," William Friedland wrote, "that there is little 'rural' society left in the United States." In fact, he believed, "instead of differences that demarcate rural and urban, there is now an increased homogeneity between metro and nonmetro locations."[1] He published those words in 1982.

In the following decade, as the American countryside continued to change, Emery Castle threw up his analytic hands trying to arrive at any firm, useful definition of rural and concluded: "One viable alternative remains—to consider the rural as an essential component of a predominantly urban society. Twenty-five percent of the nation's population and 97 percent of the nation's space is to be found there. Our conclusion, therefore, is that the rural is an important and diverse component of urban life."[2] On first reading, that statement is merely underwhelming. Pause over it, though, and it becomes more extraordinary. After all our collective investment in the very notion of rural—the political rhetoric, the cultural imaginings, the economic subsidies, and the rest—after all that, those who think long and hard about rural America have concluded that it is an adjunct, a subset, of urban life. Rural as a kind of neighborhood in the vast national city.

Yet, certainly at an economic level, this seems unarguable. There have been a few examples, perhaps, of rural communities establishing themselves as self-sufficient and independent farming communities— some New England towns in the eighteenth century, Amish settlements in the nineteenth. But on the whole, the economics of rural America have always been connected to urban centers: urban markets for rural products; urban capital for rural expansion. Land as a financial asset to be bought, sold, and mortgaged; the products of that land turned into commodities also bought and sold. In a 1995 study of a ghost town in Kansas, Joseph Hickey concluded that Kansas—and the West more broadly—"were never 'isolated frontiers' but were from the beginning rural hinterlands of cities such as Chicago and St. Louis."[3]

Nor is there much real evidence that the United States developed genuinely distinctive rural societies or cultures—certainly not to the extent found on every other continent—again with perhaps a few exceptions. In the 1930s, a handful of Americans "discovered" that America did have its own folk traditions in certain isolated pockets, and at the same moment, a group of artists during the interwar years promoted an American "regionalism," arguing that America's genuine culture grew out of its distinctive regions rather than its mongrel cities. We might remember the painters best—Thomas Hart Benton, John Steuart Curry, Grant Wood—and Wood took it upon himself to broadcast the movement in a 1935 manifesto fittingly titled *The Revolt against the City*. In it he announced that artistic inspiration came "in the distinctly rural districts of America," and thundered that "cities were far less typically American than the frontier area whose power they usurped." That was a bit disingenuous, given that Wood continued to sell his work through the Associated American Artists group based in New York City.[4]

None of those who wanted to find a genuine, authentic folk culture in this country searched more energetically than the Lomaxes—father John and son Alan. Even they, however, saw their frenetic efforts to collect folk songs as a salvage operation. "Although the spread of machine civilization is rapidly making it hard to find folk singers," the two wrote in their magisterial *American Ballads and Folk Songs* (1934), "ballads are yet sung in this country."[5] That sense of racing against the clock also motivated the WPA's slave narrative project, published in 1941 and subtitled *A Folk History of Slavery in the United States from Interviews with Former Slaves*.[6]

Those projects make a nice juxtaposition with the most aggressive defense of a distinctive rural way of life during the interwar decades. The group of southerners who called themselves the Agrarians published their own angry manifesto, *I'll Take My Stand*, in 1930. A collection of poets and professors centered at Vanderbilt University—none of them had ever touched a plow—they offered the South and its rural world as a healthy alternative to the industrialized, urbanized mainstream of American life. Only in the South did a distinctive, Jeffersonian way of life hang on, they insisted, and one of them, Donald Davidson, accused Abraham Lincoln of ruining that Jeffersonian idyll. "If Lincoln was a supporter of the Jeffersonian notion of a body of free and self-reliant farmers," Davidson wrote in 1938, "then why did he fight the South?"[7] The jaw drops to read that today, and even at the time, when Jim Crow presided iron fisted over the South, many reviewers, even those sympathetic to regionalism, blanched with embarrassment. If rural southern life, built on slavery and maintained through segregation, was the best example of rural culture America had to offer . . . well, that didn't help the cause much. But putting aside the grotesque and willful blindness to racial issues that the Agrarians indulged in, the dichotomy they posited—the rural southern ways of life in opposition to the urban northern way—is simply wrong. Far from creating a kind of American feudalism, slavery sat at the very center of American capitalism as it developed in the first half of the nineteenth century.[8]

The Lomaxes, the Regionalists, and the rest swam against a consensus that though European peasants, living in the same communities over many generations, had produced genuine and distinctive rural folkways, America had no real peasantry and thus had developed no authentic rural culture. Their work, and the work of other folklorists, however, has not really made a persuasive case.

Certainly, Richard Hofstadter wasn't convinced that the United States had ever created a "folk." Twenty years after the folklore vogue began, he noted: "In a very real and profound sense [what] the United States failed to develop . . . is a distinctly *rural* culture." He went on to be more specific about what he meant: "If a rural culture means an emotional and craftsmanlike dedication to the soil, a traditional and pre-capitalist outlook, a tradition-directed rather than a career-directed type of character, and a village community devoted to ancestral ways and habitually given to communal action, then the prairies and plains never had one."[9] There may be much to quibble with here—and Hofstadter conceded that maybe a genuine rural culture had developed in a few places, mostly east of the Appalachians—but, I think, little with which to seriously argue.

Another way to think about rural, however, is as the difference between place and space, and you might have noticed that I have primarily used the latter to describe the areas I've examined. The term *place* tends to connote specificity, authenticity, and stability. We talk about the place where this or that happened; we yearn for a sense of place; space, on the other hand, is an abstraction: empty space, outer space. Places also imply belonging and rootedness. Space implies none of those things. That's why when people seem distracted and disconnected from where they are we call them "spacey." In 1995 the urbanist Dolores Hayden published an influential book titled *The Power of Place*, implying that place has the capacity to generate its own force. By contrast, power acts upon space. Rural spaces in America are exactly that: spaces, not places. The geographer David Harvey sees the dichotomy between space and place as what he calls a "tension between place-bound fixity and spatial mobility."[10] Spaces don't embody sets of values or ideologies; they conceal them. Certainly, American rural spaces conceal, as I have argued, four powerful forces of American modernity. Those forces have acted upon rural space to no less a degree than they have metropolitan parts of the country. Indeed, often even more so.

In surveying rural America, it seems to me that the United States has produced rural space—in both the productive and ideological sense—in great abundance, but precious few rural places. My suspicion is that we regularly confuse the two. As we stare out at (or imagine) rural space, we think we are seeing "place," with all the cultural baggage with which that notion is freighted. Metropolitan Americans may need to see it that way so they can imagine an alternative to their own lives, while rural Americans themselves want to believe that they and they alone carry the torch of Jeffersonian placeness—independent, sustained by nurturing and intimate communities, governing themselves through face-to-face democracy. The rural anger toward metropolitan America that has been a defining feature of our recent politics, I suspect, comes to a boil when the fictions of rural place crash up against the realities of rural space.

This disconnect, not quite visible, lurks just below the surface of how we understand and discuss rural America. Rural America suffers from an emptiness, not of the sort I described at the outset but rather one of explanation. One that would bridge the chasm between myth and reality in any satisfying way and resolve the tension between fixity and mobility. Here's how David Foster Wallace, himself a product of downstate Illinois, described it: "Rural Midwesterners live surrounded by unpopulated land, marooned in a space whose emptiness is both physical and spiritual. It is not just people you get lonely for. You're alienated from the very space around you, for here the land is not an environment but a commodity. The land is basically a factory. You live in the same factory you work in. You spend an enormous amount of time with the land, but you're still alienated from it in some way."[11] Emptiness and its attendant alienation are decidedly not what we want to believe about rural America despite the novelists, journalists, and most recently economists who have pointed this out.

If there is no "rural" in any meaningful economic or cultural sense (and certainly not for a century, at least), how then to think about those "nonmetropolitan" areas that cover such a vast portion of the national map? At the end of the previous century, John Fraser Hart pointed us in a useful direction. "The traditional rural-urban dichotomy has become a continuum," he observed, and that continuum "has no unambiguous 'natural' break."[12] He wrote that almost exactly a century after the Census Bureau announced that there was no longer any frontier on the American map, and the coincidence is worth pausing over briefly.

The very idea of the nineteenth-century frontier was deeply flawed, and arguably deeply destructive to begin with. Frederick Jackson Turner, who did more than anyone to establish the way we have discussed the frontier, defined it as "an area of free land," as if it weren't occupied by anyone before settlers moved into it.[13] Most significantly, this conception helped erase Native people from the national map. It also contributed to the myth that the rural spaces that filled up that "free land" were white spaces. In Turner's conception, European settlers turned the "free land" of the wilderness into settled space and in so doing created "Americans." Black and brown people are simply absent from Turner's deeply influential conceptualization. Further, the definition of what distinguished a settled area from a frontier area in the Census Bureau's point of view—two or more white inhabitants per square mile—was a measure of population density. So too is Hart's notion of continuum, which hearkens back to the sociologist Louis Wirth's 1938 definition of density as one of the core characteristics of an urban area. Wirth argued, perhaps a bit tautologically, that the more dense a city becomes, "the more accentuated the characteristics associated with urbanism will be."[14]

Therefore, rather than thinking of the country as split between metropolitan and nonmetropolitan areas, we might be better off putting our residential patterns on Hart's continuum and mapping by density. At the far end of it, dense cities such as San Francisco (19,000 people per square mile) and Boston (14,000-plus); at the other, sparsely populated places such as Perry County, Kentucky (83 people per square mile), and McHenry County, North Dakota (just under 3). Flip Wirth's formula around and we can conclude that the less dense a place is, the less urban it will be.

Density, according to Wirth, brings with it a number of urban things: a greater variety of jobs, a larger number of social interactions, the creation of groups to help like-minded individuals negotiate the complex urban terrain. It also puts different kinds of people into close contact with one another. Those frequent, necessary interactions among heterogeneous people fostered what Wirth called "the broadest tolerance" among "a motley of peoples," which makes urban life possible in the first place.[15]

Density and heterogeneity have consistently been among the features of urban life that have scared nonurban Americans the most. Anti-urbanites have always recognized the link between density and diversity and have recoiled from it. That reaction is an enduring American trope.[16] Rural America is not racially or ethnically homogenous—not today and not in the past—but it is more so than metropolitan America. That contrast creates the imaginative space to pretend that rural America—"real America"—is white. And whiteness has always been a central part of our rural mythology. Further, density also necessitates a wider web of social interactions and dependencies than is true in less-dense environments. That interdependence, too, is something anti-urbanites have railed against. As Ralph Woods, the champion of industrial decentralization, put the contrast in 1939: "Agriculture is primarily an individualistic way of life. . . . Urban life, on the other hand, is essentially a co-operative existence."[17] Cooperation, for Woods, was not a good thing. Therefore, if there is a correlation between density, heterogeneity, and social tolerance, perhaps we need to ask whether lower-density residential patterns breed less tolerance; and if less-dense living fosters a sense—however true it may or may not be—of individualistic independence, then do less-dense environments make it harder for people to imagine a larger common good or feel larger social obligations?

In my observations and in my researches, people who do see themselves as rural define themselves as *against* the city rather than as affirmatively "rural." In 1958, the sociologists Arthur Vidich and Joseph Bensman noticed that even rural grievances were, essentially, urban in nature: "Even when the rural community attacks the urban mass society, the nature of the attack, its intensity and the situations which bring it forth are, in large part, the products of urban mass society. Rural life then can be seen as one area in which the dynamics of modern urban mass society are worked out." Half a century later, the Roanoke County Board of Supervisors in Virginia found themselves embroiled in a variation of this anger. In 2010, they attempted to adopt a series of policies under the umbrella of "sustainability," only to find themselves attacked by members of the right-wing Tea Party movement, which was strong in that rural county. It left supervisor Charlotte Moore flummoxed: "The Tea Party people say they want non-polluted air and clean water and everything we promote and support. . . . I really don't know what they want."[18]

In essence, what many aggrieved rural people seem to want are the benefits of urban society without the density and diversity of urban living. In this sense, rural is reduced to what the city is not. Without a positive, proactive vision of what a rural future might be, some number of Americans who live in ostensibly rural places marinate in a sense of loss and perpetual disappointment. Call it an absence of narrative coherence, and it may sting even more than the more measurable losses. Those latter are all real enough. Jobs lost in coal mines; family farms folded up and sold off to larger and larger ag conglomerates. Main Street stores shuttered and abandoned, the local high school closed and merged with another one forty-five minutes away, the freight depot that saw its last train rumble through in the early 1970s—all palpably part of the lived experience of many rural Americans. And this has been the case for roughly a century now.

That sense of narrative loss, however, centers on the conviction that the link between what the landscapes of rural America once were and what they are now has been broken. Whatever sense of place the term *rural* once engendered, it has largely evaporated. And it hasn't been replaced with anything satisfying or sustaining. Many Americans, still, project onto rural America their yearning for tight-knit community, for self-reliance and independence, neighborliness, and simpler, slower living; but that fantasy cannot accommodate the realities of life in many parts of rural America, nor does it take into account the thorough extent to which the military, industry, corporations, and suburbia have shaped rural space.

That's a tough circle to square, and certainly an expensive one. Rather than revisiting the fatigued debates over the meaning of "rural values" or whether rural folk really are more decent and hardworking than the rest of Americans, let's acknowledge that life in lower-density environments is simply more costly in a host of ways. In a nation that has made a fetish of economic efficiency, it is remarkable that we have not tallied the inefficiencies of the rural life we continue to extoll: the expense of providing basic services that people now expect, the costs of labor market distortions where jobs are few and very far between, the time it takes out of each day to live life spread over wide distances.

Much of rural America is poor, but that poverty combined with the inefficiency of living at lower density helps explain why rural Americans require as much government aid as they do.

In April 2021, the Washakie County Ambulance Service, a volunteer operation serving eight thousand county residents spread across over two thousand square miles in Wyoming, had to cease operation. Like so many other volunteer services in low-density places, it had run out of money and volunteers. Fortunately, it was taken over by a regional health system based in Cody, nearly 100 miles away from Worland, the county seat. Phillip Franklin, the director of that ambulance service, put the situation matter of factly: "Someone is always going to have to subsidize rural America."[19] It is a fair question, I think, to ask to what extent and to what end the rest of the country is obligated to subsidize low-density living.

We also need to reckon with another consequence of low-density living: it requires more energy. That not only drives up the costs of rural living—as I write this, gasoline prices hover at $5 per gallon— but it means that rural people produce more greenhouse gases than urbanites. Measured in terms of climate change, cities are "greener" than rural areas, counterintuitive though that feels. New York City, if it were its own state, would rank thirteenth in population but fifty-first in per capita energy consumption.[20] If the nation—and I recognize just how conditional that "if" is—is going to confront the climate crisis, we will have to think seriously about the carbon costs of living at low densities. Meanwhile, the country music singer Hailey Whitters warbles in "Boys Back Home," her unintentionally risible paean to the glories of rural masculinity, that real men wouldn't ever drive an electric car to crowds of cheering fans.

The Jeffersonian fantasy lives, despite how few people have ever experienced that vision of yeoman independence for themselves. None other than Henry Kissinger rhapsodized in these tones in his memoirs: "In no other country are personal relations so effortless as in small-town America. Nowhere else is there to be found the same generosity of spirit and absence of malice."[21] It isn't clear that the Harvard–DC–New York–located Kissinger ever spent any time in an American small town (or ever read *Peyton Place* for that matter), but that's hardly the point. Late in the nineteenth century, as the historian Paul Sandul has traced, California boosters dreamed of the "agriburb"—a form of suburbia that would combine proximity to urban areas with agricultural production in places such as Ontario and Orangevale. Early in the twenty-first century, more than one hundred years later, ambitious developers in Colorado and elsewhere began to market projects they called "Agriburbia," which sounded an awful lot like those California projects: a suburban subdevelopment with space for crops and horses. "We are trying to figure out a way to facilitate a more Jeffersonian type of living," explained the real estate "visionary" Matthew Redmond. "You can be a computer programmer," he went on, "but you still own a steward lot in an Agriburbia subdivision and produce fruits and vegetables for commercial reasons or for your own use."[22] The dream doesn't die hard—it doesn't die at all.

ACKNOWLEDGMENTS

In 2016, I became an accidental expert.

A year and a half earlier, I had published a book that examined what I called the "anti-urban tradition" in American life and traced its impact on policy and places across the twentieth century. I wanted to explore what I saw as a central American paradox: we are a highly urbanized nation filled with people who dislike their cities. I consider myself an urban historian and wanted the book to be a contribution to that conversation.

Then came the presidential campaign of 2016—a vertiginous and surreal fever dream that went on for what seemed like forever and ended with a result as unthinkable as it was unlikely. During the campaign and in the months that followed the election, some people discovered my book and read it as an exploration of the "urban-rural divide" that the election seemed to have exposed. The red-blue map that serves as a color-coded shorthand for our politics told the story. Hillary Clinton only won 487 counties across the country, a scant 15 percent of the total, and yet still won three million more votes in the popular tally. Even more astounding, the counties she won accounted for, by some estimates, more than 60 percent of the nation's GDP. In other words, Clinton won in the places where most Americans actually live and where the economy prospers. But because of the way rural voters are overrepresented by the Electoral College—itself a part of that anti-urban tradition I explored in my book—the loser of the popular vote wound up in the White House. In 2016, it appeared, rural America took its revenge on the rest of us for having been ignored, or left behind, or otherwise insulted.

So in 2016 and 2017, I found myself interviewed by journalists to explain this fissure in American politics. I was asked to write op-ed pieces about the urban-rural divide; I was invited to lecture several times on the same issue. It was the topic of the moment in American politics, even as many of us scratched our heads trying to figure out how the biggest huckster to come out of New York City since P. T. Barnum (and whose only exposure to life outside the Big Apple had come on golf courses) could be taken up as the savior of rural America.

In truth, I didn't actually know much about rural America or its history, but I fielded the questions as gamely as I could, prepared some lecture slides, and promised myself that someday I really would look into all of this further. After all, I live now in a tiny midwestern town surrounded by corn and soybean fields, and I teach in an only slightly larger midwestern town surrounded by soybean and corn fields. I should know about things rural. This book is an attempt to fulfill that promise.

I started working on this project in 2019 and had a full itinerary of archival trips planned for the summer of 2020. Events, of course, intervened, and I had to reconceive the research accordingly. Which is to say: this is a Covid book, and the pandemic shaped not only how I did my work but how I felt about it as I did it. There's no escaping that, and so best to acknowledge it forthrightly.

Yet even though I was unable to do much traveling, I still managed to accumulate a great many debts to archivists and others, a number of whom bent over backward to assist me even from a distance.

A profound thank-you to Christo Datini at the Archives and Special Collections, General Motors; to the staff at Benson Ford Research Center; to Lauren Dreger at the Ford Motor Company Archives; to Elizabeth Gruber at the Marquette (MI) Regional History Center; to Andrea Field of the Naperville (IL) Heritage Society; to Mary Scheonborn at the University of Minnesota Libraries; to Jane Bailey at the Shelby County (OH) Historical Society; and to Kim Jurkovic at the Dover (OH) Historical Society. Historians always lean on archivists and librarians to do our work, but the fact these people went to such lengths to help me under such extraordinary circumstances reminds me of just how indispensable they are.

Given those circumstances, it was even more fun than usual once I was able to work in archives in person. A thanks to the staff at the Spruance Library of the Bucks County (PA) Historical Society; to John Wickett, Richfield (MN) Historical Society; and to Darryl Sannes, Brooklyn (MN) Historical Society. They all welcomed me generously and provided enormous help.

I also imposed on a number of friends and colleagues for their thoughts, advice, direction, and encouragement. I owe a beer (or something stronger) to Bryant Simon, Clay Howard, David Steigerwald, Bart Elmore, Dan Amsterdam, Catherine McNicol Stock, and Ying Zhang. Closer to home I am also indebted to a number of colleagues at Miami University, including Jacky Johnson, Jenny Presnell, James Rubenstein, and Stephen Gordon. Conversations I had with two remarkable students have informed this book in all sorts of way, and it has been gratifying to watch as Eric Rhodes and Jacob Bruggeman have ceased to be my students and become colleagues. Eric's reading of part 4 was particularly astute. Another student of mine, Abigail Kussow, convinced me that my original title for this book was terrible. Andrew Offenburger, a fine historian and himself a child and student of rural America, put up with my endless talking about this book in his office on an almost weekly basis and did so without ever throwing me out. I'm grateful to Tim Mennel at the University of Chicago Press who believed in this project at the beginning when it was only a half-baked set of ideas, and then muscled the manuscript into shape at the end.

My father, Peter, once again managed to function as both unabashed cheerleader and sharp-eyed critic, as he has throughout my career. His grandson, Zachary, also read the entire manuscript, made some crucial suggestions about how to reorganize it, and stepped in to help with research for part 2. My wife, Angela Brintlinger, read every word of this, though given her own schedule, I'm not entirely sure how she managed to do it. Among the many joys she brings me is the desire simply to keep up with her.

NOTES

PREFACE

1. See Farrell, *Billionaire Wilderness*. Better, see Ian Frazier's lacerating review of this book: Frazier, "The Plushbottoms of Teton County." For a report on the OSU research, see Grabmeier, "There's No Longer One Rural America."

2. Castle, "The Forgotten Hinterlands," 9; Hart, "'Rural' and 'Farm' No Longer Mean the Same," 76.

3. Quoted in Hart, "'Rural' and 'Farm' No Longer Mean the Same," 63.

4. That scale was probably already in the process of changing. It certainly is now. See Schuman, "China's Small Farms Are Fading."

5. Centner, *Empty Pastures*, 14.

6. I should acknowledge a terrific book by the same title, though I came across it after I wrote this preface: R. Douglas Hurt's *The Big Empty: The Great Plains in the Twentieth Century*.

INTRODUCTION

1. J. B. Jackson, *The Necessity for Ruins*, 120.

2. Rural Health Information Hub, "Suicide in Rural Areas."

3. "Special Report: Covering the Meth Epidemic." See also Reding, *Methland*.

4. Case and Deaton, *Deaths of Despair*.

5. In 2018, Robert Wuthnow, perhaps our most distinguished sociologist of rural America, published a book examining the state of rural America and titled it *The Left Behind*, underscoring this now conventional wisdom.

6. See, for example, Frakt, "A Hospital Die-Off."

7. Bailey, *Country Life Movement*, 1.

8. "Decline in Rural Population," 615.

9. To take one example of this dilemma, David Danbom's book *Born in the Country* is subtitled *A History of Rural America* but, in fact, is almost entirely about agriculture and the farm economy.

10. US Census Bureau, *Historical Statistics of the United States*, 580.

11. C. M. Wilson, *Landscape of Rural Poverty*, 51. For the 1900 figure, see Fite, *American Agriculture and Farm Policy*, 3. Who actually owned the land is harder to figure out. Some of it was surely owned privately and rented out by people who no longer wanted to farm (or who owned more land than they could farm themselves); some of it was probably owned by banks or insurance companies who had foreclosed on property during the Great Depression.

12. Beck and Forster, *Six Rural Problem Areas*, 24.

13. Ganzel, "Shrinking Farm Numbers."

14. Shaults, "Creeping Ugliness of Small Towns," 17–18.

15. To underscore this point, I note that Wuthnow subtitled his 2018 book *Decline and Rage in Small-Town America*.

16. C. M. Wilson, *Landscape of Rural Poverty*, 19.

17. F. S. Fitzgerald, "Early Success," 87.

18. Hurt, *The Big Empty*, 98.

19. *The People Left Behind*, ix.

20. See US Department of Agriculture, National Agricultural Statistics Service, *Price Program*, chapter 4.

21. Both figures are taken from Dudley, *Debt and Dispossession*, 151.

22. For example, M. Williams, "Many Ohio Towns Left Behind."

23. Hofstadter, *Age of Reform*, 24–25.

24. Hofstadter, 25.

25. Clark, "Agrarian Context of American Capitalist Development," 18.

26. Levy, "The Mortgage Worked the Hardest," 39, 41.

27. Griswold, *Farming and Democracy*, 8, 15; USDA report quoted on 15–16. More recent scholarly work has certainly confirmed Griswold's insight, though in ways he could never have foreseen. The federal government was central, for example, in creating a tourist infrastructure for the rural West and for creating the "modern" South. And, of course, military spending may have altered both regions more profoundly than anything else. See Schulman, *From Cotton Belt to Sunbelt*; Nash, *The Federal Landscape*; and Markusen et al., *The Rise of the Gunbelt*.

28. Watts, *Reading the Landscape of America*, 220; Atherton, *Main Street on the Middle Border*, 336, 355.

29. Vidich and Bensman, *Small Town in Mass Society*, 104.

30. Watts, *Reading the Landscape of America*, 126–29.

31. Unidentified interview quoted in Wuthnow, *The Left Behind*, 99.

32. Centner, *Empty Pastures*, 2.

33. CNN, "Biden Lashes Out."

34. Brooks, "What Rural America Has to Teach Us."

35. Hickey, *Ghost Settlement on the Prairie*, 252.

36. Danbom, *Born in the Country*, 205.

37. Wuthnow, *The Left Behind*, 4.

38. Dudley, *Debt and Dispossession*, 4–5, 109, 127.

39. The resource curse theory began to circulate in the early 1990s associated with the economist Jeffrey Sachs.

40. Scott, *Seeing Like a State*, 2.

41. Hart, *The Look of the Land*, 3.

42. Hoganson, *The Heartland*, 302.

PART ONE

---

1. Zelinsky, "Asserting Central Authority," 345–46. Wilbur Zelinsky writes that trying to do a complete history of the USACE "would fill a large volume to overflowing" (345–46). The pun may or may not have been intended.

2. *Report on Agriculture and Rural Prosperity*, 38.

3. See the three "Nike Site" files in the Walter Havighurst Special Collections, Miami University. Thanks to Jacky Johnson for putting me on to these.

CHAPTER ONE

---

1. "Principal Facts Concerning the First Transcontinental Army Motor Transport Expedition, Washington to San Francisco July 7 to September 6, 1919," box 967, PPF 1075, President's Personal File, Dwight D. Eisenhower's Records as President, Eisenhower Presidential Library.

2. Kissel quoted in "U.S. Army Motor-Truck Train," 550.

3. Quoted in *Alliance (NE) Herald*, "Army Train Is Enroute."

4. "Principal Facts Concerning the First Transcontinental Army Motor Transport Expedition."

5. "Principal Facts Concerning the First Transcontinental Army Motor Transport Expedition."

6. Quoted in *Alliance (NE) Herald*, "Army Train Is Enroute."

7. Evinger, *Directory of U.S. Military Bases Worldwide*, 91.

8. DeVoto, "The Easy Chair," 61; USACE public affairs officer, pers. comm., August 30, 2020; US Army Corps of Engineers, "Multipurpose Waterway Development."

9. Nelson quoted in Drew, "Dam Outrage," 51.

10. Sherrill, "The Pork-Barrel Soldiers," 180; cost figures from Drew, "Dam Outrage," 57.

11. E. Peterson, "Army Engineers Imposing Flood-Control Ideas," 12.

12. E. Peterson, "Army Engineers Imposing Flood-Control Ideas," 12; Robinson, "Tuttle Creek Tragedy." For more on the fight against the corps over the Tuttle Creek project, see Genandt, "The People Be Damned."

13. For more on the community fights against the Tuttle Creek project and the nearby Milford dam project, see Hanson, "If the Lord's Willing and the Creek Don't Rise."

14. Morgan, *Dams and Other Disasters*, 370.

15. Morgan, 370–71.

16. Rich, "Rolling Along," 6.

17. See Brazos River Authority, "Why So Many Man-Made Lakes in Texas?" For a discussion of the creation of Lake Conroe in Montgomery County, Texas, see Baker, *Bulldozer Revolutions*, chapter 4.

18. Sanders, "After the Flood," 93.

19. Sanders, 98.

20. Morgan, *Dams and Other Disasters*, 317.

21. The Arthur Morgan Papers contain a great deal of material about this campaign. See Arthur Morgan Papers, VIII Special Projects, S Seneca Indians/Kinzua Dam, Antiochiana, Olive Kettering Library, Antioch College.

22. Morgan, *Dams and Other Disasters*, 317.

23. Copy of letter in Arthur Morgan Papers, VIII Special Projects, S Seneca Indians/Kinzua Dam, Antiochiana, Olive Kettering Library, Antioch College.

24. Roosevelt, "My Day, June 7, 1961."

25. *New York Times*, "Justice for the Senecas."

26. E. Wilson, "Second Look at Kinzua"; and Clark's letter in response, *Washington Post*, January 30, 1960. The editorial ran unattributed but appears to be excerpted from Wilson's book *Apologies to the Iroquois*, which was published later in 1960.

27. Morgan, *Dams and Other Disasters*, 316–67.

28. John F. Kennedy to Basil Williams, August 9, 1961, box 14, Resources: Kinzua Dam, 1961: 7 July–19 December, General File, 1954–1964, White House Staff Files of Lee C. White, Presidential Papers, Papers of John F. Kennedy, John F. Kennedy Presidential Library.

29. The Seneca Nation appealed the district court ruling to the 2nd circuit court, which affirmed it. Seneca Nation of Indians v. United States of America, 338 F.2d 55 (2d Cir. 1964).

30. Quoted in Diaz-Gonzalez, "The Complicated History of the Kinzua Dam."

31. 95 Cong. Rec. A4284 (1949) (statement of Rep. Lemke).

32. I have taken these examples, and the quotes, from "American Indians of the Army Corps of Engineers," unpublished, undated manuscript (Arthur Morgan? Late

1960s?), Arthur Morgan Papers, VIII Special Projects, S Seneca Indians/Kinzua Dam, Antiochiana, Olive Kettering Library, Antioch College.

33. US Army Corps of Engineers, "Kinzua Dam & Allegheny Reservoir."

CHAPTER TWO

1. Liggett, "What Is the Matter with Our Army?," 462.

2. Liggett, 462.

3. See South, "10 US Military Bases."

4. Lewis, *On the Edge of the Black Waxy*, 11–12.

5. Poage quoted in Edwards, "Land Acquisition in Coryell County," 20.

6. Lewis, *On the Edge of the Black Waxy*, 12.

7. I have taken this summary of the Camp Hood land takings from Sylvia Ann Edwards's marvelous MA thesis, "Land Acquisition for the Formation of Camp Hood."

8. Chapin et al., *In the Shadow of a Defense Plant*, 73.

9. Schulman, *From Cotton Belt to Sunbelt*, 95; Sparrow, *Warfare State*.

10. Friedman, "The Drama in Temple," 521–22.

11. Lewis, *On the Edge of the Black Waxy*, 28, 38, 68.

12. See *Fifty Years of Excellence*.

13. Rogers, "Ike Orders Probe of Segregated Schools"; *Crusader*, "NAACP Protests Slow Integration."

14. This story was widely reported. See, for example, *Miami News*, "Ike Told of Negro GIs' Peril."

15. *New Pittsburgh Courier*, "Fort Hood Group Blasts GI Jim Crow."

16. *Pittsburgh Courier*, "Army Jails GI 'Sit-Ins.'"

17. Arnold, "3 Soldiers Hold News Conference."

18. Markusen et al., *The Rise of the Gunbelt*; statistics from 11–12.

19. Faulkner quoted in Schulman, *From Cotton Belt to Sunbelt*, 135.

20. Lewis, *On the Edge of the Black Waxy*, 38.

21. Stockton, Hardwick, and Dale, *An Economic Survey of Killeen, Texas*, 7.

22. Stockton, Hardwick, and Dale, vii.

23. *Hearing before the Real Estate and Military Construction Subcommittee of the Committee on Armed Services*, 83rd Cong. 2 (1953) (statement of Maj. Gen. L. L. Doan, commanding general, First Armored Division).

24. *Hearing before the Real Estate and Military Construction Subcommittee of the Committee on Armed Services*, 83rd Cong. 7 (1953) (statement of Roy Smith, president of First National Bank, Killeen, TX).

25. For this discussion, I have drawn from *Hearing before the Real Estate and Military Construction Subcommittee of the Committee on Armed Services*, 83rd Cong. 11, 18 (1953).

26. Boroff, "Fort Hood: Sparta Goes Suburban," 48.

27. Boroff, 48.

28. Boroff, 48.

CHAPTER THREE

1. Evinger, *Directory of U. S. Military Bases Worldwide*; Stebbins, "America's Largest Military Bases."

2. Shaw, *Locating Air Force Base Sites*, 89.

3. Sorenson, *Shutting Down the Cold War*, 10; *Ideal Base Study* is referred to in Shaw, *Locating Air Force Base Sites*, 103–4.

4. Sorenson, *Shutting Down the Cold War*, 10.

5. J. B. Jackson, *The Necessity for Ruins*, 12.

6. R. L. Polk & Co., *Marquette City and County Directory*. For the list of mines, see 42–47.

7. See n.a., "Michigan's Upper Peninsula Iron Ore Industry," n.p. (1957). See also Robert Reed, "Michigan Iron Mines," typescript from the Michigan Department of Conservation, 1957. Both documents were provided by the Marquette Regional History Center.

8. Stetson, "New Span Sparks Boom."

9. Hailey, "Michigan's North Beckons Business"; Stetson, "Upper Michigan Asks for Job Aid."

10. *L'Anse (MI) Sentinel*, "To All Residents of Baraga County" (ad); *Oxford (MI) Leader*, "From the Office of Senator Ferguson."

11. Biolo, "Details of Proposed AF Lease Bared."

12. Nash, *The Federal Landscape*, 85.

13. Hurt, *The Big Empty*, 161. ICBMs required arid soil to keep their fuel moisture free. The Great Plains provided that dry soil in vast abundance.

14. Kuletz, *Tainted Desert*, 39. See also Heefner, *The Missile Next Door*, especially the introduction. Heefner's book focuses largely on South Dakota and is a terrific study of the interaction between decision makers and those who had to live with those decisions.

15. *Mining Journal*, "Sawyer Airport Part of Perimeter Defense." The *Mining Journal* dutifully printed Lewis's speech in its entirety.

16. *Milwaukee Journal*, "Marquette Learning to Live with Airmen"; *Mining Journal*, "Sawyer Base Grew"; *Mining Journal*, "Sawyer Pumps $45 Million"; *Daily Mining Gazette*, "K. I. Sawyer Peninsula's Third Largest Community."

17. *Chicago Tribune*, "Negro Airmen Invade Town in Michigan"; *Arizona Tribune* (Phoenix), "Racial Battle Stirs City."

18. Vik, "Sawyer Blacks List 'Demands.'"

19. J. Hicks, "Treated Better in South."

20. *Port Huron (MI) Times Herald*, "Alarm System Fixed."

21. Associated Press, "Ellsberg, Berrigan Arrested"; Fitzpatrick, "Practice for Peace."

22. "Individual Department of Defense Installation and Activity Reduction,

Realignment and Closure Actions by State," box 11, folder "Defense—Military Base Realignments and Closures," John Marsh Files, Gerald Ford Presidential Library, https://www.fordlibrarymuseum.gov/library/document/0067/1562941.pdf.

23. See *U.S. News & World Report*, "Midwest's Last Frontier"; and Jimmy Carter to Sec. of Defense, memo re: Project ELF (SEAFARER), marked "Administratively Confidential," container 63, folder 2/16/78, Office of Staff Secretary, Presidential Files, Jimmy Carter Presidential Library and Museum, https://www.jimmycarterli brary.gov/digital_library/sso/148878/63/SSO_148878_063_08.pdf.

24. *U.S. News & World Report*, "Midwest's Last Frontier."

25. For a more nuanced explanation of Congress's failure to close military bases, see F. Thompson, "Why America's Military Base Structure Cannot Be Reduced."

26. The BRAC process has been summarized by a number of scholars. I have relied on Mayer, "Closing Military Bases (Finally)." Needless to say, BRAC is not totally immune from political pressures. See Koven, "Closings and the Politics-Administration Dichotomy." For base closure/realignment numbers, see Sorenson, *Shutting Down the Cold War*, 1.

27. Quoted in Flesher, "Residents Say Town a Goner If Base Closes."

28. Quoted in Flesher.

29. *Mining Journal*, "Farewell Barbeque."

30. Quoted in D. Peterson, "Proposed Military Base Cutbacks."

31. *Electric Utility Week*, "In Face of Load Loss."

32. Quoted in D. Peterson, "Proposed Military Base Cutbacks."

33. Hultquist and Petras, "Examination of Economic Impacts of Closures," 158.

34. White House Press Secretary, "Economic Renewal"; "Statement of Barry W. Holman, Director Defense Capabilities and Management," August 28, 2001, GAO-01-1054, https://www.gao.gov/assets/gao-01-1054t.pdf.

35. "Statement of Holman."

36. Press Release, Senator Carl Levin, June 5, 1998, provided by the Marquette Regional History Center; White House Press Secretary, "Economic Renewal."

37. *South Bend (IN) Tribune*, "Population Swells in Northern Michigan."

38. Associated Press, "Declining Enrollment Common in Michigan Schools."

39. Associated Press, "Demolition Starts on 36 Structures."

40. Pratt, "Down and Out in Purest Michigan."

41. Quoted in G. Peterson and Halberg, "Closure Affects More Than Jobs."

42. US Environmental Protection Agency, "National Priorities List (NPL) Sites."

43. See "K.I. Sawyer Air Force Base (Gwinn, Marquette County)," Michigan PFAS Action Response Team, Michigan.gov, content last updated November 6, 2020, https://www.michigan.gov/pfasresponse/0,9038,7-365-86511_82704-452822--,00 .html. Sawyer was part of a study a national study to look at water contamination

around military bases. Though the study was completed by 2018, its release was stalled by the Trump Administration because one aide worried that it would cause a "public relations nightmare." See Spangler, "Kildee."

44. BeVier, "Town Feels Betrayed by Government."

POSTSCRIPT

1. *Report on Agriculture and Rural Prosperity*, 37.

2. See Westheider, *Fighting on Two Fronts*, and Appy, *Working Class War*.

3. One 1967 study of Korean War soldiers found that soldiers from the "lower classes" and from "rural backgrounds" were overrepresented in infantry units because, according to military sources, the infantry required "limited educational preparation." See Morris Janowitz, "American Democracy and Military Service," *Transaction*, March 1967. Likewise, during Vietnam there seems to have been a slightly larger than average enlistment rate for young men from small towns. If they were not drafted, farm boys and city kids did not enlist at the same rates. See J. Johnston and Bachman. *Young Men and Military Service*, 106.

4. Philipps and Arango, "Who Signs Up to Fight?"; *Report on Agriculture and Rural Prosperity*, 38.

5. *Report on Agriculture and Rural Prosperity*, 38.

6. See Mittelstadt, *Rise of the Military Welfare State*.

7. Cancian and Dubois, *Base Realignment and Closure (BRAC) Roundtable*; Kurta quoted in Philipps and Arango, "Who Signs Up to Fight?"

8. Officials estimated that 215,000 Oklahoma men were eligible for the draft in 1917. Only 115,000 registered. Of those, however, 80,000 claimed an exemption. In other words, only 15 percent of those 215,000 registered as willing to serve in the army. Oklahoma Historical Society, "World War I."

9. See Stock, *Nuclear Country*.

10. Stock, introduction. Stock's book examines South Dakota politics specifically, but I believe her conclusions can be applied to other rural states.

11. Lutz, *Homefront*, 3.

12. NPR, "Small Towns Absorb the Toll of War"; Smee et al., "Critical Concerns in War Veteran–Forensic Interface."

13. See Stock, *Nuclear Country*. Statistics from a 2007 AP/Ipsos poll cited in Associated Press, "Small Towns Hit Hard by War."

14. Quoted in Lears, "Orthodoxy of the Elites."

PART TWO

1. *Rural Economic Development in the 1980s*, 1.

CHAPTER FOUR

1. West Virginia Center on Budget and Policy, "State of Rural West Virginia."

2. To understand this industrial transformation, see Deborah Fitzgerald's indispensable book borrowing that slogan, *Every Farm a Factory*.

3. This story received national press attention, including Fausset and Jordan, "Georgia Chicken Town Reels after Disaster."

4. A. J. Wright, "Recent Changes in the Concentration of Manufacturing," 146.

5. See, for example, Danbom, *The Resisted Revolution*.

6. Tugwell, *The Democratic Roosevelt*, 24, 207.

7. Roosevelt and commentator quoted in Woods, *America Reborn*, 296–97.

8. See Gilbert, "Agrarian Intellectuals in a Democratizing State," 215.

9. Noyes, "War Orders and Decentralization," 3.

10. Tugwell, *The Democratic Roosevelt*, 207.

11. Figures from Keck, "Reevaluating the Rural Electrification Administration," 39. Richard Hirsh argues that efforts to bring electricity to rural areas had begun in the 1920s, undertaken by private power companies and even some land-grant universities. This prequel to the New Deal achieved some success as well. See Hirsh, "Shedding New Light on Rural Electrification."

12. Tugwell, *The Democratic Roosevelt*, 207.

13. Woods, *America Reborn*, 320.

14. These figures are from A. J. Wright, "Recent Changes in Manufacturing," 147.

15. A. J. Wright, 166.

16. "Dispersal through Growth," *Challenge* 3 (1954): 50.

17. Austin, "Steel Men Oppose Idea."

18. "Statement of Hon. Pat McCarran," 5.

19. "Dispersal through Growth," 53.

20. "Statement of Hon. Pat McCarran," 5.

21. "Statement of Hon. Pat McCarran," 6.

22. Sparrow, *Warfare State*, 249.

23. Austin, "Steel Men Oppose Idea." See also "Statement of Hon. Pat McCarran," 2–8.

24. Austin, "Steel Men Oppose Idea"; Melamid, "Economic Aspects of Industrial Dispersal," 312.

25. *New York Times*, "Plan Dispersal Spurned by House."

26. *Industrial Dispersion Guidebook for Communities*, 1.

27. *Wall Street Journal*, "Industrial Dispersal."

28. Stark, "Machinists Fight Plant Dispersal."

29. Walz, "Americans Go West, but to Factory."

30. *U.S. News & World Report*, "Why Factories Are Taking to the Country," 72.

31. Kahn quoted in *Industrial Buildings*, 44.

32. *Industrial Buildings*, 44 (Kahn), 36 (Ferguson).

33. High, *Industrial Sunset*, 83.

34. High, 74–75.

35. High, 84.

36. Neuhoff, *Trends in Industrial Location*, 7–9.

37. High, *Industrial Sunset*, 84–85. See also *Impact of Industry*, n.p.

38. Leak, "Rural Plant Sites," 64; Wrigley, "Small Cities Can Help Revitalize," 58–59; Schiller "America's Dying Small Towns," 199.

39. Broadway, "From City to Countryside."

40. Dwight D. Eisenhower, "Annual Message to the Congress on the State of the Union," January 12, 1961, online by Gerhard Peters and John T. Woolley, the American Presidency Project, https://www.presidency.ucsb.edu/documents/annual-message-the-congress-the-state-the-union-7.

41. For an assessment of Eisenhower's farm policy, see Schapsmeier and Schapsmeier, "Eisenhower and Agricultural Reform." Edward and Frederick Schapsmeier note that Eisenhower wanted to reform the price support system rather than scrap it altogether, because he knew that would be politically toxic.

42. Petrushka, "The Rural Development Program," 8.

43. For this discussion, I have relied on Petrushka, "The Rural Development Program."

44. Volpe quoted in *U.S. News & World Report,* "A Helping Hand for Smaller Towns," 95.

45. Summers et al., *Industrial Invasion of Nonmetropolitan America*, v.

46. *U.S. News & World Report*, "Why Factories Are Taking to the Country," 72.

47. Talmadge, "A Strategy for Survival," 62; Swanson, "Myth of Urbanism," 34.

48. *A New Life for the Country*, 6.

49. See Talmadge, "A Strategy for Survival."

50. Quoted in US Congress, *Explanation of the Rural Development Act of 1972*, 7.

51. Quoted in US Congress, *Explanation of the Rural Development Act of 1972*, 22. Talmadge's reassurances have certainly proved to be a bit of wishful thinking. Economic development at the state and local level involves as often as not poaching existing firms from other places. In the 1970s, for example, at least seventy companies moved from Minnesota to South Dakota alone. See English, "How Small Towns Steal Jobs," 61.

52. Quoted in US Congress, *Explanation of the Rural Development Act of 1972*, 7.

53. Quoted in US Congress, *Explanation of the Rural Development Act of 1972*, 7. See also Wrigley, "Small Cities Can Help Revitalize," 58–59.

54. Hansen, "Factors Determining the Location of Industrial Activity," 5–8.

55. Quoted in US Congress, *Explanation of the Rural Development Act of 1972*, 12.

56. Talmadge, "A Strategy for Survival," 62, 65.

57. Quoted in US Congress, *Explanation of the Rural Development Act of 1972*.

58. Maddox, *Toward a Rural Development Policy*, 8.

59. Summers et al., *Industrial Invasion of Nonmetropolitan America*, vi.

60. Summers et al., 3–4.

61. Summers et al., 3–4. In fact, local communities had been offering "inducements" to industry since the 1930s. Lewis Atherton counted 130 such plants that had been subsidized locally in Wisconsin between 1930 and 1945. See Atherton, *Main Street on the Middle Border*, 343.

62. Morgan, *Industries for Small Communities*, 3.

63. Hansen, "Factors Determining the Location of Industrial Activity," 19. See also Henderson, "Rebuilding Rural Manufacturing."

64. Hansen, "Factors Determining the Location of Industrial Activity," 16, 24.

65. Talmadge, "A Strategy for Survival," 64.

66. Clawson, "The Future of Nonmetropolitan America," 107; Maddox, *Toward a Rural Development Policy*, iv; figures on farm and nonfarm population taken from Maddox, 2.

67. Gallup figures cited in Hansen, "Factors Determining the Location of Industrial Activity," 9.

CHAPTER FIVE

1. *The Decentralization Story*, Benson Ford Research Center, the Henry Ford, accession 422, box 2, 1952, 1.

2. In fact, Henry Ford II was brought back from the Pacific theater to run the company. Thanks to James Rubenstein for alerting me to Ford's wartime situation. Pers. comm., November 5, 2021.

3. *Wall Street Journal*, "Ford to Build Metal Stamping Plant"; *Detroit Free Press*, "Ford to Add Glass Plant in Nashville"; *Detroit Times*, "Ford Union Starts Move to 'Save Jobs.'" These and others were found in a clippings file titled "Decentralization Materials," Benson Ford Research Center, the Henry Ford. Thanks to Lauren Dreger for finding them for me.

4. Neuhoff, *Trends in Industrial Location*, 26.

5. Hurley, "Automotive Industry: Study in Industrial Location," 10–11.

6. Untitled, undated typescript, DN 1238, box 3, folder 10, Archives & Special Collections, GM Heritage Center, Sterling Heights, MI.

7. Here I rely on two documents in the GM archives: DN 1238, box 3, folder 5; and DN 1238, box 3, folder 3, Lordstown Collection, Archives & Special Collections, GM Heritage Center. The former is a typescript chronology for the Lordstown plant up to 1973; the latter records notes taken in 1984 as someone tried to track the history and fate of that first car.

8. *Youngstown (OH) Vindicator*, "Chevrolet to Build World's Biggest Auto Plant."

9. The speech and O'Keefe's memo are in box 1, folder 1, Lordstown Collection, Archives & Special Collections, GM Heritage Center.

10. "Remarks of Semon E. Knudsen," groundbreaking ceremonies at Lordstown, Ohio, September 29, 1964, Lordstown Collection, Archives & Special Collections, GM Heritage Center.

11. "Remarks of Semon E. Knudsen."

12. Murphy, "The Rural-Urban Balance," 55–56.

13. Murphy, "The Rural-Urban Balance," 55–56; "Testimony from Gov. Bruce King," in *Rural Development*, 1–2.

14. Whang, "Lordstown: GM's Dream Turns into a Nightmare." This was a UPI story that was widely reprinted.

15. Fritchey, "'Lordstown Syndrome' Survives Strike."

16. *Arizona Republic* (Phoenix), "Blue No More."

17. See Rubenstein, *The Changing US Auto Industry*, 238. The fight between the UAW and GM over the southern strategy was reported widely in the press in the late 1970s. See, for example, *Dispatch* (Moline, IL), "General Motors, UAW Clash over Southern Strategy." GM abandoned their gambit to hire nonunion workers by 1980.

18. Quoted in Rubenstein, *The Changing US Auto Industry*, 211.

19. *Ohio Farmer*, "A Good Record."

20. These comments were reported widely, though there is no record that the term *co-prosperity* sent a chill down anyone's spine. See *Dayton (OH) Daily News*, "Honda Dealing for Plant in Ohio."

21. *Marysville (OH) Journal-Tribune*, "Honda to Build Near Marysville." The Japanese word is *ohayō*.

22. Quoted in *Marysville (OH) Journal-Tribune*.

23. Quoted in *Newark (OH) Advocate*, "Honda Expanding Operations in Ohio."

24. Rubenstein, *The Changing US Auto Industry*, 251.

25. Roger Lentz, interview by Zachary Brintlinger-Conn, August 16, 2021, Shelby County (OH) Historical Society.

26. In fact, as of 2021, Honda operated unionized plants in thirteen of the sixteen countries where it has a footprint.

27. G. Johnson, *I Just Want to Tell You the Truth*, 5.

28. Quoted in *Newark (OH) Advocate*, "Honda Expanding Operations in Ohio."

29. Lentz, interview by Brintlinger-Conn.

30. *Reuters*, "Trump Warns U.S. May Cut Off GM Subsidies."

31. The story broke in June 2020 by the *Business Journal* of Youngstown, Ohio, in partnership with ProPublica. See O'Brien, "Republicans and Democrats Agree."

32. Quoted in *Business Journal* (Youngstown, OH), "DeWine Predicts Exciting Reaction."

33. For a nice riff on this theme, see Zelinsky, "Asserting Central Authority," 411–12.

34. Hansen, "Factors Determining the Location of Industrial Activity," 5–8.

35. Hansen, 27.

36. Talmadge, "A Strategy for Survival," 64–65.

37. *Better Country: A Strategy for Rural Development*, 16.

38. Wilkerson, "Trends in Rural Manufacturing," 43; Henderson, "Rebuilding Rural Manufacturing." Henderson's report paints an upbeat picture of a manufacturing rebound in rural areas, driven largely by the export of processed foods and fossil fuels.

39. See Green, "Deindustrialization of Rural America."

40. Venkataramani et al., "Association between Plant Closures and Opioid Mortality."

41. Cottrell, "Death by Dieselization," 358.

42. Cottrell, 359.

43. Cottrell, 359.

PART THREE

1. Usselman, "Still Visible," 584.

2. Actually, I have a pretty good idea. The history of business is on offer in virtually no American business schools. See Conn, *Nothing Succeeds Like Failure*.

3. Chandler, *The Visible Hand*, 5–6.

4. Chandler, 209.

5. R. Wright, "Capitalism and the Rise of Corporation Nation," 149.

CHAPTER SIX

1. See Elmore, "Environmental History of an American Bank."

2. See Raney, "Business Organization and Corporate Farming."

3. Isett and Miller, *The Social History of Agriculture*, 153.

4. "Handout D: Mary Elizabeth Lease Speech 1890," Bill of Rights Institute, https://billofrightsinstitute.org/activities/handout-d-mary-elizabeth-lease-speech-1890.

5. For starters, see Steinberg, *Down to Earth*; White, *Railroaded*; and Worster, *Rivers of Empire*.

6. I owe a particular debt to my friend and colleague Andrew Offenberger and his class Raiders of the Lost Archive for help with this section, especially Alyssa Thrasher, Daniel Staton, Jack Deletto, and Max Parduhn.

7. Environmental Working Group, "Subtotal, Farming Subsidies."

8. Mahon, "History of Riceland Foods."

9. Capper, "Farm Bloc Action Required."

10. *Little River (County, AK) News*, "Agricultural Department."

11. See *Fort Worth Star-Telegram*, "Farm Bureau Sends Quiz to Candidates."

12. Quoted in *Willmar (MN) Tribune*, "Will You Stick."

13. 61 Cong. Rec. H1033 (1921) (statement of Rep. Volstead); 62 Cong. Rec. S2057 (1922) (statement of Sen. Capper).

14. Quoted in *Coconino Sun* (Flagstaff, AZ), "Scope of the Cooperative Movement."

15. Coolidge had already made his support known before this December speech. See, for example, *Brownsville (TX) Herald*, "President Favors Co-operative Marketing." His speech was reported widely. See, for one example, *Healdsburg (CA) Enterprise*, "President Coolidge Urges Co-operative Marketing."

16. Jenkins quoted in *New York Times*, "Two Concerns Quit Merger Plan."

17. See United States v. Borden Co., 308 U.S. 188 (1939). For coverage of the ruling, see Henning, "Supreme Court Orders Milk Case Trial."

18. Colfax, "Many Plans for Aid to Farmers."

19. Gaumnitz quoted in *Omaha Guide*, "Farm Cooperatives and National Affairs."

20. *Worcester (MD) Democrat*, "Cooperatives and Consumers."

21. See Mahon, "History of Riceland Foods."

22. Lauck, "Corporate Farming Debate in the Midwest," 140. See also Pawley, *The Nature of the Future*.

23. See Harl, "Corporation—Present and Proposed Restrictive Legislation"; and Raup, "Corporate Farming in the United States." For Minnesota statistics, see Dowell, *Corporate-Owned Farm Land in Minnesota*, 24.

24. Crossman, "Research into Problems of Corporate Farming."

25. Quoted in *Des Moines (IA) Register*, "California Irrigation Project."

26. Sanderson, "Corporate System at Issue."

27. Quoted in Hatfield, "Freeman Orders Study of Corporations' Farm Role."

28. Quoted in *Corporation Farming: Hearings*, 1–2.

29. Quoted in *Corporation Farming: Hearings*, "Statement of Ben H. Radcliffe," 18.

30. Quoted in Muhm, "Super-Corporate Farm Assailed."

31. Harl, "Corporation—Present and Proposed Restrictive Legislation," 1247–48.

32. Quoted in Getz, "Pierre-spective: Family Farm Act."

33. *Lincoln (NE) Journal Star*, "Populist Discontent."

34. *Lincoln (NE) Journal Star*. "Full Text of Initiative 300."

35. *Lincoln (NE) Journal Star*, "Prudential Will Add $100,000."

36. This story was reported widely. See, for example, *South Bend (IN) Times*, "Corporations Buying Farms."

37. Krause, *Corporate Farming, 1969–1982*, iii.

38. *Rapid City (SD) Journal*, "Family Farm Act Approved."

39. J. L. Jones, "An Editor's Outlook"; Heins, "Iowa Lags in Corporation Farm Development."

40. Harl, "Corporation—Present and Proposed Restrictive Legislation," 1257; Curtis Jensen, "South Dakota Family Farm Act of 1974," 596–97.

41. Quoted in E. Smith, "America's Richest Farms and Ranches," 529.

42. Quoted in *New Republic*, "Who's the Farmers' Friend?," 5.

43. Quoted in Kloppenberg, *First the Seed*, 136.

44. Quoted in *New Republic*, "Who's the Farmers' Friend?," 6.

45. There is a nice symmetry here. As Deborah Fitzgerald points out, the fear that the Soviet Union would dump cheap grain onto the world market in the 1920s

"indicated that industrialized agriculture had come of age." D. Fitzgerald, *Every Farm a Factory*, 178.

46. *U.S. News & World Report*, "Why a Food Scare," 15.

47. *New Republic*, "Who's the Farmers' Friend?," 6.

48. Quoted in Pollan, *The Omnivore's Dilemma*, 54.

49. Quoted in Farnsworth, "Butz Tells Rome Conference Food Is Tool."

50. For a discussion of the US-USSR "farm race," see Hamilton, *Supermarket USA*.

51. Conkin, *A Revolution Down on the Farm*, 72–75.

52. J. Davis, "Economics of the Ever-Normal Granary," 21.

53. Fite, *American Agricultural and Farm Policy*, 19.

54. Pollan narrates this story nicely; see *The Omnivore's Dilemma*, 48–54.

55. J. Davis, "Economics of the Ever-Normal Granary," 20.

56. Quoted in *Des Moines (IA) Tribune*, "Nixon Signs Compromise Farm Bill."

57. See US Government Accountability Office, "Farm Programs." The program of direct payments was tweaked in subsequent farm bills, then eliminated altogether in the 1996 bill, only to be restored in 2002.

58. *Harvard Business School Bulletin* 41 (1955).

59. Heady, "The Agriculture of the U.S.," 121.

60. Heady, 121, 127.

61. For a history of this love affair, see Mart, *Pesticides, A Love Story*. Michelle Mart's thesis is that a heightened awareness of environmental issues in the 1960s and 1970s did little to dampen the enthusiasm for these chemicals.

62. Quoted in Mart, 213.

63. See Scott, *Seeing Like a State*, especially the introduction.

64. Lamm, "Banking and the Agricultural Problems of the 1980s"; Dudley, *Debt and Dispossession*, 9, 33, 151. See also *Rural Economic Development in the 1980s*, 3; and Wenk and Hardesty, "Effects of Rural-to-Urban Migration," 76.

65. Nugent, *The Tolerant Populists*, 43.

66. See Levy, "The Mortgage Worked the Hardest," 47.

67. Dudley, *Debt and Dispossession*, 5, 90.

68. See Smarsh, *Heartland*; and Westover, *Educated*. For more on the recent experience of farmwomen, see Jack, *The Midwest Farmer's Daughter*.

69. Quoted in Pollan, *The Omnivore's Dilemma*, 55.

70. Etter, "Farmers Wonder If Boom Is Bubble."

CHAPTER SEVEN

1. Lebhar, *Chain Stores in America*, 247–49.

2. For references to "death sentence," see Scroop, "The Anti-Chain Store Movement," especially notes 32 and 33.

3. *Austin (TX) American,* "Chain Store Tax Drive Re-opened."

4. *Excise Tax on Retail Stores,* 23.

5. See Lebhar, *Chain Stores in America,* 261.

6. See Lebhar, 53–54.

7. *Keep Market Street Open,* 79.

8. *Excise Tax on Retail Stores,* 602–71.

9. *Excise Tax on Retail Stores,* 189.

10. See Brinkley, *The End of Reform.*

11. Quoted in Winkler, *Five and Ten,* 132.

12. *Sioux City (IA) Journal,* "Woolworth's Nickel Idea."

13. Winkler, *Five and Ten,* 52.

14. Quoted in A. Isenberg, *Downtown America,* 99.

15. *Daily Herald* (Provo, UT), "Wonderful Growth of Golden Rule Syndicate"; Curry, *Creating an American Institution,* 78–79.

16. Curry, 111, 135.

17. *Daily Herald* (Provo, UT), "Wonderful Growth of Golden Rule Syndicate."

18. In 1916, Penney gave an interview to Charles Hurdn, printed as Hurdn, "How Penney Chain Finds and Trains Profit-Making 'Partners.'"

19. Woolworth's opened a massive store in central Boston in 1970. At that point there seems to have been only one other Woolworth's in town, though the retailer was operating five thousand stores nationwide. See Barmash, "Woolworth Set to Open Largest Store."

20. Quoted in Curry, *Creating an American Institution,* 250–51.

21. Quoted in A. Isenberg, *Downtown America,* 100.

22. In her 1975 essay "On the Mall," Joan Didion recalls taking a business school course in "Shopping Center Theory." She wrote of it: "One thing you will note about shopping-center theory is that you could have thought of it yourself, and a course in it will go a long way toward dispelling the notion that business proceeds from mysteries too recondite for you and me." Didion, "On the Mall," 184.

23. J. Walter Thompson Company, preface to *Retail Shopping Areas,* iii.

24. See Winkler, *Five and Ten,* 141.

25. *St. Joseph (MO) Gazette,* "Eastern Firm to Locate Here"; and *St. Joseph (MO) New-Press,* "Opening of New Store."

26. *Davis County (UT) Clipper,* "J. C. Penney Purchases Chain Store System."

27. Winkler, *Five and Ten,* 70.

28. See survey information in A. Isenberg, *Downtown America,* 98.

29. J. Harvey, "Lucky Mart's Luck Ran Out."

30. Curry, *Creating an American Institution,* 289.

31. A. Isenberg, *Downtown America,* 262.

32. *Philadelphia Inquirer,* "Employees Tour Penney Store."

33. McDonald, "How They Minted the New Penney."

34. *Daily Reporter* (Dover, OH), "Downtown Needs Cited by Dover Businessman";

DeGraw, "Help Asked for Dover's Downtown"; Eaton, "Penney's Building Sells for $66,000."

35. *Herald and Review* (Decatur, IL), "Has Sold Out."

36. *Herald and Review* (Decatur, IL), "Woolworth Closing Stuns Residents."

37. *Herald and Review* (Decatur, IL), "Woolworth Closing Stuns Residents."

38. Midland quoted in Shurtleff and Aoyagi, "Archer Daniels Midland: Work with Soy."

39. For starters, see Reich and Bearman, *Working for Respect*; Copeland and Labuski, *The World of Wal-Mart*; Lichtenstein, *The Retail Revolution*; and Moreton, *To Serve God and Wal-Mart*.

40. C. Turner, *My Father's Business*, 100–101; K. Fisher, "Big Fish in Small Ponds," 278; Wahba, "'If Walmart and 7-Eleven Had a Baby . . .'"

41. Quoted in Garino, "Dollar General, Wary of Losers."

42. Brown, "Southern Chains Draw a Bead"; Ta, "Dollar General Flourishes."

43. *Beatrice (NE) Daily Sun*, "Dollar General Opens Local Store."

44. C. Turner, *My Father's Business*, 151, 207.

45. Corwin, "Dollar General," 44.

46. The reference is to Luke 2:49: "Why did you seek Me? Did you not know that I must be about My Father's business?"

47. C. Turner, *My Father's Business*, 111.

48. C. Turner, 188. Turner tells the story of the SEC investigation. It forced him to step down from the company. But he seems oblivious that those spectacular years in the late '90s reflect books that the company had cooked. See 227–35.

49. Quoted in Garino, "The Music Is Not Piped In"; *Business Week*, "How Dollar General Sells Cheaper"; *Stores*, "Dollar General: Locked into Niche," 28.

50. Blyskal, "Renegade Retailers," 66; *Business Week*, "How Dollar General Sells Cheaper," 73.

51. Quoted in Barrett, "When Walmart Leaves Town." See also M. Hicks, *The Local Economic Impact of Wal-Mart*.

52. Ta, "Dollar General Flourishes."

53. *Fortune*, "Companies to Watch"; *Stores*, "Dollar General: Locked into Niche," 28; Faircloth, "Value Retailers Go Dollar for Dollar."

54. Berner, "Penny Pinchers Propel a Retail Star."

55. Faircloth, "Value Retailers Go Dollar for Dollar"; Berner, "Penny Pinchers Propel a Retail Star."

56. *Discount Store News*, "Dollar General Opens Third Inner City Store."

57. I have taken much of this from Alec MacGillis's excellent piece, "The Dollar Store Deaths."

58. Whaley quoted in MacGillis, "The Dollar Store Deaths."

59. C. Turner, *My Father's Business*, 204.

60. See US Department of Labor, "History of Violations."

61. Quoted in Moreton, *To Serve God and Wal-Mart*, 93.

62. MacGillis, "The Dollar Store Deaths."

63. Vasos quoted in MacGilllis, "The Dollar Store Deaths."

64. Quoted in Garino, "The Music Is Not Piped In."

65. Quoted in *Stores*, "Dollar General: Locked into Niche," 28.

PART FOUR

1. Take, for example, Golden Valley, Minnesota, a near-western suburb of Minneapolis. There the city government is sponsoring a racial justice project called "Just Deeds," which, among other things, encourages homeowners to examine their deeds to see whether they contain racially restrictive language. If so, the city then offers help to have the language removed. See "Just Deeds Project," City of Golden Valley, accessed November 17, 2022, https://www.goldenvalleymn.gov/452/Just-Deeds-Project#:~:text=Just%20Deeds%20is%20a%20program,change%20to%20promote%20racial%20equity.

2. According to lore, Clinton wrote that song specifically about Washington, DC.

3. Kruse, *White Flight*, 245.

CHAPTER EIGHT

1. Olson and Lyson, *Under the Blade*, 24. For this discussion I have relied on Olson and Lyson, *Under the Blade*, chapter 1.

2. In 1975, John Kasarda noted that studies of suburban growth had not taken into account annexation. As a result, he claimed, these studies were marred by a "systematic bias which artificially inflates central city growth and understates suburban growth." Kasarda, "Differential Patterns of Growth," 44.

3. Olson and Lyson, 25–28.

4. Some scholars argued—and still do—that suburbanization is essentially an urban phenomenon. I disagree, and certainly in the mid-twentieth century, my own assessment was that suburban development was an attempt to create something different, and indeed, anti-urban.

5. Quoted in Fuller, "Builders Just Nibble at Land."

6. Figures cited in Popper, *Politics of Land-Use Reform*, 28; and Keeanga-Yamahtta Taylor, *Race for Profit*, 57.

7. Census data reported in *U.S. News & World Report*, "Cities Crowding—Countryside Losing," 76–78; E. W. Jones, "Farm Labor and Public Policy," 12.

8. W. Thompson, *Migration within Ohio*, 82, 93.

9. Hawley, *Intrastate Migration in Michigan*, 193.

10. Bogue, *Metropolitan Decentralization*, 10, 14, 16.

11. It had first used the metropolitan area concept in 1905 and has refined the 1949 definition several times since. See US Census Bureau, "Metropolitan Areas."

12. Census numbers cited in Martin, "Ecological Change in Satellite Rural Areas," 74.

13. Clark, "Agrarian Context of American Capitalist Development," 37.

14. Whetten, "Suburbanization as a Field," 321.

15. Moore and Barlowe, *Effects of Suburbanization upon Rural Land Use*, 5.

16. Press and Hein, *Farmers and Urban Expansion*, 27.

17. *Detroit Free Press*, "Josephine Chapman, 59, Attorney and Homemaker."

18. See the statistics compiled by Freeman, *A Haven and a Hell*, 104.

19. Quoted in Nieland, "Brooklyn Park's Fields Growing Houses."

20. I have taken the information about Richfield and quotations here from the transcripts of oral histories conducted by the Minnesota Historical Society c. 2006–7 and housed at the Richfield Historical Society. For Brooklyn Park, see the oral interviews in the Brooklyn Historical Society files. See also Hoisington, *The Brooklyns*.

21. Fishman, *Bourgeois Utopias*.

22. Streeter, "The Rural Dilemma and Challenge," 4.

23. *Time*, "Okies of the '60s," 31; *Newsweek*, "Wanna Go Home," 30; G. Johnson, "Denizens of Rural Slums," 14.

24. Gregory, *The Southern Diaspora*, 85.

25. Berger, *Working-Class Suburb*, ix, 93; Nicolaides, *My Blue Heaven*, 43. Likewise, in his study of Los Angeles, Mike Davis describes "boomtown Fontana" as filled with "industrialized Okies." M. Davis, *City of Quartz*, 398–99.

26. Knoke and Henry, "Political Structure of Rural America," 56.

27. Rodehaver, "Fringe Settlement as a Two-Directional Movement," 57. As with so much of the sociological research about rural areas and the suburbs, discussions of the "fringe" quickly revealed definitional conundrums. E.g., "An examination of studies of the rural-urban fringe indicates that major problems have been created by the lack of a concise definition of the area." Kurtz and Eicher, "Fringe and Suburb," 32.

28. Maitland and Knebel, "Rural to Urban Transition," 29.

29. University of Pennsylvania Institute for Urban Studies, *Accelerated Urban Growth in a Metropolitan Area*, ix, 2, 7, 17.

30. Keyso was among those who helped shut the plant down in the early 1990s. See Russakoff, "The American Dream." See also "Andrew James Keyso," obituary, *Republican and Herald* (Pottsville, PA), January 22, 2013.

31. There is a set of faded snapshots of Yesenosky's wife, Bertha, and their children in their new Levittown house. See box 11, folder 11, Levittown Community Collection, Bucks County (PA) Historical Society.

32. Ross, *The Social Trend*, 47; Carter, "The Shrinking South," 21; *Business Week*, "Why Do Arkansans Vanish?," 96–98; Carter, 22.

33. Schnore, "Metropolitan Growth and Decentralization," 6.

34. *Chicago Tribune*, "600 Homes in West Suburbs"; Kertz, "Farm Stands Still."

35. Sargent, "Urbanization of a Rural County," 1–9.

36. See University of Pennsylvania Institute for Urban Studies, *Accelerated Urban Growth in a Metropolitan Area.*

37. Quoted in Mullaney, "Giant Steel Mills Displace Farmers;" "A Steel Plant Rises Where Spinach Grew," *US Steel News,* January 1952, box 5, folder 1, Levittown Community Collection, Bucks County (PA) Historical Society.

38. University of Pennsylvania Institute for Urban Studies, *Accelerated Urban Growth in a Metropolitan Area,* 7, 17.

39. Fuller, "Builders Just Nibble at Land"; farmer quoted in Popper, *Politics of Land-Use Reform,* 212.

40. Hofstadter, *The Age of Reform,* 41.

41. Deloria, "What Tecumseh Fought For."

42. Christopher Clark notes that because selling public land was seen as such an important source of government revenue, Congress passed two laws in 1804 and 1808 that sought to restrict people from settling and to remove those "squatters" who tried. See Clark, "Agrarian Context of American Capitalist Development," 30. Of course, the fact that land speculation lay at the heart of American development was the central observation Thorstein Veblen made in his last publication, *Absentee Ownership and Business Enterprise* (1923).

43. Press and Hein, *Farmers and Urban Expansion,* 27. See also Moore and Barlowe, *Effects of Suburbanization upon Rural Land Use,* 11, 17; Lewis, *On the Edge of the Black Waxy,* 19–21. For more on this topic, see also Clarence Jensen, "Discussion: Economic Conflicts," 155–57.

44. Moore and Barlowe, *Effects of Suburbanization upon Rural Land Use,* 17.

45. Queen and Carpenter, "From the Urban Point of View," 111; University of Pennsylvania Institute for Urban Studies, *Accelerated Urban Growth in a Metropolitan Area,* ix.

46. E. Fisher, "Township Seeks Funds," in news clippings, Levittown Community Collection, Bucks County (PA) Historical Society; Mullaney, "Giant Steel Mills Displace Farmers."

47. See Hoisington, *The Brooklyns,* 167; and Keillor, "My Boyhood Home."

CHAPTER NINE

1. See "Eva Dombrowski," obituary, *Pottsville Republican,* December 2, 1981. I have used Ancestry.com for information about Adam Dombrowski.

2. *Bristol (PA) Daily Courier,* "Protest Over Negro Family Ends Meeting."

3. *Pottsville (PA) Republican,* "Brabazon-McMenamin Wedding at Mayfair."

4. *Levittown (PA) Times,* "Bentcliff Is Fined, Put on Probation."

5. Blee, *Women of the Klan.* I have not been able to track several of the others, so the number of rural Levittowners on this list might well be higher.

6. *Bristol (PA) Daily Courier,* "Myers Case Courtroom Phase Ends." For more on this story, see *Bristol (PA) Daily Courier,* "Letter Turns Up—Three Years Late."

7. Press and Hein, *Farmers and Urban Expansion*, 2, 21.

8. Brademas, "Fringe Living Attitudes," 77.

9. Quoted in F. Johnson, *Richfield: Minnesota's Oldest Suburb*, 79–80. See also Harlow's own memoir, *Without Fear or Favor*.

10. Sargent, "Urbanization of a Rural County," 1.

11. Zimmer and Hawley, "Local Government as Viewed by Fringe Residents," 365.

12. This was a much-discussed issue, especially in the scholarship of the 1950s. See, for example, S. C. Smith, "Economic Conflicts in the Rural-Urban Fringe."

13. Zimmer and Hawley, "Local Government as Viewed by Fringe Residents," 370.

14. Zimmer and Hawley, 365–66.

15. Moore and Barlowe, *Effects of Suburbanization upon Rural Land Use*, 25, 29.

16. Gans, *Levittowners*, 17, 19, 88, 99.

17. F. Johnson, *Richfield: Minnesota's Oldest Suburb*, 72, 75.

18. Friedberger, "The Rural-Urban Fringe," 504–5.

19. Moore and Barlowe, *Effects of Suburbanization upon Rural Land Use*, 29. Farmers might have worried about how zoning could be used against them, but new suburbanites often used zoning as a way to exclude nonwhite and/or lower-class people from moving in by prohibiting apartment buildings, public housing, and more. See D. Freund, *Colored Property*.

20. University of Pennsylvania Institute for Urban Studies, *Accelerated Urban Growth in a Metropolitan Area*, 2.

21. Solove, "Problem on the Fringe," 125.

22. See Solove, 136–38.

23. Quoted in Streeter, "The Rural Dilemma and Challenge," 4.

24. Quoted in Elsner, "Farmer Plows On." The story made national news when the *New York Times* picked it up on June 9; see D. Johnson, "As Farm Meets Suburb." Perhaps because of this press attention, the charges were withdrawn, and Dettmering never got his day in court.

25. Quoted in D. Johnson, "As Farm Meets Suburb."

26. See Hayden, *Building Suburbia*.

27. Roberts, "Growing Potatoes in Brooklyn Park," 27.

28. Salamon, *Newcomers to Old Towns*, 10, 177.

29. Salamon, 10.

30. Ogg, *Naperville: A Brief History*.

31. *Naperville (IL) Clarion*, "Mayor Zaininger Tells Aims of Administration."

32. *Naperville (IL) Clarion*, "Future Goal—to Preserve Gracious Rural Living."

33. *Newsweek*, "What's Happening to Our Town?," 28.

34. *Newsweek*, 29.

35. Newman, "A Way of Life," B1.

36. "Herbert H. Walbaum, 94," obituary, *Chicago Tribune*, October 12, 2004. Full disclosure: My wife is descended from the Walbaums, and she first told me these stories.

CONCLUSION

1. For a rural sociologist, this observation amounted to a professional dilemma. As he continued: "Hence, there is no longer any basis in the United States, if there ever was in the past, for a rural sociology." Friedland, "The End of Rural Society and the Future of Rural Sociology," 590, 593.

2. Castle, "Overview," 497.

3. Hickey, *Ghost Settlement on the Prairie*, 13. This relationship between urban center and rural hinterland was most thoroughly explored by William Cronon in his hugely influential book *Nature's Metropolis*.

4. For more on this, see Conn, *Americans against the City*, 119–22; Wood quoted on 120.

5. For the "discovery" of the American folk, see Conn, *Americans against the City*, 114–19. Lomax quoted there.

6. The project has been digitized by the Library of Congress in the collection "Born in Slavery: Slave Narratives from the Federal Writers' Project, 1936 to 1938," https://www .loc.gov/collections/slave-narratives-from-the-federal-writers-project-1936-to-1938 /about-this-collection/.

7. D. Davidson, *The Attack on Leviathan*, 216.

8. For starters, see Baptist, *The Half Has Never Been Told*; Beckert, *Empire of Cotton*; and Beckert and Rockman, *Slavery's Capitalism*. Some of this recent scholarship caught up with the pioneering and largely ignored work of Eric Williams, published in 1944; see E. Williams, *Capitalism and Slavery*.

9. Hofstadter, *Age of Reform*, 43.

10. Lefebvre, *The Production of Space*, 8–9; D. Harvey, *Justice, Nature and the Geography of Difference*, 296. See also W. J. T. Mitchell's useful summary discussion of this in "Preface to the Second Edition," in *Landscape and Power*.

11. Wallace, "Ticket to the Fair," 38.

12. Hart, "'Rural' and 'Farm' No Longer Mean the Same," 71.

13. F. J. Turner, "Significance of the Frontier."

14. Wirth, "Urbanism as a Way of Life," 9.

15. Wirth, 20.

16. See Conn, *Americans against the City*, especially the introduction.

17. Woods, *America Reborn*, 77.

18. Vidich and Bensman, *Small Town in Mass Society*, 105; Kaufman and Zernike, "Activists Fight Green Projects."

19. Watkins, "Out of Money and Volunteers."

20. This issue is explored provocatively in Owen, "Green Manhattan." He makes that case that "everywhere should be more like New York" (111–21).

21. Kissinger, *Years of Renewal*, 28. Kissinger wrote those fatuous lines to introduce his discussion of Gerald Ford, a man who embodied the nation's "simplest values."

22. See Sandul, *California Dreaming*; Redmond quoted on 208.

BIBLIOGRAPHY

Agnew, Eleanor. *Back from the Land: How Young Americans Went to Nature in the 1970s, and Why They Came Back*. Chicago: Ivan R. Dee, 2004.

Alliance (NE) Herald. "Army Train Is Enroute to the Pacific Coast." July 17, 1919.

Appy, Christian. *Working Class War: American Combat Soldiers and Vietnam*. Chapel Hill: University of North Carolina Press, 1993.

Archer, John, Paul Sandul, and Katherine Solomonson, eds. *Making Suburbia: New Histories of Everyday America*. Minneapolis: University of Minnesota Press, 2015.

Arizona Republic (Phoenix). "Blue No More." September 13, 1974.

Arizona Tribune (Phoenix). "Racial Battle Stirs City." September 15, 1961.

Arnold, Martin. "3 Soldiers Hold News Conference to Announce They Won't Go to Vietnam." *New York Times*, July 1, 1966.

Associated Press. "Declining Enrollment Common in Michigan Schools." September 3, 2011.

———. "Demolition Starts on 36 Structures at Ex-Sawyer AFB." June 24, 2013.

———. "Ellsberg, Berrigan Arrested in Separate Demonstrations." April 10, 1982.

———. "Small Towns Hit Hard by War." CBS News, November 7, 2020. https://www.cbsnews.com/news/small-towns-hit-hard-by-war/.

Atherton, Lewis. *Main Street on the Middle Border*. Bloomington: Indiana University Press, 1954.

Austin, Kenneth. "Steel Men Oppose Idea of Dispersal." *New York Times*, July 2, 1944.

Austin (TX) American. "Chain Store Tax Drive Re-opened." January 15, 1940.

Bailey, Liberty Hyde. *The Country Life Movement in the United States*. New York: Macmillan, 1916.

Baker, Andrew. *Bulldozer Revolutions: A Rural History of the Metropolitan South*. Athens: University of Georgia Press, 2018.

Baptist, Edward. *The Half Has Never Been Told: Slavery and the Making of American Capitalism*. New York: Basic Books, 2014.

Barmash, Isadore. "Woolworth Set to Open Its Largest Store." *New York Times*, September 11, 1970.

Barrett, Brian. "When Walmart Leaves Town." *New Yorker*, January 30, 2016. https://www.newyorker.com/business/currency/when-walmart-leaves-town.

Beasley, Norman. *Main Street Merchant: The Story of the J. C. Penney Company*. New York: McGraw-Hill Book Company, Inc., 1948.

Beatrice (NE) Daily Sun. "Dollar General Opens Local Store." September 21, 1992.

Beauregard, Robert. *When America Became Suburban*. Minneapolis: University of Minnesota Press, 2006.

Beck, P. G., and M. C. Forster. *Six Rural Problem Areas: Relief—Resources—Rehabilitation*. Washington, DC: Works Progress Administration Division of Social Research, Research Monograph I, 1935.

Beckert, Sven. *Empire of Cotton: A Global History*. New York: Penguin Random House, 2014.

Beckert, Sven, and Seth Rockman, eds. *Slavery's Capitalism: A New History of America's Economic Development*. Philadelphia: University of Pennsylvania Press, 2016.

Berger, Bennett. *Working-Class Suburb: A Study of Auto Workers in Suburbia*. Berkeley: University of California Press, 1968.

Berner, Robert. "Penny Pinchers Propel a Retail Star." *Wall Street Journal*, March 20, 1998.

Better Country: A Strategy for Rural Development in the 1980s. Washington, DC: United States Department of Agriculture, 1983.

BeVier, Thomas. "Town Feels Betrayed by Government." *Detroit News*, March 14, 1993.

Biolo, Bob. "Details of Proposed AF Lease Bared at Public Meet." *Mining Journal*, January 19, 1955.

Blee, Kathleen. *Women of the Klan: Racism and Gender in the 1920s*. Berkeley: University of California Press, 1991.

Blum, Albert. "The Farmer, the Army and the Draft." *Agricultural History* 38 (1964): 34–42.

Blyskal, Jeff. "Renegade Retailers," *Forbes*, May 24, 1982.

Bogue, Donald. *Metropolitan Decentralization: A Study of Differential Growth*. Oxford: Scripps Foundation for Research in Population Problems, 1951.

Boroff, David. "Fort Hood: Sparta Goes Suburban." *Harper's Magazine*, January 1, 1964.

Brademas, Thomas. "Fringe Living Attitudes." *Journal of the American Institute of Planners* (Spring 1956): 75–82.

Brazos River Authority. "Why Are There So Many Man-Made Lakes in Texas?" *Water School* (blog), n.d., accessed May 20, 2020. https://www.brazos.org/About-Us /Education/Water-School/ArticleID/433.

Brinkley, Alan. *The End of Reform: New Deal Liberalism in Recession and War.* New York: Vintage Books, 1996. First published 1995 by Alfred A. Knopf.

Bristol (PA) Daily Courier. "Letter Turns Up—Three Years Late." October 8, 1959.

———. "Myers Case Courtroom Phase Ends." December 12, 1957.

———. "Protest Over Negro Family Ends Meeting." August 15, 1957.

Broadway, Michael. "From City to Countryside: Recent Changes in the Structure and Location of the Meat and Fish-Processing Industries." In *Any Way You Cut It: Meat Processing and Small-Town America*, ed. Donald D. Stull, Michael J. Broadway, and David Griffith, 17–40. Lawrence: University of Kansas Press, 1995.

Brooks, David. "What Rural America Has to Teach Us." *New York Times*, March 22, 2019.

Brown, Dave. "Southern Chains Draw a Bead on Iowa." *Des Moines (IA) Register*, May 21, 1989.

Brownsville (TX) Herald. "President Favors Co-operative Marketing." August 3, 1925.

Brunner, Edmund Des., and Irving Lorge. *Rural Trends in Depression Years.* New York: Columbia University Press, 1937.

Business Journal (Youngstown, OH). "DeWine Predicts Exciting Reaction to Lordstown Motors Reveal." June 24, 2020.

Business Week. "How Dollar General Sells Cheaper Than Anyone." July 21, 1975.

———. "Why Do Arkansans Vanish?" April 12, 1958.

Cancian, Mark, and Raymond Dubois. *Base Realignment and Closure (BRAC) Roundtable.* Washington, DC: Center for Strategic & International Studies, September 2017.

Capper, Arthur. "Farm Bloc Action Required to Avoid Grave Economic Crisis U. S., Capper Says." *Duluth (MN) News Tribune*, August 13, 1922.

Carter, Hodding. "The Shrinking South." *Look*, March 4, 1958.

Case, Anne, and Angus Deaton. *Deaths of Despair and the Future of Capitalism.* Princeton, NJ: Princeton University Press, 2020.

Castle, Emery. "The Forgotten Hinterlands." In *The Changing American Countryside: Rural People and Places*, ed. Castle, 3–10. Lawrence: University of Kansas Press, 1995.

———. "Overview." In *The Changing American Countryside: Rural People and Places*, ed. Castle, 495–502. Lawrence: University of Kansas Press, 1995.

Centner, Terence J. *Empty Pastures: Confined Animals and the Transformation of the Rural Landscape.* Urbana: University of Illinois Press, 2004.

Chandler, Alfred. *The Visible Hand: The Managerial Revolution in American Business.* Cambridge, MA: Harvard University Press, 1977.

Chapin, F. Stuart, Jr., Theodore W. Wirths, Alfred M. Denton Jr., and John C. Gould. *In the Shadow of a Defense Plant: A Study of Urbanization in Rural South Carolina.* Chapel Hill: Institute for Research in Social Science, 1954.

Charles, Daniel. *Lords of the Harvest: Biotech, Big Money, and the Future of Food*. New York: Basic Books, 2001.

Chicago Tribune. "Negro Airmen Invade Town in Michigan." September 11, 1961.

———. "600 Homes in West Suburbs." January 16, 1955.

Clark, Christopher. "The Agrarian Context of American Capitalist Development." In *Capitalism Takes Command: The Social Transformation of Nineteenth-Century America*, ed. Michael Zakim and Gary J. Kornblith, 13–38. Chicago: University of Chicago Press, 2012.

Clawson, Marion. "The Future of Nonmetropolitan America." *American Scholar* 42 (Winter 1972–73): 102–9.

CNN. "Biden Lashes Out at Palin's 'Pro-America' Comment." Updated October 17, 2008. http://www.cnn.com/2008/POLITICS/10/17/campaign.wrap/index.html.

Coates, Peter, Tim Cole, Marianna Dudley, and Chris Pearson. "Defending Nation, Defending Nature? Militarized Landscapes and Military Environmentalism in Britain, France, and the United States." *Environmental History* 16, no. 3 (July 2011): 456–91.

Coconino Sun (Flagstaff, AZ). "The Scope of the Cooperative Movement." August 1, 1924.

Colfax, Harden. "Many Plans for Aid to American Farmers." *Evening Star* (Washington, DC), August 19, 1928.

Conkin, Paul. *A Revolution Down on the Farm: The Transformation of American Agriculture Since 1929*. Lexington: University of Kentucky Press, 2008.

Conn, Steven. *Americans against the City: Anti-urbanism in the 20th Century*. New York: Oxford University Press, 2014.

———. *Nothing Succeeds Like Failure: The Sad History of American Business Schools*. Ithaca, NY: Cornell University Press, 2019.

Copeland, Nicholas, and Christine Labuski, *The World of Wal-Mart: Discounting the American Dream*. New York: Routledge, 2013.

Corporation Farming: Hearings before the Subcommittee on Monopoly of the Select Committee on Small Business, United States Senate. Washington, DC: Government Printing Office, 1968.

Corwin, Pat. "Dollar General, A Basics Category Killer." *Discount Merchandiser* 33 (September 1993).

Cottrell, W. F. "Death by Dieselization: A Case Study in the Reaction to Technological Change." *American Sociological Review* 16 (1951): 358–65.

Cox, Karen, and Sarah E. Gardner, eds. *Reassessing the 1930s South*. Baton Rouge: Louisiana State University Press, 2018.

Cronon, William. *Nature's Metropolis: Chicago and the Great West*. New York: W. W. Norton, 1992.

Crossman, B. D. "Research into Management Problems of Corporate Farming." *Journal of Farm Economics* 35 (1953): 953–61.

Crusader. "NAACP Protests Slow Integration of Army Schools." October 2, 1953.

Curry, Mary Elizabeth. *Creating an American Institution: The Merchandising Genius of J. C. Penney*. New York: Garland, 1993.

Daily Herald (Provo, UT). "Wonderful Growth of Golden Rule Syndicate of Stores." July 6, 1911.

Daily Mining Gazette. "K. I. Sawyer Peninsula's Third Largest Community." October 19, 1979.

Daily Reporter (Dover, OH). "Downtown Needs Cited by Dover Businessman." January 25, 1977.

Danbom, David B. *Born in the Country: A History of Rural America*. Baltimore: Johns Hopkins University Press, 2017 (1995).

———. *The Resisted Revolution: Urban America and the Industrialization of Agriculture, 1900–1930*. Ames: Iowa State University Press, 1979.

Davidson, Claud, and Thomas Bell, "A Methodological Inquiry into the Determination of the Rural-Urban Interface." *Western Journal of Agricultural Economics* 1 (1977): 187–90.

Davidson, Donald. *The Attack on Leviathan: Regionalism and Nationalism in the United States*. Chapel Hill: University of North Carolina Press, 1938.

Davis, Joseph. "The Economics of the Ever-Normal Granary." *Journal of Farm Economics* 20 (1938): 1–21.

Davis, Mike. *City of Quartz: Excavating the Future in Los Angeles*. New York: Verso, 1990.

Davis County (UT) Clipper. "J. C. Penney Purchases Large Chain Store System Owned by Johnson & Stevens." October 28, 1927.

Dayton (OH) Daily News. "Honda Dealing for Plant in Ohio." September 27, 1977.

DeGraw, Ed. "Help Asked for Dover's Downtown." *Daily Reporter* (Dover, OH), January 20, 1977.

Deloria, Philip. "What Tecumseh Fought For." *New Yorker*, November 2, 2020.

Des Moines (IA) Register. "California Irrigation Project." June 11, 1966.

Des Moines (IA) Tribune. "Nixon Signs Compromise Farm Bill." August 10, 1973.

Detroit Free Press. "Ford to Add Glass Plant in Nashville." July 15, 1955.

———. "Josephine Chapman, 59, Attorney and Homemaker." February 23, 1997.

Detroit Times. "Ford Union Starts Move to 'Save Jobs.'" March 11, 1957.

DeVoto, Bernard. "The Easy Chair: One Hundred Year Plan." *Harper's*, August 1, 1950.

Diaz-Gonzalez, Maria. "The Complicated History of the Kinzua Dam and How It Changed Life for the Seneca People." *Allegheny Front*, February 12, 2020. https://www.alleghenyfront.org/the-complicated-history-of-the-kinzua-dam-and-how-it-changed-life-for-the-seneca-people/.

Dickerman, G. S. "The Drift to the Cities." *Atlantic Monthly*, September 1913, 349–52.

Didion, Joan. "On the Mall." In *The White Album*. New York: Simon and Schuster, 1979.

Discount Store News. "Dollar General Opens Third Inner City Store." October 7, 1996.

Dispatch (Moline, IL). "General Motors, UAW Clash over Southern Strategy." April 1, 1976.

Dowell, A. A. *Corporate-Owned Farm Land in Minnesota, 1936–1940*. University of Minnesota Agricultural Experiment Station, 1940.

Drew, Elizabeth. "Dam Outrage." *Atlantic*, April 1970, 51–62.

Dudley, Kathryn Marie. *Debt and Dispossession: Farm Loss in America's Heartland*. Chicago: University of Chicago Press, 2000.

Eaton, Jim. "Penney's Building Sells for $66,000." *Daily Reporter* (Dover, OH), September 29, 1977.

Edwards, Sylvia Ann. "Land Acquisition in Coryell County, Texas, for the Formation of Camp Hood, 1942–1945: A Civilian Perspective." Master's thesis, Baylor University, 1988.

Electric Utility Week. "In Face of Load Loss, Mich. Utility Closing Plant, Shifting Workers." July 26, 1993.

Elmore, Bart. "The Environmental History of an American Bank." *Environmental History* 27 (2022): 113–39.

Elsner, David. "Farmer Plows On as Neighbors Toss and Turn Him In." *Chicago Tribune*, May 31, 1990.

English, Carey. "How Small Towns Steal Jobs from the Cities." *U.S. News & World Report*, March 21, 1983.

Environmental Working Group. "Subtotal, Farming Subsidies in the United States, 1995–2020." EWG's Farm Subsidy Database, n.d. https://farm.ewg.org/top_recips.php?fips=00000&progcode=totalfarm&regionname=theUnitedStates.

Etter, Lauren. "Farmers Wonder If Boom in Grain Prices Is a Bubble." *Wall Street Journal*, January 31, 2008.

Evinger, William, ed. *Directory of U.S. Military Bases Worldwide*. Phoenix: Oryx Press, 1995.

Excise Tax on Retail Stores: Hearings Before a Subcommittee of the Committee on Ways and Means, House of Representatives. Washington, DC: Government Printing Office, 1940.

Faircloth, Anne. "Value Retailers Go Dollar for Dollar." *Fortune*, July 6, 1998.

Farnsworth, Clyde. "Butz Tells Rome Conference Food Is Tool in Kit of American Diplomacy." *New York Times*, November 17, 1974.

Farrell, Justin. *Billionaire Wilderness: The Ultra-wealthy and the Remaking of the American West*. Princeton, NJ: Princeton University Press, 2020.

Fausset, Richard, and Miriam Jordan. "A Georgia Chicken Town Reels after a Plant Disaster." *New York Times*, January 29, 2021.

Fifty Years of Excellence: Fort Hood 50th Anniversary. Washington, DC: Department of the Army, 1992.

Fisher, Elizabeth. "Township Seeks Funds to Purchase Farm Site." *Bucks County (PA) Courier Times*, March 14, 2000.

Fisher, Kenneth. "Big Fish in Small Ponds." *Forbes*, June 26, 1989.

Fishman, Robert. *Bourgeois Utopias: The Rise and Fall of Suburbia*. New York: Basic Books, 1987.

Fite, Gilbert C. *American Agriculture and Farm Policy since 1900*. Publication no. 59. Washington, DC: American Historical Association, 1964.

Fitzgerald, Deborah. *Every Farm a Factory: The Industrial Ideal in American Agriculture*. New Haven, CT: Yale University Press, 2003.

Fitzgerald, F. Scott. "Early Success." In *The Crack-Up*. New York: New Directions, 1993.

Fitzpatrick, Jim. "Practice for Peace." *Clare (MI) Sentinel*, August 31, 1983.

Flesher, John. "Residents Say Upper Michigan Town a Goner If Base Closes." Associated Press, March 12, 1993.

Flynn, John. *Country Squire in the White House*. New York: Doubleday, Doran, 1940.

Fortune. "Companies to Watch." August 26, 1991.

Fort Worth Star-Telegram. "Farm Bureau Sends Quiz to Candidates for Senate and House." September 12, 1920.

Frakt, Austin. "A Hospital Die-Off Hits Rural America Hard." *New York Times*, October 30, 2018.

Frazier, Ian. "The Plushbottoms of Teton County." *New York Review of Books*, December 17, 2020, 18–22.

Freeman, Lance. *A Haven and a Hell: The Ghetto in Black America*. New York: Columbia University Press, 2019.

Freund, David. *Colored Property: State Policy and White Racial Politics in Suburban America*. Chicago: University of Chicago Press, 2007.

Freund, Rudolf. "Military Bounty Lands and the Origins of the Public Domain." *Agricultural History* 20 (1946): 8–18.

Friedberger, Mark. "The Rural-Urban Fringe in the Late Twentieth Century." *Agricultural History* 74 (2000): 502–14.

Friedland, William. "The End of Rural Society and the Future of Rural Sociology." *Rural Sociology* 47 (1982): 589–608.

Friedman, Morris. "The Drama in Temple." *New Republic*, October 22, 1945.

Fritchey, Clayton. "'Lordstown Syndrome' Survives Strike." *Democrat and Chronicle*, April 9, 1972.

Fuller, Ernest. "Builders Just Nibble at N.W. Suburb Land." *Chicago Tribune*, August 1, 1955.

Gans, Herbert. *The Levittowners: Ways of Life and Politics in a New Suburban Community*. New York: Columbia University Press, 1967, 1982.

Ganzel, Bill. "Shrinking Farm Numbers." Wessels Living History Farm, 2007. Accessed February 14, 2020. https://livinghistoryfarm.org/farminginthe50s/life_11.html.

Garino, David. "Dollar General Corp., Wary of Losers, Starts to Turn Around Two New Units." *Wall Street Journal*, April 12, 1978.

———. "The Music Is Not Piped In, but Earnings Seem That Way at Dollar General Corp." *Wall Street Journal*, December 27, 1971.

Genandt, James. "The People Be Damned: The Tale of Tuttle Creek." Master's thesis, Emporia State University, 1988.

Getz, Jack. "Pierre-spective: Family Farm Act." *Rapid City (SD) Journal*, January 31, 1974.

Gilbert, Jess. "Agrarian Intellectuals in a Democratizing State: A Collective Biography of USDA Leaders in the Intended New Deal." In *The Countryside in the Age of the*

Modern State: Political Histories of Rural America, ed. Catherine McNicol Stock and Robert D. Johnston, 213–39. Ithaca, NY: Cornell University Press, 2001.

Grabmeier, Jeff. "There's No Longer One Rural America—Could There Be Five?" *Ohio State News*, January 13, 2022. https://news.osu.edu/theres-no-longer-one -rural-america--could-there-be-five/.

Green, Gary Paul. "Deindustrialization of Rural America." *Local Development & Society* 1 (2020): 15–25.

Gregory, James. *The Southern Diaspora: How the Great Migrations of Black and White Southerners Transformed America*. Chapel Hill: University of North Carolina Press, 2005.

Griswold, A. Whitney. *Farming and Democracy*. New York: Harcourt, Brace, 1948.

Hailey, Foster. "Michigan's North Beckons Business." *New York Times*, July 26, 1954.

Hamilton, Shane. *Supermarket USA: Food and Power in the Cold War Farms Race*. New Haven, CT: Yale University Press, 2018.

———. *Trucking Country: The Road to America's Wal-Mart Economy*. Princeton, NJ: Princeton University Press, 2008.

Hansen, Niles. "Factors Determining the Location of Industrial Activity in Metropolitan and Nonmetropolitan Areas." Discussion Paper No. 50, July 1972. In *Studies in Nonmetropolitan Economic Development and Poverty*, 3–28. Austin: Center of Economic Development, University of Texas at Austin, 1972.

———. *Rural Poverty and the Urban Crisis: A Strategy for Regional Development*. Bloomington: Indiana University Press, 1970.

Hanson, Robin. "'If the Lord's Willing and the Creek Don't Rise': Flood Control and the Displaced Rural Communities of Irving and Broughton, Kansas." *Great Plains Quarterly* 30 (2010): 251–69.

Harl, Neil. "Corporation—Present and Proposed Restrictive Legislation." *Business Lawyer* 25 (1970): 1247–58.

Harlow, LeRoy. *Without Fear or Favor: The Odyssey of a City Manager*. Provo, UT: Brigham Young University Press, 1977.

Hart, John Fraser. *The Look of the Land*. Englewood Cliffs: Prentice Hall, 1975.

———. "'Rural' and 'Farm' No Longer Mean the Same." In *The Changing American Countryside*, ed. Emery Castle, 63–76. Lawrence: University of Kansas Press, 1995.

———. "Small Towns and Manufacturing." *Geographical Review* 78 (1988): 272–87.

Harvey, David. *Justice, Nature and the Geography of Difference*. Cambridge: Blackwell, 1996.

Harvey, Joyce. "Lucky Mart's Luck Ran Out." *Lancaster (OH) Eagle-Gazette*, September 14, 2015.

Hatfield, Larry. "Freeman Orders Study of Corporations' Farm Role." *Gazette* (Cedar Rapids, IA), December 18, 1967.

Hathaway, Dale. "Migration from Farms and Its Meanings." *Monthly Labor Review* 83 (February 1960): 136–40.

Hawley, Amos. *Intrastate Migration in Michigan: 1935–1940*. Ann Arbor: University of Michigan Press, 1953.

Hayden, Dolores. *Building Suburbia: Green Fields and Urban Growth, 1820–2000*. New York: Pantheon Books, 2003.

———. *The Power of Place: Urban Landscapes as Public History*. Cambridge, MA: MIT Press, 1995.

Heady, Earl O. "The Agriculture of the U.S." *Scientific American* 235 (September 1976): 106–27.

Healdsburg (CA) Enterprise. "President Coolidge Urges Co-operative Marketing." December 10, 1925.

Heefner, Gretchen. *The Missile Next Door: The Minuteman in the American Heartland*. Cambridge, MA: Harvard University Press, 2012.

Heins, Ed. "Iowa Lags in Corporation Farm Development." *Des Moines (IA) Register*, October 17, 1965.

Henderson, Jason. "Rebuilding Rural Manufacturing." In *The Main Street Economist*. Kansas City, MO: Federal Reserve Bank of Kansas City, 2012.

Henning, Arthur Sears. "Supreme Court Orders Chicago Milk Case Trial." *Chicago Tribune*, December 5, 1939.

Herald and Review (Decatur, IL). "Has Sold Out." March 10, 1904.

———. "Woolworth Closing Stuns Residents." September 18, 1990.

Hewes, Leslie. *The Suitcase Farming Frontier: A Study in the Historical Geography of the Central Great Plains*. Lincoln: University of Nebraska Press, 1973.

Hickey, Joseph. *Ghost Settlement on the Prairie: A Biography of Thurman, Kansas*. Lawrence: University of Kansas Press, 1995.

Hicks, Jim. "Treated Better in South, Says Negro in N.D." *Minneapolis Star-Tribune*, November 12, 1961.

Hicks, Michael. *The Local Economic Impact of Wal-Mart*. Youngstown, NY: Cambria Press, 2007.

Higbee, Edward. *Farms and Farmers in an Urban Age*. New York: 20th Century Fund, 1963.

High, Steven. *Industrial Sunset: The Making of North America's Rust Belt, 1969–1984*. Toronto: University of Toronto Press, 2003.

High, Steven, and David W. Lewis. *Corporate Wasteland: The Landscape and Memory of Deindustrialization*. Ithaca, NY: ILR Press, an imprint of Cornell University Press, 2007.

Hirsch, Arnold. *Making the Second Ghetto: Race and Housing in Chicago, 1940–1960*. Cambridge: Cambridge University Press, 1983.

Hirsh, Richard. "Shedding New Light on Rural Electrification: The Neglected Story of Successful Efforts to Power Up Farms in the 1920s and 1930s." *Agricultural History* 92 (2018): 296–327.

Hofstadter, Richard. *The Age of Reform: From Bryan to F.D.R.* New York: Knopf, 1955.

Hoganson, Kristin L. *The Heartland: An American History*. New York: Penguin Press, 2019.

Hoisington, Daniel J., ed. *The Brooklyns: A History of Brooklyn Center and Brooklyn Park Minnesota*. New York: Brooklyn Historical Society, 2001.

Hultquist, Andy, and Tricia L. Petras. "An Examination of Local Economic Impacts of Military Base Closures." *Economic Development Quarterly* 26 (2012): 151–61.

Hunter, Liggett. "What Is the Matter with Our Army? Its Alienation from the People." *Independent*, February 29, 1912.

Hurdn, Charles. "How Penney Chain Finds and Trains Profit-Making 'Partners.'" *Dickinson (ND) Press*, June 3, 1916.

Hurley, Neil. "The Automotive Industry: A Study in Industrial Location." *Land Economics* 35 (1959): 1–14.

Hurt, R. Douglas. *The Big Empty: The Great Plains in the Twentieth Century*. Tucson: University of Arizona Press, 2011.

The Impact of Industry in a Southern Rural County. Charlottesville: University of Virginia Bureau of Population and Economic Research, 1956.

Industrial Buildings: The Architectural Record of a Decade. New York: F. W. Dodge Corporation, 1951.

Industrial Dispersion Guidebook for Communities. Washington, DC: Government Printing Office, 1952.

Isenberg, Alison. *Downtown America: A History of the Place and the People Who Made It*. Chicago: University of Chicago Press, 2004.

Isenberg, Nancy. *White Trash: The 400-Year Untold History of Class in America*. New York: Penguin Books, 2016.

Isett, Christopher, and Stephen Miller. *The Social History of Agriculture: From the Origins to the Current Crisis*. New York: Rowan & Littlefield, 2017.

Is Your Plant a Target? Washington, DC: National Security Resources Board, 1951.

Jack, Zachary Michael. *The Midwest Farmer's Daughter: In Search of an American Icon*. West Lafayette, IN: Purdue University Press, 2012.

Jackson, John Brinckerhoff. *The Necessity for Ruins*. Amherst: University of Massachusetts Press, 1980.

Jackson, Kenneth. *Crabgrass Frontier: The Suburbanization of the United States*. New York: Oxford University Press, 1985.

Jensen, Clarence. "Discussion: Economic Conflicts in the Rural-Urban Fringe: A Problem of Metropolitan Organization." *Proceedings of the Annual Meeting* (Western Farm Economics Association) 31 (1958): 155–57.

Jensen, Curtis. "The South Dakota Family Farm Act of 1974: Salvation or Frustration for the Family Farmer?" *South Dakota Law Review* 20 (1975): 575–97.

Johnson, Dirk. "As Farm Meets Suburb, Sides Clash." *New York Times*, June 9, 1990.

Johnson, Frederick. *Richfield: Minnesota's Oldest Suburb*. Richfield: Richfield Historical Society, 2008.

Johnson, Gerald. "Denizens of Rural Slums." *New Republic*, May 23, 1960.

Johnson, Gerald. *I Just Want to Tell You the Truth.* Bloomington, IN: AuthorHouse, 2010.

Johnston, Jerome, and Jerald Bachman. *Young Men and Military Service.* Ann Arbor: Institute for Social Research, University of Michigan, 1972.

Jones, E. Walton. "Farm Labor and Public Policy." *Monthly Labor Review* 91 (March 1968): 12–15.

Jones, Jenkin Lloyd. "An Editor's Outlook." *Iowa City Press-Citizen,* February 6, 1965.

J. Walter Thompson Company. *Retail Shopping Areas.* New York: J. Walter Thompson Company, 1927.

Kasarda, John. "Differential Patterns of City and Suburban Growth in the United States." *Journal of Urban History* 2 (1975): 43–66.

Kaufman, Leslie, and Kate Zernike. "Activists Fight Green Projects, Seeing U.N. Plot." *New York Times,* February 4, 2012.

Keck, Richard. "Reevaluating the Rural Electrification Administration: A New Deal for the Taxpayer." *Environmental Law* 16 (1985): 39–89.

Keep Market Street Open. New York: Institute of Distribution, 1940.

Keillor, Garrison. "My Boyhood Home." In *Brooklyn Park.* New York: Brooklyn Park Economic Development Authority, 1994.

Kertz, Jane. "Farm Stands Still while City Moves In around It." *Chicago Tribune,* November 25, 1956.

Kissinger, Henry. *Years of Renewal.* New York: Simon and Schuster, 1999.

Kloppenburg, Jack Ralph, Jr. *First the Seed: The Political Economy of Plant Biotechnology.* Madison: University of Wisconsin Press, 1988.

Knoke, David, and Constance Henry. "Political Structure of Rural America." *Annals of the American Academy of Political and Social Science* 429 (1977): 51–62.

Koven, Steven. "Base Closings and the Politics-Administration Dichotomy Revisited." *Public Administration Review* 52 (1992): 526–31.

Krause, Kenneth. *Corporate Farming, 1969–1982.* Washington, DC: USDA Economic Research Service, 1987.

Krausz, N. G. P. "Corporate Organization of Family Farms." *Journal of Farm Economics* 40 (1958): 1624–33.

Kruger, David Delbert. "Earl Corder Sams and the Rise of J. C. Penney." *Kansas History* 35 (2012): 164–85.

Kruse, Kevin. *White Flight: Atlanta and the Making of Modern Conservatism.* Princeton, NJ: Princeton University Press, 2005.

Kuletz, Valerie. *Tainted Desert: Environmental and Social Ruin in the American West.* New York: Routledge, 1998.

Kurtz, Richard, and Joanne Eicher. "Fringe and Suburb: A Confusion of Concepts." *Social Forces* 37 (1958): 32–37.

Kushner, David. *Levittown: Two Families, One Tycoon, and the Fight for Civil Rights in America's Legendary Suburb.* New York: Walker, 2009.

La Chappelle, Peter. *I'd Fight the World: A Political History of Old-Time, Hillbilly, and Country Music.* Chicago: University of Chicago Press, 2019.

Lamm, Brian. "Banking and the Agricultural Problems of the 1980s." Chapter 8 of *History of the Eighties: Lessons for the Future*, vol. 1: *An Examination of the Banking Crises of the 1980s and Early 1990s*. Washington, DC: FDIC Division of Research and Statistics, 1997. https://www.fdic.gov/bank/historical/history/259_290.pdf.

L'Anse (MI) Sentinel. "To All Residents of Baraga County." Advertisement, February 17, 1954.

Lassiter, Matthew. *The Silent Majority: Suburban Politics in the Sunbelt South*. Princeton, NJ: Princeton University Press, 2006.

Lauck, Jon. *American Agriculture and the Problem of Monopoly: The Political Economy of Grain Belt Farming, 1953–1980*. Lincoln: University of Nebraska Press, 2000.

———. "The Corporate Farming Debate in the Post–World War II Midwest." *Great Plains Quarterly* 18 (1998): 139–53.

Leak, Robert. "Rural Plant Sites Are Marketable and Profitable." *Nation's Business*, September 1969.

Lears, Jackson. "Orthodoxy of the Elites." *New York Review of Books*, January 14, 2021.

Lebhar, Godfrey. *Chain Stores in America: 1859–1959*. New York: Chain Store Pub. Corp., 1959.

Lefebvre, Henri. *The Production of Space*. Oxford: Blackwell, 1991.

Levittown (PA) Times. "Bentcliff Is Fined, Put on Probation." February 27, 1958.

Levy, Jonathan. "The Mortgage Worked the Hardest: The Fate of Landed Independence in Nineteenth-Century America." In *Capitalism Takes Command: The Social Transformation of Nineteenth-Century America*, ed. Michael Zakim and Gary J. Kornblith, 39–68. Chicago: University of Chicago Press, 2012.

Lewis, Oscar. *On the Edge of the Black Waxy: A Cultural Survey of Bell County, Texas*. St. Louis: Washington University Studies, 1948.

Lichtenstein, Nelson. *The Retail Revolution: How Wal-Mart Created a Brave New World of Business*. New York: Metropolitan Books, 2009.

Liggett, Hunter. "What Is the Matter with Our Army? Its Alienation from the People." *Independent*, February 29, 1912.

Lincoln (NE) Journal Star. "Full Text of Initiative 300." October 3, 1982.

———. "Populist Discontent." October 29, 1982.

———. "Prudential Will Add $100,000." October 28, 1982.

Little River (County, AK) News. "Agricultural Department." July 10, 1920.

Littlewood, Thomas B. *Soldiers Back Home: The American Legion in Illinois, 1919–1939*. Carbondale: Southern Illinois University Press, 2004.

Lutz, Catherine. *Homefront: A Military City and the American 20th Century*. Boston: Beacon Press, 2002.

MacGillis, Alec. "The Dollar Store Deaths." *New Yorker*, July 6 and 13, 2020.

Maddox, James. *Toward a Rural Development Policy*. Washington, DC: National Planning Association, 1973.

Mahon, J. C. "The History of Riceland Foods." *Craighead County Historical Quarterly* 17 (Summer 1979): 10–17.

Maitland, Sheridan, and Stanley Knebel. "Rural to Urban Transition." *Monthly Labor Review* 91 (June 1968): 28–32.

Markusen, Ann, Peter Hall, Scott Campbell, and Sabina Deitrick. *The Rise of the Gunbelt: The Military Remapping of Industrial America.* New York: Oxford University Press, 1991.

Mart, Michelle. *Pesticides, a Love Story: America's Enduring Embrace of Dangerous Chemicals.* Lawrence: University of Kansas Press, 2015.

Martin, Walter. "Ecological Change in Satellite Rural Areas." In *The Suburban Community,* ed. William M. Dobriner, 67–85. New York: G. P. Putnam's Sons, 1958.

———. *The Rural-Urban Fringe: A Study in Adjustment to Residence Location.* Eugene: University of Oregon Press, 1953.

Marysville (OH) Journal-Tribune. "Honda to Build Near Marysville." October 11, 1977.

Mayer, Kenneth. "Closing Military Bases (Finally): Solving Collective Dilemmas through Delegation." *Legislative Studies Quarterly* 20 (1995): 393–413.

McDonald, John. "How They Minted the New Penney." *Fortune,* July 1967.

Melamid, Alexander. "Economic Aspects of Industrial Dispersal." *Social Research* 23 (1956): 311–22.

Miami News. "Ike Told of Negro GIs' Peril." September 9, 1957.

Michigan PFAS Action Response Team. "K.I. Sawyer Air Force Base (Gwinn, Marquette County)." Michigan.gov, n.d. Accessed November 9, 2021. https://www.michigan.gov/pfasresponse/0,9038,7-365-86511_82704-452822--,00.html.

Milwaukee Journal. "Marquette Learning to Live with Airmen." September 2, 1960.

Mining Journal. "Farewell Barbeque." August 27, 1994.

———. "Sawyer Airport Part of Perimeter Defense, AF Secretary Declares." July 30, 1954.

———. "Sawyer Base Grew into U.P.'s Fourth Largest City." May 29, 1970.

———. "Sawyer Pumps $45 Million Annually into the U.P. Economy." February 22, 1973.

Mitchell, W. J. T., ed. "Preface to the Second Edition." In *Landscape and Power,* vii–xii. Chicago: University of Chicago Press, 2002.

Mittelstadt, Jennifer. *The Rise of the Military Welfare State.* Cambridge, MA: Harvard University Press, 2015.

Moore, E. H., and Raleigh Barlowe. *Effects of Suburbanization upon Rural Land Use.* Lansing: Michigan State University Agricultural and Applied Science, 1955.

Moreton, Bethany. *To Serve God and Wal-Mart: The Making of Christian Free Enterprise.* Cambridge, MA: Harvard University Press, 2009.

Morgan, Arthur. *Dams and Other Disasters.* Boston: Porter Sargent, 1971.

———. *Industries for Small Communities.* Yellow Springs, OH: Community Service, 1953.

Muhm, Don. "Super-Corporate Farm Assailed." *Des Moines (IA) Tribune,* March 21, 1968.

Mullaney, Thomas. "Giant Steel Mills Displace Farmers." *New York Times,* January 31, 1951.

Muller, Peter O. "The Evolution of American Suburbs: A Geographical Interpreta-
    tion." *Urbanism Past & Present* 4 (Summer 1977): 1–10.
Murphy, W. B. "The Rural-Urban Balance." *Vital Speeches* 32 (1965): 55–56.
Myers, Jill Ogden. "The Suburbanization of Anderson Township, Hamilton County,
    Ohio." MA Thesis, Miami University, 1969.
Naperville (IL) Clarion. "Future Goal—to Preserve Gracious Rural Living." In "Naper-
    ville: First in DuPage and First in Progress," insert, November 6, 1958.
————. "Mayor Zaininger Tells Aims of Administration." In "Naperville: First in Du-
    Page and First in Progress," insert, December 1960.
Nash, Gerald D. *The Federal Landscape: An Economic History of the Twentieth-Century
    West.* Tucson: University of Arizona Press, 1999.
Nelson, Lowry. *Rural Sociology: Its Origins and Growth in the United States.* Minne-
    apolis: University of Minnesota Press, 1969.
Neuhoff, Malcolm. *Trends in Industrial Location.* New York: National Industrial Con-
    ference Board, 1952.
Newark (OH) Advocate. "Honda Expanding Operations in Ohio." July 9, 1984.
*A New Life for the Country: The Report of the President's Task Force on Rural Develop-
    ment.* Washington, DC: Government Printing Office, 1970.
Newman, Lisa. "A Way of Life Is on Verge of Riding Off into Sunset." *Chicago Tribune,*
    October 26, 1991.
New Pittsburgh Courier. "Fort Hood Group Blasts GI Jim Crow." May 13, 1961.
New Republic. "Who's the Farmers' Friend?" December 4, 1971.
Newsweek. "Wanna Go Home." August 5, 1963.
————. "What's Happening to Our Town?" August 15, 1988.
New York Times. "Justice for the Senecas." June 12, 1961.
————. "Plan Dispersal Spurned by House." July 12, 1951.
————. "Two Concerns Quit Grain Merger Plan." July 9, 1925.
Nicolaides, Becky. *My Blue Heaven: Life and Politics in the Working-Class Suburbs of
    Los Angeles, 1920–1965.* Chicago: University of Chicago Press, 2002.
Nieland, Alma. "Brooklyn Park's Fields Growing Houses Now." *Minneapolis Star,*
    June 17, 1977.
Noyes, C. E. "War Orders and Decentralization." *Editorial Research Reports 1941,*
    vol. 1.
NPR. "Small Towns Absorb the Toll of War." Morning Edition, February 20, 2007.
Nugent, Walter. *The Tolerant Populists: Kansas Populism and Nativism.* Chicago: Uni-
    versity of Chicago Press, 2013 (1963).
O'Brien, Dan. "Republicans and Democrats Agree: GM Should Pay Back the Tax-
    payers of Ohio." *Business Journal* (Youngstown, OH), July 1, 2020. https://www
    .propublica.org/article/republicans-and-democrats-agree-gm-should-pay-back
    -the-taxpayers-of-ohio.
Ogg, Bryan. *Naperville: A Brief History.* Charleston, SC: History Press, 2018.
Ohio Farmer. "A Good Record." March 7, 1895.

Oklahoma Historical Society. "World War I." *Encyclopedia of Oklahoma History and Culture*, n.d. https://www.okhistory.org/publications/enc/entry.php?entry =WO024.

Olson, Richard, and Thomas Lyson, ed. *Under the Blade: The Conversion of Agricultural Landscapes*. Boulder, CO: Westview Press, 1999.

Omaha Guide. "Farm Cooperatives and National Affairs." October 31, 1936.

Outlook. "The Bureau of Rural Organization." July 5, 1913, 498.

———. "The Decline in Rural Population." November 19, 1910, 614–15.

———. "U.S. Army Motor-Truck Train on Trans-Continental Demonstration Tour." August 9, 1919, 550–53.

Owen, David. "Green Manhattan." *New Yorker*, October 18, 2004.

Oxford (MI) Leader. "From the Office of Senator Homer Ferguson." July 30, 1954.

Pawley, Emily. *The Nature of the Future: Agriculture, Science, and Capitalism in the Antebellum North*. Chicago: University of Chicago Press, 2020.

Pencak, William. *For God and Country: The American Legion, 1919–1941*. Boston: Northeastern University Press, 1989.

The People Left Behind: A Report by the President's National Advisory Commission on Rural Poverty. Washington, DC: Government Printing Office, 1967.

Peterson, Dean. "Proposed Military Base Cutbacks Would Hit Local Areas the Hardest, Credit Analysts Say." *Bond Buyer*, March 22, 1993.

Peterson, Elmer. "The Army Engineers Are Imposing Their Flood-Control Ideas on Creeks!" *Saturday Evening Post*, February 23, 1952.

Peterson, Greg, and Jon Halberg. "Closure Affects More Than Jobs." *Mining Journal*, March 29, 1993.

Petrushka, Ann Traylor. "The Rural Development Program: A Historical Assessment of Rural Policy under the Eisenhower Administration and Its Application to the 'Farm Crisis' of the 1980s." Master's thesis, Kansas State University, 1988.

Philadelphia Inquirer. "Employees Tour Penney Store at King of Prussia." August 14, 1963.

Philipps, Dave, and Tim Arango. "Who Signs Up to Fight? Makeup of U.S. Recruits Shows Glaring Disparity." *New York Times*, January 10, 2020.

Pitrone, Jean Maddern. *F. W. Woolworth and the American Five and Dime: A Social History*. Jefferson, NC: McFarland, 2003.

Pittsburgh Courier. "Army Jails GI 'Sit-Ins,' CORE Appeals to JFK." May 6, 1961.

Pollan, Michael. *The Omnivore's Dilemma: A Natural History of Four Meals*. New York: Penguin Random House, 2006.

Popper, Frank. *The Politics of Land-Use Reform*. Madison: University of Wisconsin Press, 1981.

Port Huron (MI) Times Herald. "Alarm System Fixed." November 28, 1979.

Pottsville (PA) Republican. "Brabazon-McMenamin Wedding at Mayfair." August 3, 1948.

Pratt, Chastity. "Down and Out in Purest Michigan." *Bridge Magazine*, June 21, 2016.

Press, Charles, and Clarence Hein. *Farmers and Urban Expansion: A Study of a Michigan Township*. Washington, DC: Farm Economics Division, Economic Research Service, US Department of Agriculture, 1962.

Queen, Stuart, and David Carpenter. "From the Urban Point of View." *Rural Sociology* 18 (1953): 102–8.

Raney, Mark. "Business Organization and Corporate Farming." *Journal of ASFMRA* 24 (1960): 15–24.

Rapid City (SD) Journal. "Family Farm Act Approved." February 1, 1974.

Raup, Philip. "Corporate Farming in the United States." *Journal of Economic History* 33 (1973): 274–90.

Reding, Nick. *Methland: The Death and Life of an American Small Town*. New York: Bloomsbury USA, 2009.

Reich, Adam, and Peter Bearman. *Working for Respect: Community and Conflict at Walmart*. New York: Columbia University Press, 2018.

Report to the President of the United States from the Task Force on Agriculture and Rural Prosperity. Washington, DC: United States Department of Agriculture, 2017.

Reuters. "Trump Warns U.S. May Cut Off GM Subsidies after Job Cuts." November 27, 2018.

Rich, Nathaniel. "Rolling Along." *New York Review of Books*, October 7, 2021.

R. L. Polk & Co. *Marquette City and County Directory*. Detroit, 1895.

Roberts, Norene. "Growing Potatoes in Brooklyn Park." *Hennepin History*, Fall 1994.

Robinson, James. "The Tuttle Creek Tragedy." *Manhattan (KS) Tribune News*, July 14, 1955.

Rodehaver, Myles. "Fringe Settlement as a Two-Directional Movement." *Rural Sociology* 12 (1947): 49–57.

Rogers, Jeanne. "Ike Orders Probe of Segregated Schools at Fort Belvoir and Other Posts in South." *Washington Post*, March 20, 1953.

Roosevelt, Eleanor. "My Day, June 7, 1961." *The Eleanor Roosevelt Papers Digital Edition*, 2017. Accessed November 10, 2022. https://www2.gwu.edu/~erpapers/my day/displaydoc.cfm?_y=1961&_f=md004960.

Ross, Edward Alsworth. *The Social Trend*. New York: Century, 1923.

Rubenstein, James. *The Changing US Auto Industry*. London: Routledge, 1992.

Rural Development: 1971—A Year of Listening and Watching the Development of the Growing Consensus That Something Must Be Done for the People of the American Countryside. Printed for the Senate Committee on Agriculture and Forestry. Washington, DC: Government Printing Office, 1972.

Rural Economic Development in the 1980s: A Summary. Information Bulletin No. 533. Washington, DC: US Department of Agriculture, Agriculture and Rural Economy Division, Economic Research Service, 1987.

Rural Health Information Hub. "Suicide in Rural Areas." In the *Rural Suicide Prevention Toolkit*. Last reviewed May 9, 2022. https://www.ruralhealthinfo.org /toolkits/suicide/1/rural.

Russakoff, Dale. "The American Dream, Fired Up and Melted Down." *Washington Post*, April 12, 1992.

Salamon, Sonya. *Newcomers to Old Towns: Suburbanization of the Heartland*. Chicago: University of Chicago Press, 2003.

Sanders, Scott. "After the Flood." In *Earthworks*, 93–100. Bloomington: Indiana University Press, 2012.

Sanderson, Veryl. "Corporate System at Issue." *Courier* (Waterloo, IA), August 27, 1967.

Sandul, Paul. *California Dreaming: Boosterism, Memory, and Rural Suburbs in the Golden State*. Morgantown: West Virginia University Press, 2014.

Sargent, Charles. "Urbanization of a Rural County." In *Research Bulletin*. Lafayette, IN: Purdue University Research Station, September 1970.

Schapsmeier, Edward, and Frederick Schapsmeier. "Eisenhower and Agricultural Reform: Ike's Farm Policy Legacy Appraised." *American Journal of Economics and Sociology* 51 (1992): 147–59.

Schiller, Ronald. "America's Dying Small Towns: Tragedy or Opportunity?" *Reader's Digest*, July 1972, 199–204.

Schnore, Leo. "Metropolitan Growth and Decentralization." In *The Suburban Community*, ed. William M. Dobriner, 3–20. New York: G. P. Putnam's Sons, 1958.

Schoenfeld, Eugen. "Small-Town Jews' Integration into Their Communities." *Rural Sociology* 35 (1970): 175–90.

Schroeter, John, Azzeddine M. Azzam, and J. David Aiken. "Anti-corporate Farming Laws and Industry Structure: The Case of Cattle." *American Journal of Agricultural Economics* 88 (2006): 1000–1014.

Schulman, Bruce J. *From Cotton Belt to Sunbelt: Federal Policy, Economic Development, and the Transformation of the South, 1938–1980*. New York: Oxford University Press, 1991.

Schuman, Michael. "China's Small Farms Are Fading. The World May Benefit." *New York Times*, October 6, 2018.

Scott, James C. *Seeing Like a State: How Certain Schemes to Improve the Human Condition Have Failed*. New Haven, CT: Yale University Press, 1998.

Scroop, Daniel. "The Anti-Chain Store Movement and the Politics of Consumption." *American Quarterly* 60 (2008): 925–49.

Selected Studies of Migration since World War II: Proceedings of the Thirty-Fourth Annual Conference of the Milbank Memorial Fund. New York: Milbank Memorial Fund, 1958.

Shallat, Todd. *Structures in the Stream: Water, Science, and the Rise of the U.S. Army Corps of Engineers*. Austin: University of Texas Press, 1994.

Shaults, Dan. "The Creeping Ugliness of Small Towns." *Focus/Midwest*, June 1962, 16–18.

Shaw, Frederick J., ed. *Locating Air Force Base Sites: History's Legacy*. Washington, DC: Air Force History and Museums Program, 2004.

Sherrill, Robert. "The Pork-Barrel Soldiers." *Nation*, February 14, 1966.

Shortridge, James. *The Middle West: Its Meaning in American Culture*. Lawrence: University of Kansas Press, 1989.

Shurtleff, William, and Akiko Aoyagi. "Archer Daniels Midland Company (1929–Mid 1980s): Work with Soy." In "History of Soybeans and Soyfoods, 1100 B.C. to the 1980s," unpublished manuscript. Available at Soyinfo Center, accessed July 7, 2021. https://www.soyinfocenter.com/HSS/archer_daniels_midland.php.

Sioux City (IA) Journal. "Woolworth's Nickel Idea." October 11, 1912.

Smarsh, Sarah. *Heartland: A Memoir of Working Hard and Being Broke in the Richest Country on Earth*. New York: Scribner, 2018.

Smee, Daniel, Shoba Sreenivasan, Thomas Garrick, James McGujire, Danial Dow, and Daniel Woehl. "Critical Concerns in Iraq/Afghanistan War Veteran-Forensic Interface: Veterans Treatment Court as Diversion in Rural Communities." *American Academy of Psychiatric Law* 41 (2013): 256.

Smith, Everett. "America's Richest Farms and Ranches." *Annals of the Association of American Geographers* 70 (1980): 528–41.

Smith, Stephen C. "Economic Conflicts in the Rural-Urban Fringe: A Problem of Metropolitan Organization." *Proceedings of the Annual Meeting* (Western Farm Economics Association) 31 (1958): 144–55.

Solove, Ronald. "Problem on the Fringe: Conflict in Urban-Rural Transition Areas." *Ohio State Law Journal* 31 (1970): 125–39.

Sorenson, David. *Shutting Down the Cold War: The Politics of Military Base Closure*. New York: St. Martin's Press, 1998.

South, Jeff. "10 US Military Bases Are Named after Confederate Generals." *Conversation*, September 27, 2018. https://theconversation.com/10-us-military-bases-are-named-after-confederate-generals-103137.

South Bend (IN) Times. "Corporations Buying Farms." August 4, 1968.

South Bend (IN) Tribune. "Population Swells in Northern Michigan." March 10, 1996.

Spangler, Todd. "Kildee: Release Report on Military Base Toxins." *Detroit Free Press*, May 16, 2018.

Sparrow, James T. *Warfare State: World War II Americans and the Age of Big Government*. New York: Oxford University Press, 2011.

"Special Report: Covering the Meth Epidemic in Rural America." Institute for Rural Journalism, July 2005. http://www.uky.edu/CommInfoStudies/IRJCI/reports/reportsmeth.htm.

Spectorsky, A. C. *The Exurbanites*. Philadelphia: J. B. Lippincott, 1955.

Stark, Louis. "Machinists Fight Plant Dispersal." *New York Times*, December 7, 1949.

"Statement of Hon. Pat McCarran, Senator from Nevada." In *Decentralization of Heavy Industry: Hearings before a Subcommittee of the Committee on Interstate Commerce*, 2–8. Washington, DC: Government Printing Office, 1946.

Stebbins, Samuel. "America's Largest Military Bases." *24/7 Wall St.*, November 7, 2019, last updated June 10, 2020. https://247wallst.com/special-report/2019/11/07/americas-largest-military-bases-2/.

Steinberg, Ted. *Down to Earth: Nature's Role in American History*. New York: Oxford University Press, 2000.

Stetson, Damon. "New Span Sparks Boom in Michigan." *New York Times*, July 17, 1956.

———. "Upper Michigan Asks for Job Aid: Peninsula Requires Outside Help to Check Decline." *New York Times*, November 11, 1959.

St. Joseph (MO) Gazette. "Eastern Firm to Locate Here." March 31, 1901.

St. Joseph (MO) New-Press. "Opening of New Store." November 10, 1904.

Stock, Catherine McNicol. *Nuclear Country: The Origins of the Rural New Right*. Philadelphia: University of Pennsylvania Press, 2020.

Stockton, John, Olin Hardwick Jr., and Alfred Dale. *An Economic Survey of Killeen, Texas*. Austin: Bureau of Business Research, University of Texas.

Stores. "Dollar General: Locked into the Low-Income Niche." May 1996.

Streeter, C. P. "The Rural Dilemma and Challenge." In *Rural Urban Fringe Conference Proceedings*, ed. John Quinn and N. G. P. Krauss, 3–6. Champaign: University of Illinois Department of Agricultural Economics, 1967.

Sugrue, Thomas. *The Origins of the Urban Crisis: Race and Inequality in Postwar Detroit*. Princeton, NJ: Princeton University Press, 1996.

Summers, Gene F., Sharon D. Evans, Frank Clemente, E. M. Beck, and Jon Minkoff. *Industrial Invasion of Nonmetropolitan America: A Quarter Century of Experience*. New York: Praeger, 1976.

Swanson, Gordon. "The Myth of Urbanism." *Education Digest* 36 (September 1970): 34–35.

Ta, Linh. "Dollar General Flourishes in Rural Iowa While Towns Fight for Grocery Stores." *Iowa Capital Dispatch*, March 31, 2020.

Talmadge, Herman. "A Strategy for Survival of the Countryside." *Nation's Business*, September 1972.

Taylor, Keeanga-Yamahtta. *Race for Profit: How Banks and the Real Estate Industry Undermined Black Homeownership*. Chapel Hill: University of North Carolina Press, 2019.

Thompson, Fred. "Why America's Military Base Structure Cannot Be Reduced." *Public Administration Review* 48 (1988): 557–63.

Thompson, Warren. *Migration within Ohio, 1935–1940*. Oxford: Scripps Foundation for Research in Population Problems, 1951.

Time. "Okies of the '60s." April 20, 1962.

Town and Country. "The Re-arrangement of Army Posts: Our Scattered Army a Menace to Efficient Service." May 19, 1906.

Tugwell, Rexford. *The Democratic Roosevelt: A Biography of Franklin D. Roosevelt.* Garden City, NY: Doubleday, 1957.

Turner, Carl, Jr. *My Father's Business: The Small-Town Values That Build Dollar General into a Billion-Dollar Company.* Nashville: Center Street, 2018.

Turner, Frederick Jackson. "The Significance of the Frontier in American History." *Annual Report of the American Historical Association* (1893): 197–227. https://www.historians.org/about-aha-and-membership/aha-history-and-archives/historical-archives/the-significance-of-the-frontier-in-american-history-(1893).

University of Pennsylvania Institute for Urban Studies. *Accelerated Urban Growth in a Metropolitan Area: A Study of Urbanization, Suburbanization and the Impact of the Fairless Works Plant in Lower Bucks County, Pennsylvania.* Philadelphia: University of Pennsylvania Institute for Urban Studies with the cooperation of the Bureau of Urban Research, Princeton University, 1954.

US Army Corps of Engineers. "Kinzua Dam & Allegheny Reservoir." Pittsburgh District, n.d., accessed July 16, 2020. https://www.lrp.usace.army.mil/missions/recreation/lakes/kinzua-dam-allegheny-reservoir/.

———. "Multipurpose Waterway Development." In *The U.S. Army Corps of Engineers: A Brief History*, n.d., accessed September 26, 2020. https://www.usace.army.mil/About/History/Brief-History-of-the-Corps/Multipurpose-Waterway-Development/.

US Census Bureau. *Historical Statistics of the United States, Colonial Times to 1970.* Washington, DC: Government Printing Office, 1975.

———. "Metropolitan Areas." Last revised December 8, 2021. https://www.census.gov/history/www/programs/geography/metropolitan_areas.html.

US Congress. *Explanation of the Rural Development Act of 1972, Public law 92-419: Remarks of Herman E. Talmadge, Chairman of the Committee on Agriculture and Forestry, United States Senate.* Senate Committee on Agriculture and Forestry. Washington, DC: Government Printing Office, 1972.

US Department of Agriculture, National Agricultural Statistics Service. *Price Program: History, Concepts, Methodology, Analysis, Estimates, and Dissemination.* Washington, DC, 2011. https://www.nass.usda.gov/Surveys/Guide_to_NASS_Surveys/Prices/Price_Program_Methodology_v11_03092015.pdf.

US Department of Labor. "History of Violations: Dollar General Continues to Put Workers at Risk; Company Faces $321K in Penalties after Recent Alabama Inspection." OSHA News Release Region 4, December 13, 2021.

US Environmental Protection Agency. "National Priorities List (NPL) Sites—by State." N.d. Accessed July 20, 2020. https://www.epa.gov/superfund/national-priorities-list-npl-sites-state.

US Government Accountability Office. "Farm Programs: Direct Payments Should Be Reconsidered." GAO-12-640, July 3, 2012. https://www.gao.gov/products/gao-12-640.

U.S. News & World Report. "Cities Crowding—Countryside Losing." May 7, 1962.

———. "A Helping Hand for Smaller Towns." November 22, 1971.

———. "Midwest's Last Frontier: Upper Peninsula." April 30, 1979.

———. "Why a Food Scare in a Land of Plenty?" July 16, 1973.

———. "Why Factories Are Taking to the Country." June 17, 1963.

Usselman, Steven. "Still Visible: Alfred Chandler's *The Visible Hand*." *Technology and Culture* 47 (2006): 584–96.

Vance, Sandra, and Roy Scott. *Wal-Mart: A History of Sam Walton's Retail Phenomenon*. New York: Twayne Publishers, 1994.

Varenne, Hervé. *Americans Together: Structured Diversity in a Midwestern Town*. New York: Teachers College Press, 1977.

Veblen, Thorstein. *Absentee Ownership and Business Enterprise*. New York: B. W. Huebsch, 1923.

Venkataramani, Atheendar S., Elizabeth F. Bair, Rourke L. O'Brien, and Alexander C. Tsai. "Association between Automotive Assembly Plant Closures and Opioid Mortality in the United States." *JAMA Internal Medicine* 180, no. 2 (February 2020): 254–62.

Vidich, Arthur, and Joseph Bensman. *Small Town in Mass Society: Class, Power, and Religion in a Rural Community*. Princeton, NJ: Princeton University Press, 1968 (1958).

Vik, Dean. "Sawyer Blacks List 'Demands.'" *Mining Journal*, April 16, 1974.

Wahba, Phil. "'It Walmart and 7 Eleven Had a Baby...'" *Fortune*, June 1, 2019, 142–48.

Wallace, David Foster. "Ticket to the Fair." *Harper's*, July 1994.

Wall Street Journal. "Ford to Build Metal Stamping Plant Near Chicago Heights, Ill." July 7, 1955.

———. "Industrial Dispersal." February 25, 1955.

Walz, Jay. "Americans Go West, but to Factory, Not Farm." *New York Times*, October 10, 1948.

Watkins, Ali. "Out of Money and Volunteers, Rural Ambulances Drift to a Dead End." *New York Times*, April 26, 2021.

Watts, May Theilgaard. *Reading the Landscape of America*. New York: Collier, 1975.

Wenk, DeeAnn, and Constance Hardesty, "The Effects of Rural-to-Urban Migration on the Poverty Status of Youth in the 1980s." *Rural Sociology* 58 (1993): 76–92.

Westheider, James. *Fighting on Two Fronts*. New York: New York University Press, 1997.

Westover, Tara. *Educated*. New York: Random House, 2018.

West Virginia Center on Budget and Policy. "State of Rural West Virginia." Blog post, 2018. Accessed June 1, 2020. https://wvpolicy.org/state-of-rural-west -virginia/.

Whang, Roy. "Lordstown: GM's Dream Turns into a Nightmare." *Mansfield (OH) News Journal*, March 23, 1972.

Whetten, Nathan. "Suburbanization as a Field for Sociological Research." *Rural Sociology* 16 (1951): 319–30.

White, Richard. *Railroaded: The Transcontinentals and the Making of Modern America*. New York: Norton, 2011.

White House Office of the Press Secretary. "Economic Renewal: Community Reuse of Former Military Bases." Press release, April 21, 1999. https://clintonwhitehouse6. archives.gov/1999/04/1999-04-21-report-on-community-reuse-of-former-military -bases.html.

Wilkerson, Chad. "Trends in Rural Manufacturing." In *New Directions in Manufacturing: Report of a Workshop (2004)*. Washington, DC: National Academies Press, 2004.

Williams, Eric. *Capitalism and Slavery*. Chapel Hill: University of North Carolina Press, 1944.

Williams, Mark. "Many Ohio Towns Left Behind Despite Stronger Economy." *Columbus Dispatch*, December 16, 2018.

Willmar (MN) Tribune. "Will You Stick." March 2, 1921.

Wilson, Charles Morrow. *The Landscape of Rural Poverty: Corn Bread and Creek Water*. New York: Henry Holt, 1940.

Wilson, Edmund. "Second Look at Kinzua." *Washington Post*, January 24, 1960.

Winkler, John. *Five and Ten: The Fabulous Life of F. W. Woolworth*. New York: R. M. McBride, 1940.

Wirth, Louis. "Urbanism as a Way of Life." *American Journal of Sociology* 44 (1938): 1–24.

Wood, Robert C. *Suburbia: Its People and Their Politics*. Boston: Houghton Mifflin, 1959.

Woods, Ralph. *America Reborn: A Plan for Decentralization of Industry*. London: Longmans, Green, 1939.

Worcester (MD) Democrat. "Cooperatives and Consumers." February 22, 1935.

Worster, Donald. *Rivers of Empire: Water, Aridity, and the Growth of the American West*. New York: Pantheon Books, 1986.

Wright, Alfred J. "Recent Changes in the Concentration of Manufacturing." *Annals of the Association of American Geographers* 35 (1945): 144–66.

Wright, Richard. "Capitalism and the Rise of Corporation Nation." In *Capitalism Takes Command: The Social Transformation of Nineteenth-Century America*, ed. Michael Zakim and Gary J. Kornblith, 145–68. Chicago: University of Chicago Press, 2012.

Wrigley, Robert, Jr. "Small Cities Can Help to Revitalize Rural Areas." *Annals of the American Academy of Political and Social Science* 405 (January 1973): 55–64.

Wuthnow, Robert. *The Left Behind: Decline and Rage in Small-Town America*. Princeton, NJ: Princeton University Press, 2018.

———. *Remaking the Heartland: Middle America since the 1950s*. Princeton, NJ: Princeton University Press, 2011.

Youngstown (OH) Vindicator. "Chevrolet to Build World's Biggest Auto Assembly Plant at Lordstown." February 17, 1956.

Zelinsky, Wilbur. "Asserting Central Authority." In *The Making of the American Landscape*, ed. Michael P. Conzen, 329–56. New York: Routledge, 2010.

Zimmer, Basil, and Amos Hawley. "Local Government as Viewed by Fringe Residents." *Rural Sociology* 23 (1958): 363–70.

INDEX

University of Minnesota Agricultural
Experiment Station, 151
University of Nebraska, 13
University of Pennsylvania, 225–26, 228
University of Texas, Bureau of Business
Research, 48
University of Wisconsin, 109, 222
Upper Peninsula, MI, mining, 55–56,
62
USACE. *See* United States Army Corps
of Engineers (USACE)
USAF. *See* United States Air Force
(USAF)
USDA. *See* United States Department
of Agriculture (USDA)
U.S. Steel, Fairless Works plant, 223,
225–26, 228, 237

Vasos, Todd, 199
Vidich, Arthur, 254
Visible Hand, The (Chandler), 137–38
Volpe, John, 104
Volstead, Andrew, 146

Walbaum, Herb, 245–46
Walker Manufacturing, 142
Wallace, David Foster, 252
Wallace, George, 161, 221, 232
Wallace, Henry, 163, 164, 177
Walmart, 140, 190, 191, 193, 195–96, 199
Walton, Sam, 190
Washakie County (WY) Ambulance
Service, 256
Watts, May, 11
Wechsler, Lewis, 231
Wells Fargo, 141
Westover, Tara, 171
West Point, 26, 31

Whaley, Nan, 198
Whetten, Nathan, 214–15
White Sands Missile Range, 52
Whitney Dam, 29, 32
Whyte, William, 243
WIFE (Women Involved in Farm Eco-
nomics), 155
Williams, Basil, 34
Wilson, Charles Morrow, 7
Wilson, Edmund, 35
Winesburg, Ohio (Anderson), 213, 229
W. K. Kellogg Foundation, viii
Women Involved in Farm Economics
(WIFE), 155
Wood, Grant, 249; *The Revolt against
the City*, 249
Woods, Ralph, 91, 254
Woolworth, Frank Winfield, 178–79,
182; and Jefferson County, NY, 179
Woolworth's, 140, 174, 178, 183; and De-
catur, IL, 188–90; and Erie, PA, 179;
and Greensboro, NC, 188; and Lan-
caster, OH, 185–86; and Lancaster,
PA, 179; store closings, 188
Works Progress Administration (WPA):
Division of Social Research, 6; *Slave
Narratives: A Folk History of Slavery
in the United States*, 249
World Food Conference (1974), 162
WPA. *See* Works Progress Administra-
tion (WPA)
Wuthnow, Robert, 14

Yesenosky, Joseph, 223
York Iron Company, 55

Zaininger, William, 242–43
Zimmer, Basil, 235